D1522885

Our
EXODUS

M. M. SILVER

Our EXODUS

Leon Uris and the Americanization
of Israel's Founding Story

Wayne State University Press   Detroit

14 13 12 11 10   5 4 3 2 1

Library of Congress Cataloging-in-Publication Data

Silver, Matthew.

Our Exodus : Leon Uris and the Americanization of Israel's founding story / M. M. Silver.

p. cm.

Includes index.

ISBN 978-0-8143-3443-0 (cloth : alk. paper)

1. Uris, Leon, 1924–2003. 2. Uris, Leon, 1924–2003. Exodus. 3. Jews—United States—
Attitudes toward Israel. I. Title.

PS3541.R46Z88 2010

813'.54—dc22

2010002650

Publication of this book was made possible through the generosity of the Bertha M.
and Hyman Herman Endowed Memorial Fund.

Designed and typeset by Maya Rhodes

Composed in The Sans and Sabon

For Mel

Contents

Introduction

The divorce of history from literature has been as calamitous for Jewish as for general historical writing, not only because it affects the very image of the past that results. Those who are alienated from the past cannot be drawn to it by explanation alone; they require evocation as well.

—Yosef Hayim Yerushalmi, *Zakhor: Jewish History and Jewish Memory*, 100

I believe it will be like a breath of spring air for the American people to meet Mr. Ari Ben Canaan, the fighting Jew who won't take shit from nobody.

—Leon Uris in a letter to his father, June 25, 1956

IT TOOK THE JEWS close to 1,900 years, after the destruction of the Second Temple, to reestablish a state of their own in the land of Israel. It took them fifty years, after Theodor Herzl convened the first Zionist Congress, to convert the Jewish statehood program into a reality. It took them ten years, after the declaration of Israel's establishment in May 1948, to explain the founding rationale and circumstances of the Jewish state in terms readily apprehensible to masses of fair-minded persons around the globe. This last ten-year period—the story of how the Jews told their biggest modern story—remains uncharted territory, virtually a secret history.

Curiously, little attention has been paid to the way Israel's founding story was packaged and popularized for the world at large. After centuries of messianic yearning and decades of concentrated political activity, the Jews had a complicated, inspiring story to tell. Its successful telling did not defy cultural logic. In view of the sickening facts of the genocidal murder of six million Jews, innumerable readers and movie watchers around the globe were predisposed to welcome a narrative about Jewish recovery and renewal in Israel. Still, combining the basic facts and spiritual intangibles of Israeli statehood into one popular story was not an easy feat. The story was comprised of astonishing contrasts—the contrast between the devastating vulnerability of the Holocaust in Europe and the improbable, impressive victory over Arab antagonists in the 1948 War of Independence, the contrast between statelessness and statehood, and the contrast between the secular pioneering ethos of the new state of Israel and the religious, ancient contours of the land of Israel. Synthesizing these and many other polarities posed a daunting creative challenge. How that challenge was overcome is the story of this book.

Israel's founding purposes and circumstances were not immediately comprehensible outside of the band of communal kibbutz and moshav farmers, Palmach and Irgun fighters, and Labor Zionist and Revisionist Zionist politicians who established the Jewish state. These aims and realities had to be translated into a 1950s popular culture idiom of postwar affluence and free world democracy. We can be fooled into thinking that this project of popularizing Israel's founding is easy to understand in retrospect because it was carried out by a text, Leon Uris's novel *Exodus,* whose characterization of heroic Israeli striving versus abominable antagonism was manifestly overdrawn. Simple formulas might indeed help stories circulate among mass audiences, but a satisfactory explanation of why a particular account of a historical event captivates hundreds of thousands of readers cannot hinge on a subjective judgment about the level of sophistication in the handling of character or plot. In fact, a series of overlapping questions regarding *Exodus*'s success have been left lingering since its publication half a century ago because no obvious answers to them were available.

Leon Uris persuasively associated Israel's founding with forces of democratic freedom in the postwar world, and for as long as Cold War modes of thinking prevailed, his narrative appeared to encapsulate absolute truth about the rectitude of the Jewish state. The chaotic, morally confusing realities that mounted in Israel in the 1980s and after (two demoralizing Lebanon wars, two Palestinian intifada uprisings, a prolonged, embittering dispute about the disposition of territories occupied by Israel after the 1967 Six Days' War) appeared to deviate sharply from the uplifting, idealistic ethos evoked by the conventional story of Israel's founding. By the twenty-first century, new criticisms of the Jewish state were consolidating rapidly; the most poignant, thought-provoking critique was leveled by a group of "post-Zionist" Israeli scholars and thinkers who themselves had been weaned on the accepted narrative of their country's founding, and who claimed that they could no longer live with its contents.[1]

Many post-Zionist claims about Israel's founding circumstances stirred immediate controversy, and remain in dispute. However, these researchers' well-documented revisions of crucial topics of the 1948 war, such as the mass exodus of about 700,000 Palestinians, irreversibly changed understandings of Israel's founding.[2] This altered view of the birth of the Jewish state has serious implications on many levels. Among other things, it dislodges us from dogmatic views about Israel's founding, the most intriguing event in modern Jewish history, and it encourages us to reflect about how we originally came to think about the Jewish state. Historians have a vantage point for asking how a country's founding story was first strung together only after it has started to unravel.

This project of reexamining where our own founding assumptions about Israel's birth came from can make a vitally important contribution to our understanding of modern Jewish identity and experience. In fact, the fundamental contention of this book is that Israel's meaning in world culture can best be assessed by looking at how people have been telling stories about the country and analyzing what motivated them to thread various patches of reality into one narrative or another. This methodology of treating Israel's founding story with analytic rigor—as though the telling of the story *is* the story[3]—helps us make headway past problematic, and ultimately unproductive, binary polarities between the "real" facts of 1948 and "mythic" perceptions of Israel's founding.

In study and discussion of Israeli history we have reached an exasperating situation in which historians presume to have in their warehouse possession of the true facts of the 1948 war (and other pivotal moments in the ongoing dispute), whereas everyone else is thought to be in the thrall of distorted narratives. This analytic hierarchy is dubious on many grounds. For one thing, it assumes that historians have adequate access to all parts of the bewildering array of on-the-ground viewpoints that constituted the 1948 experience, when in fact the leading Israeli new historians or post-Zionists confess to being unable to obtain or interpret Arab source materials.[4]

For another thing, the current thinking assumes that historians are somehow impervious to "mythic" nationalist perceptions of heroism or travail, when in fact they are, by their own admission, extremely responsive in their work to familiar 1948 narratives.[5]

Most telling of all, even when a reasonable degree of empirical agreement is reached on particularly contentious subjects, wide gaps of disagreement persist as to what the facts really mean. Arguments continue because identity investments in a historical experience such as Israel's founding go well beyond the results of an empirical evaluation of their facts. The facts *are* important (as this study argues, one important reason why Israel's conventional founding narrative had staying power was that its crafters did their homework, and grounded many, though not all, of their images in reality). Ultimately, however, differences in interpretation about Israel and its origins are dictated by conflicting identity needs rather than merely technical issues relating to the acquisition and assortment of facts.

That a dead end has been reached in the Zionist/post-Zionist pyrotechnics about the facts of 1948 is evidenced by the increasingly recondite disquisition about Plan D (*tochnit dalet*), a military blueprint devised by Jewish army (Haganah) officers several weeks before Israel's statehood declaration, which endorsed "operations against enemy settlements."[6] Historians who agree about the basic facts related to the mass Arab exodus and Plan D—that is, scholars who concur that Haganah pressure exerted against villagers and urban residents was an important contributor to the spiral of panic and flight, and that Plan D was never executed systematically but rather left to the discretion of local commanders as they assessed specific circumstances in the field—disagree vehemently about the possibility that Zionist leaders harbored a "master plan" for the expulsion of Palestinians. Bickering about the moral meaning of Plan D and the mass Palestinian departure, these historians all but admit that their subject of interest is not what Israelis or Arabs really did in 1948, but rather perceptions of what Israelis or Arabs are really like. Thus, University of Exeter scholar Ilan Pappé makes a striking statement in a debate ostensibly devoted to the effects of Plan D. As it turns out, it makes no difference to him that what he characterizes as a master plan for expulsion was never really executed on the ground. "In the final analysis," Pappé explains, "if I plan to throw someone out of his flat, the fact that he had left before I had a chance to expel him in no way alters the fact of my intention."[7]

When historians march the words *fact* and *intention* together in the same short row it is a strong indication that they are not really worried about actual events and results. Instead, trying to sort out their own, or others', images of what historical subjects were like, they are working in the realm of perception.

Diametrically opposite things said about the 1948 war and Israel's founding can each have a reasonable degree of factual certainty. I am firmly attached to Israel's victory in that war, and, as an unthinking reflex response, I would be inclined to regard as madness any attempt to dispute the reality of the tangible benefits (a political state, a viable framework for Jewish nation building) accrued to the Jews as a result of this victory. Nonetheless, a factually reasonable case denigrating the reality of Israel's victory can be presented by pointing out that a large portion of the war's Palestinian refugee losers, and their descendants, have adamantly refused to settle permanently in any political construct other than pre-1948 Palestine, and that Arab states that lost the 1948 round of fighting have subsequently found ways to prevent Israel from enjoying the margin of security that is supposed to redound from military triumph. That is to say, even the most basic fact about 1948—who won the war?—is subject to perception. This being the case, the time has come for historical research to concentrate on narrative perceptions that continually give color and ethical meaning to the bare facts of Israel's founding and its subsequent history. This book tackles Leon Uris's *Exodus*, the text that, more than any other single artifact, set the narrative frames for a sympathetic worldwide understanding of modern Israel's genesis.

Exodus, a long historical novel, was enormously popular. After May 1959, it topped U.S. bestseller lists for close to five months,[8] and, in September of that year, advance paperback orders of 1.5 million copies had no precedent in publishing history.[9] The book's remarkable sales figures, coupled with the box-office success of Otto Preminger's 1960 film version of *Exodus*, regularly prompt comparisons to mass-culture landmarks, such as *Gone with the Wind*.[10] Such quantitative measures of *Exodus*'s impact are thought provoking (and we will, of course, return to them); however, they do not on their own explain why *Exodus* warrants sustained attention as a leading item in the revival of Jewish culture in the post-Holocaust world.

With a forcefulness resembling Uris's muscular prose style, *Exodus* shattered well-emplaced barriers, and blasted open new cultural possibilities. Its historical importance as a barrier breaker and cultural trailblazer should be listed succinctly.

First, a Zionist public relations coup, *Exodus* popularized the Jewish state formula in ways that had no precedent, even though Jewish nationalists had for decades honed talents in journalism and diplomacy in the hope of scoring propaganda points for their cause.

Second, *Exodus* played a vital role in the recovery of Jewish self-confidence after the devastation of the Holocaust. *Exodus*'s positive messages of Jewish revitalization and empowerment were missing in other popularized responses to the tragedy, such as the *Diary of Anne Frank* and the Eichmann trial.

Third, *Exodus* ripped open the shroud of American Jewry's silence about Israel in the 1950s. Its spirit of Jewish heroism and its images of American-Israeli union inspired American Jews to display openly their ethnic pride for the Jewish state.

Finally, fourth, while *Exodus* is a product of American Jewish history, and a book about the Jewish state, its impact on modern identity well exceeds these two centers, the United States and Israel, of post-Holocaust Jewish experience. *Exodus,* an impassioned tribute to Israel, was written by an assimilated American Jew whose target audience was Jews and fellow Americans with backgrounds roughly similar to his own; however, up to the end of the Cold War, the novel exercised an unparalleled galvanizing effect among Soviet Jews who were determined to embark on their own exodus, on a journey to the Jewish state for freedom. Uris's messages, in other words, appealed powerfully to Jews who had antithetical experiences of free world democracy and Communist oppression. *Exodus*'s history proves that images of Israel, popularized in the Cold War métier of good and bad, had a unique ability to unify Jews who faced very different political, social, and economic circumstances.

These bullet items on *Exodus*'s historical résumé are highly significant, and this study dedicates much effort to their amplification. However, *Exodus*'s place in history cannot be appropriately estimated just by weighing its specific contributions one at a time. Instead, as a story with interlocking plot parts, the *Exodus* narrative served for decades as one morally consistent guide for thinking and talking about Israel, its accomplishments and problems. Its success inculcated in the minds of hundreds of thousands of readers and movie viewers that Israel is a story with consecutive segments, that you cannot understand why the King David Hotel was bombed in

1946 by the right-wing Zionist Irgun unless you know what the British had promised the Jews under the 1917 Balfour Declaration, and what happened to Jews during the Holocaust.

This narrative taught that history mattered. The lesson can be thought of as being ironic, since it was taught by an author, Leon Uris, who was a high school dropout and who had virtually no training in Jewish subjects before he took himself through a crash course on Zionist history in the months before he drafted *Exodus*. It is also the *Exodus* novel's distinctive characteristic. Leon Uris marshaled an impressive wealth of data into his historical novel. Even more impressively, millions of readers were willing to put up with so much Jewish history, particularly in *Exodus*'s Book Two, whose over one hundred pages are packed to the gills with information about the Dreyfus Trial, Joseph Trumpeldor, the Balfour Declaration, the British White Papers, *ha'apalah* illegal immigration of Holocaust refugees, and more. Yet, however devoted Uris was to historical facts, and however much patience his readers displayed toward this improbably educational methodology in a best-seller action novel, it is indisputably the case that *Exodus* is filled with historical untruths. In fact, the enterprise of identifying the novel's historical errors dominates the few serious and engaging articles that are to be found in the woefully meager scholarly literature about *Exodus* and Uris.[11]

To some extent, this penchant for exposing what Uris got wrong results from the embittering and prolonged nature of the Arab-Jewish dispute, as well as from the anti-Arab animus of *Exodus,* which appears dated and insensitive to contemporary readers, including committed supporters of Israel. In other words, that critics want to distance themselves from the way *Exodus* relates to Arab opposition to Israel's founding is not surprising. However, scholars who are not focused on *Exodus*'s prejudicial characterization of Arabs also fasten their discussions to aspects of Israel's statehood struggle whose history Uris distorted. Thus, one researcher points out that Uris's narrative "changed history" by injecting causal connections into the politicized context of ha'apalah illegal immigration that never really existed.[12] On one level, this scholarly attachment to factual distortions in *Exodus* seems pedantic and moot. After all, the huge influence Uris's novel and its film version exerted on a mass audience is not going to by eradicated by the correction of any of its numerous errors. On another level, without spelling out the implications of their fact checking, these few skeptical assessments of *Exodus*'s ac-

Uris at his craft. Publicity photo for follow-up novel to *Exodus, Mila 18*. (Harry Ransom Humanities Research Center, the University of Texas at Austin)

curacy hint about the crucial issue: if Leon Uris was very right about some things, and very wrong about other things, does it make sense to say that *history* is what mattered about *Exodus*?

Cagily enough, this book answers that question with a resounding "yes and no." No, errors and truths contained in *Exodus*'s telling of the history of the founding of the Jewish state are not crucially significant because Uris's novel was not ultimately about the "real" Israel. Yes, the way history is presented in *Exodus* is crucially significant because the representations reflect needs, expectations, and aspirations of Jewish identity and culture in the post-Holocaust world.

Exodus conveyed reams of factual information about the Jewish state and its founding, much more data than the most talented Israeli government spokesman today could ever hope to present in hours of press conferences. However, as we seek to demonstrate in this study via an examination of authorial motivation, readers' and critics' responses, and narrative strategies of plot and character, *Exodus* utilized Israeli-Zionist terms and landscapes instrumentally, as a kind of conceptual scenery useful for the examination of identity issues important to Jews everywhere, and in the United States in particular. Leon Uris, in short, wrote a book that was primarily "about" Jewish empowerment, and secondarily about Israel.

In some respects, these two topics (empowerment and Israel) overlap. Most obviously, Uris's recognition that chronicling Israel's military triumph in 1948 would inspire Jewish, and non-Jewish, readers and put to rest lingering, post-Holocaust stereotypes about Jewish weakness and vulnerability, fully accorded with the Israelis' prideful interpretation of the implications of their state's founding. Just as surely, Uris foisted on his story of Jewish statehood identity concerns that were hardly priorities in the political culture of the young state of Israel. The heart of *Exodus* is a melodramatic romance between a Jewish Israeli, Ari Ben Canaan, and an American Protestant, Kitty Fremont. Tugging this Harlequin love affair through the pages of *Exodus,* Uris (himself married to a Danish American Christian woman) projected his own identity investment in Christian-Jewish harmony, and cleverly symbolized America's developing love affair with Israel's pioneering frontier democracy. While tawdry and sentimental in literary terms,[13] the Kitty-Ari pairing was an intriguing and inveigling mass-culture image of Judeo-Christian union in the post-Holocaust world. As such, it represented abstract issues that went well beyond the factual specifics of Israel's founding, and its palpable basis (Jewish-Christian intimacy) had virtually no internal relevance for Israel, whose Jewish majority lives without the intermarriage angst that is so familiar in American Jewish culture.

A topic like the Kitty-Ari romance, which so obviously imposes an identity concern of the Jewish Diaspora onto the story of the establishment of Jewish statehood, hedges against our ability to conclude that *Exodus* was "about" Israel. In truth, Leon Uris wrote a book about the Jewish need to feel strong after the Holocaust. His consummate formula for satisfying that need—guns and Christian good will—was applicable in some ways to Israel and not applicable in other ways. Since Israel was really used as a playing field upon which the author and his readers could work out their own identity issues, *Exodus* needed to be right about the basic dimensions of the

Jewish state, and not its specific measurements. Or, put more simply, since *Exodus* was never exactly about Israel, it did not matter that Uris was not exactly right about all the facts of its establishment.

Exodus, and the history it conveys, can and should be seen in an additional way, however. Uris's novel was never about the real Israel; but for millions of readers and viewers, and for many years, the imaginary, heroic Jewish state it describes became a reality. In this sense, analyzing the historical contents of *Exodus* is worthwhile, but not to verify or dispute their mimetic reliability. Not exactly about Israel, the "facts" in *Exodus* are staggeringly revealing measures of Jewish cultural strategies for self-presentation, and survival, in the post-Holocaust world.

In the case of a narrative dealing with the aftermath of the Holocaust and Jewish statehood, is it reasonable to expect that historical contents could have been faithful reproductions of reality? In fact, in 1958, the odds were against verisimilitude in a popular account of the founding of Israel. This book will elaborate upon the reasons why this was so, but we should note them briefly here. First, perhaps surprisingly, for sixty years after its establishment at the end of the nineteenth century, the Zionist movement had never developed tools for popularizing the rationale of the Jewish state, which meant that a writer in Uris's position lacked a pre-prepared template upon which factual information about Israel could be readily communicated. Second, ten years after Israel's founding, American Jews, and other Americans, remained far away from the Jewish state in evident political, cultural, and social senses, and it was difficult to achieve precision on a subject about which mass audiences had only a rudimentary sense of familiarity. Third, Cold War popular culture processed topics in Manichaean modes of democratic good and totalitarian evil. A writer familiar with those modes (as Uris, the scriptwriter for the 1957 film *Gunfight at the O.K. Corral,* clearly was) had the best chance of conveying Israel's statehood story to a mass audience. Popularizing Israel meant refashioning it, making it in some (but not all) ways a simpler story than it ever was.

Since this refashioned *Exodus* narrative became the real Israel for millions, limiting discussion of its historical impact to the contrast between Uris's "imagined" Israel and the "actual" founding of Israel in 1948 is not merely pedantry. That level of analysis ignores an impressive corpus of scholarship that illustrates that nationalist history and culture is primarily about imagined communities.[14] As a special example of a national entity whose well-being depends on the support of faraway Diaspora communities that can never be directly in touch with its day-to-day realities, Israel is governed by perception no less than any country in the world; and so framing analyses of its history upon mechanical oppositions between "truths" and "myths" about the Jewish state and founding is beside the point. Our focus should be upon why particular characterizations and plot twists involving the socialist kibbutz, Holocaust survivor ma'apalim, Palmach commanders, or Palestinian fighters emerged. Whose identity needs were served by these characterizations? How can storytelling about Israel mobilize energy in disparate parts of the Jewish world? What happens when extremely complicated (e.g., the modern revival of an ancient nation) or excruciating (e.g., the Holocaust) events are mass marketed in popular culture?

Of course, no study of a single text or several cultural artifacts can furnish conclusive answers to such broad questions of how Jewish or any other ethno-national identity interacts with historical memory in the modern world. Yet I hope this book shows that systematic examination of *Exodus* offers valuable insights about narrative as an agency of national reclamation in an era of mass publishing and mass media. In Jewish experience, no other single text produced after the Holocaust and Israeli statehood in 1948 so forcefully urges reevaluation of history as an issue of narrative perception.

1) Contextualizing *Exodus*

AS A HUGELY INFLUENTIAL, best-selling historical novel that was adapted as a popular film, *Exodus* can possibly be compared to familiar works in American cultural history, including Harriet Beecher Stowe's *Uncle Tom's Cabin* (which was performed on the stage) and Margaret Mitchell's *Gone with the Wind,* or perhaps works of political realism authored by John Steinbeck (a writer Uris attested to having admired).[1] These possible American comparisons will be discussed later in this book;[2] this chapter puts *Exodus* in perspective by measuring its place in Jewish contexts, particularly worldwide publicity efforts undertaken for decades by the Zionist movement and American Jewish attitudes toward Israel in the 1950s. Our argument is that even in these Jewish contexts to which it most obviously belongs, *Exodus* stands out conspicuously as a phenomenon whose unabashed pro-Israel messages and wildfire success levels have little, or no, precedent. *Exodus* is a cultural item whose black-and-white contents were easy for everyone to understand, even though they could not be put into a readily available context.

The Zionist movement waited sixty years for the publication of *Exodus.*

Virtually from the birth of organized Zionism at the end of the nineteenth century, Jewish nationalists were keenly aware of the value of publicity. Movement founder Theodor Herzl, a journalist by profession, was a master stage manager, and he devoted a considerable portion of his labors at the early Zionist Congresses toward creating a dignified Jewish collective appearance that would impress the outside world.[3] From Herzl's era through the 1920s and 1930s, a strikingly high proportion of leading Zionists were journalists. This Zionist predilection for journalism was an outgrowth of the way modern Jewish history unfolded both as an ongoing public discussion between Jews and Gentiles about the terms of political and social emancipation and between Jewish subgroups about the place of Jewish religion and tradition in a secularizing age.[4] Zionists' efforts with media organs suggested that they accorded priority to the public dissemination of information about their movement.

Despite the talents of Zionists like Herzl, Berl Katznelson, Ze'ev Jabotinsky, and many others who at stages of their careers worked extensively in journalism,[5] the Zionist movement through the period between the world wars was not particularly successful in the dissemination of its messages, symbols, and ideas. The Zionists made use of visual media—photographs, postcard etchings, slide shows, and films—to publicize images of Zionist *halutz* pioneering in the communal settlements of Eretz Israel and generally to stimulate a sense of Mandatory Palestine as a Jewish country. Whether such visual publicity work really had an impact upon the non-Jewish world is questionable—it is hard to think of an exhibition of Zionist images before World War II that captured the imagination of well-known non-Jewish thinkers and writers in Europe or the United States. Such visual publicity was innately divisive in the Jewish world, and it is hard to see how Diaspora Jews could have rallied wholeheartedly behind what the Zionists were showing to Gentiles. The Zionist images of the new Jewish man in Eretz Israel, "a bronzed farmer, in motion, working with hand implements in the field," evoked provocative normative contrasts with the old Jews of the Diaspora. As noted by Michael Berkowitz, a scholar whose research has focused largely on Zionist consciousness raising and publicity work in the West, a "substantial portion" of the Zionist photographs "documented the idea that a younger generation of national Jews was growing up stronger and healthier than they possibly could in Eastern Europe."[6] It is easy to see why publicity campaigns built around such premises failed to excite minds and hearts across the board in the Jewish world.

During the interwar period, the prestate Jewish community of Mandatory Palestine, the *Yishuv*, invested sporadically in outreach visits paid by its leading lights to Diaspora and Gentile communities in America and elsewhere.[7] More systematically, the Zionist movement craftily utilized the names and images of distinguished statesmen, scientists, and politicians, Jews and non-Jews, to enhance its luster around the globe. Visits paid by philo-Semite or pro-Zionist figures, such as Lord Balfour, to the Yishuv were widely publicized.[8] Such trips sometimes became associated with key Zionist symbols. Leopold Pilichowski's portrait of Lord Balfour's address at the inauguration of the Hebrew University of Jerusalem on Mount Scopus in 1925 exemplifies the connection between visual image making, symbolic Zionist institutions, and public relations uses of world statesmen and visits to Palestine. However, outside of circles of persons already committed to the Zionist cause, how many hearts were stirred by the Pilichowski painting? In public relations terms, the Zionist movement had some access to esteemed personalities who had distinguished international reputations, but these world icons tended not to be fully committed to Jewish national concepts, and whenever they cooperated with the Zionists, they found themselves surrounded by confusing allegations about foul play leveled by one sectarian Zionist camp against another.

One telling example in this regard is Albert Einstein's connection to the Zionist movement. During the interwar period, the world-famous physicist probably stood alone as the one figure whose words on behalf of the Zionist movement, had they been disseminated with consistency and passion, might have had worldwide impact on a scale foreshadowing the postwar sales figures and sensation stirred by Uris's *Exodus*. And the preeminent Zionist leader of the early interwar period, Chaim Weizmann, was himself a scientist who had strong connections with Einstein. In fact, in 1921, the year Einstein received the Nobel Prize for physics, Einstein arrived in the United States with Weizmann to help kick off Zionism's new worldwide fund-raising mechanism, the Keren Hayesod (Palestine Foundation Fund). The problem was that the 1921 Keren Hayesod tour became mired in volatile intramural Zionist skirmishing about philanthropy and investment strategies and practices; in Zionist history, the tour and the year are remembered as a fiasco whose low point occurred when Supreme Court justice Louis Brandeis, a committed Zionist and distinguished American, marched with his followers straight out of the organized Zionist movement, ostensibly owing to the dispute with Weizmann about the commingling of investment and charity funds.[9]

Such spectacles could not have impressed outside observers. In fact, sometimes they caused the public to focus on the personalities of Zionism's famous spokesmen and ignore the information about Jewish needs and national ambitions that they were providing. "Prof. Einstein here; Explains Relativity," proclaimed the *New York Times* when the physicist arrived in April 1921,[10] implying that his scientific theory was bigger news, if not easier to understand, than the disputes raging about the financing of the Zionist movement.

Just as commonly, Einstein was not himself around, but the Zionists found cause to use his reputation and image nonetheless. Einstein never seriously applied himself at the Hebrew University of Jerusalem, but his name was used for years to bolster the new institution's reputation and also to add weight to Weizmann's faction in a battle about the university's character as an elitist research, or student oriented, institution.[11] Sometimes, Zionists found ingenious ways to imprint the world-famous Einstein face on their pioneering landscape. Berkowitz's volume features an amusingly revealing photograph of a visiting delegation inaugurating the Einstein Forest in Palestine in 1930[12]—the physicist was unable to attend, so the well-dressed participants had themselves pictured around a photograph of Einstein in their rustic, Jewish pioneering setting.

As the Einstein example suggests, Zionists in the interwar period had within their reach some powerful publicity tools. Frustratingly, the Zionists were often too disorganized and fractious to make good use of these resources; concurrently, these famous spokesmen were not fully available or consistent about their support.

As the interwar period advanced, the painful gap between the objective accuracy of Zionist forecasts regarding Jewish needs in a world of rising anti-Semitism and the very limited ability of Zionist publicists to get their messages across in world media was acutely obvious to thoughtful Yishuv pioneers and Diaspora Zionists who dealt with publicity projects. Gershon Agron, a journalist and American Zionist who brought a briefcase full of publicity plans when he settled in Mandatory Palestine in the 1920s, wailed about the apparent impossibility of disseminating information about the Yishuv in world media. "I feel that the present neglect of these places [Yishuv sites] is an injustice to this part of the world and the Western world," the future founder of the *Jerusalem Post* wrote despondently to the *Chicago Tribune* in 1924. "As an American citizen, I feel especially that the American reader has no opportunity of familiarizing himself with conditions in this part of the world."[13]

Limits on Zionist publicity work varied according to the evolving sociopolitical character of different regional contexts during this interwar interval. In the United States during the "return to normalcy" period of the Roaring Twenties, Zionism's pessimistic analyses regarding the fate of Jewish-Christian relations and its advocacy of radical change in the settlement patterns of Jews brushed too sharply against the grain of the context's assumptions of prosperity and against the burgeoning Jewish sense of being "at home in America,"[14] to borrow Deborah Dash Moore's phrase. In Eastern Europe, where various organized Zionist groups experienced significant growth in the interwar period, the story was rather different. Anti-Semitic local environments and (as Ezra Mendelsohn notes) demoralizing effects of restrictive policies emplaced by British authorities in Palestine late in the period inhibited publicity outreach work that was, or might have been, undertaken by local Zionists.[15]

During the interwar period, the American Zionist movement's experiments with publicity work yielded negligible results. Fascinating and articulate characters, such as the ailing poetess Jessie Sampter, who rose up through the Hadassah movement and settled in Mandatory Palestine, and Maurice Samuel, who wrote and lectured on Zionism extensively after settling in the United States as a young man, tapped creatively into literary and nonfiction genres while contributing publicity materials that had formal or informal backing from the American Zionist movement.[16] Visits to Mandatory Palestine made a strong impression on some Jewish intellectuals, such as the Berlin-born writer Ludwig Lewisohn, who left America for a prolonged world tour in the mid-1920s, and whose responses to Yishuv life found expression in a powerful 1925 critique of Jewish assimilation called *Israel*. Lewisohn found pioneering Labor Zionist institutions to be stifling, but he believed that the uninhibited Jewish way of life in the Yishuv might inspire Jews everywhere in the world to shun forms of self-denial ("the highest virtue of Tel Aviv is that its example may teach Jews to be noisy everywhere in the world," Lewisohn reflected[17]). However persuasive they might have been to circles of articulate Jews and non-Jews, Zionism-influenced works like Lewisohn's *Israel* reached no more than ten or twenty thousand readers in this interwar period.[18] This lack of a mass audience for works dealing directly or indirectly with Zionist themes has led historians to downplay the significance of American Jewish writing about prestate Israel. In his standard-setting study of American

Zionism up to the Holocaust, Melvin Urofsky did not find cause to mention Zionist publicity work in the United States before 1948.[19] It is not a stretch to conclude simply that American Jewry had never produced a popular book about Zionism before Leon Uris set out to write *Exodus* in conjunction with Israel's tenth anniversary.

American Jewish publicity efforts accelerated during the Holocaust years, the period when Zionist formulas gained virtual across-the-board acceptability to mainstream American Jewish groups and organizations for the first time.[20] In this period of dire emergency, Zionist figures combined use of the mass media and organized lobbying in publicity initiatives whose impact far surpassed anything before seen in the United States. This work was highly significant, but it cannot really be contextualized on a par with what Leon Uris accomplished in *Exodus*.

The personal backgrounds and circumstances of these Holocaust-era Zionist publicists in the United States were unlike Uris's situation as an unaffiliated, assimilated American Jew. For instance, American Zionist Emanuel Neumann knew Hebrew, spent years of his adult life in the Yishuv, and was professionally employed by the Jewish nationalist movement;[21] and Hillel Kook (who assumed the name Peter Bergson in America) was a right-wing Zionist from the Yishuv who, together with cohorts, launched publicity efforts on behalf of the rescue of European Jewry whose no-holds-barred character reflected his group's disregard for norms important to American Jewry (in fact, the efficacy of the Bergson group's publicity efforts was limited by tensions and clashes with the American Jewish leadership).[22] Publicity efforts undertaken by these figures in the Holocaust era were different in tone from Uris's *Exodus*, which maintained a made-in-America feel even as it told the story of Israel's founding, and which celebrated Jewish renewal and strength.

The remarkably energetic Bergson group produced events for large audiences that engaged the talents of European and American creative luminaries. The historian Stephen Whitfield has classified works produced by the Bergson group as "pageants," defining the genre as a "hybrid of art and propaganda" that evokes the past to "stimulate communal cohesion." Ostensibly aesthetic events, continues Whitfield, pageants "are really political gestures."[23] The Bergson group's spring 1943 pageant, *We Will Never Die,* mourned the murder of millions of Jews and affirmed faith in the Jewish future while featuring a score composed by Kurt Weill and a cast of stars such as

Edward G. Robinson, John Garfield, Claude Rains, Frank Sinatra, and Burgess Meredith.[24] The *We Will Never Die* pageant was performed twice on March 9, 1943, to record audiences at Madison Square Garden and was also broadcast on the radio; when it was performed a few weeks later at Constitution Hall in Washington, Supreme Court justices and hundreds of congressmen were in the audience; Eleanor Roosevelt called the pageant "one of the most impressive and moving" productions she had ever seen (the FDR White House never produced an official endorsement for the pageant).[25] However, a planned, multicity tour of *We Will Never Die* quickly skid off the rails, partly because local hosts were deterred by the militant, right-wing Zionist politics of the Bergson group and its Committee for a Jewish Army. The pageant's creators wondered whether having put Holocaust horrors on the stage had generated any substantive rescue efforts. Weill lamented: "The pageant has accomplished nothing. . . . all we have done is make a lot of Jews cry, which is not a unique accomplishment."[26]

On the rubble of the Holocaust, the Bergson group produced one play, the 1946 one-act drama *A Flag Is Born,* which marked a transition from World War II publicity efforts on behalf of Jewish rescue toward a focus on the Jewish statehood struggle.[27] Unlike *Exodus,* this play had explicitly partisan political purposes—its backers, the Bergson group's American League for a Free Palestine (ALFP), sought revenue to purchase ships that would bring Holocaust survivors to the Holy Land, in defiance of British restrictions. Nonetheless, embedded within *A Flag Is Born* are intriguing parallels to the novel and film version of *Exodus;* and so the story of this 1946 play should be summarized briefly, as a reminder that for all its singularity, Uris's Zionist publicity coup did not emerge ex nihilo.

Ben Hecht, a well-known writer who by 1946 had under his belt coauthorship of the Pulitzer Prize–winning play *The Front Page,* along with script-writing credit for films such as *Scarface*[28] and *Spellbound,* produced the script of *A Flag Is Born* for the ALFP, after having collaborated with the Bergson group on *We Will Never Die.* The child of Russian Jewish immigrants, Hecht, like Uris, grew into young adulthood without any strong feeling for Jewish matters; with Hecht, this assimilated orientation changed sharply in 1939 in response to Hitler's savagery. In his well-known 1954 autobiography, Hecht testified that the Nazis' mass murder "brought my Jewishness to the surface."[29] In 1941, Hecht's provocative newspaper attacks on American Jewish apathy captured the attention of Hillel Kook;[30] thereafter, Hecht banged out hard-hitting publicity materials about the Nazi genocide and the imperative of Jewish rescue, and his impassioned prose became a vital asset for the Bergson group.

Much of the power of the 1946 play *A Flag Is Born* derived from despair and frustration felt by Hecht and his Bergson group peers, who knew that their wartime pleas, warnings, and frenetic activities had not yielded successful mass rescue missions. During a key moment in *A Flag Is Born*, David, a young, suicidal survivor of the Treblinka death camp, articulated Hecht's deep anger about American Jewish inaction during the Holocaust: "Where were you, Jews," David pointedly asked. "Where were you when six million Jews were being burned to death in the ovens?"

These troubling words were uttered on the stage by a twenty-two-year-old rising star, Marlon Brando. The actor, who joined the cast after having learned about "the true nature of the killing of the Jews," and who performed for minimum actors' guild wages, recalled that "Jewish girls got out of their seats and screamed and cried from the aisles" after he delivered his searing indictment concerning the murder of six million Jews.[31] Brando called *A Flag Is Born* a "powerful, well-written pageant."[32] Brando's motives, commentators have assumed, were not entirely altruistic. He was eager to appear with theater greats such as Paul Muni, a veteran of the Yiddish stage who in *A Flag Is Born* played Tevya, an elderly, ailing Holocaust survivor who, en route to Palestine, rests in a European cemetery on a Sabbath eve (praying, Tevya has visions of heroes from the Jews' ancient biblical past). In retrospect, the creative talent and backing that attracted Brando to this Jewish play appears impressive. Stella Adler, a veteran acting teacher and developer of the Stanislavski method, recruited celebrity supporters for *A Flag Is Born* (including Bob Hope, Milton Berle, Paul Robeson, and the Marx Brothers); Kurt Weill composed the score; and Metropolitan Opera tenor Mario Berini sang liturgical music.

Written and performed in a period when the Yishuv's struggle against British immigration restrictions was hitting its dramatic peak, *A Flag Is Born* dipped into American iconography to legitimate Zionist claims against British policy in these late hours of the Mandate. Utilizing analogies to the American Revolution, which the *Exodus* novel and film subsequently drummed into the minds of millions of readers and viewers, ALFP publicity work for the play proclaimed,

"It's 1776 in Palestine!"[33] Drawing comparisons between American democratic freedom fighting and the Zionist statehood struggle, the production of *A Flag Is Born* presaged techniques utilized by Uris and *Exodus*. A similar point can be made about the way Tevya's visions in *A Flag Is Born* allude to biblical heroes and episodes to vivify long-standing Jewish attachment to Eretz Israel—this, too, anticipated a key technique of *Exodus,* whose author (as we shall see) judged that the book's "nicest" marketing strategy was to play up "biblical connections." More broadly, the Bergson group's use of celebrity artists and celebrity patrons for dramas about very serious Jewish subjects foreshadowed *Exodus*'s journey to the silver screen, on which stars such as Paul Newman, Eva Marie Saint, and Sal Mineo acted as heroes fighting for the establishment of the Jewish state.

Exceeding the original production plan, *A Flag Is Born* was performed 120 times on Broadway, over a ten-week period, and then hit stages in five other cities. Reviews were mostly supportive, and the play reportedly raised, in ticket revenue and accompanying donations, about $1 million.[34] Hillel Kook's recollections about use of the play's revenue are ambiguous,[35] but proceeds from *A Flag Is Born* are said to have been used to purchase a four-hundred-ton former yacht, the SS *Abril,* which was renamed the SS *Ben Hecht* and used in a valiant attempt to transport six hundred Holocaust survivors to Mandatory Palestine (the passengers, along with the twenty-one-man crew of mostly American volunteers, were corralled at sea by the British, and sent to Cyprus and Acre). These impressive results paid tribute to the prolific energy of the Bergson group; and in a loose sense, this successful dramatization of Israel's founding struggle previewed *Exodus*. Ultimately, however, the comparison between a 105-minute, one-act, three-character play written and performed in the interval between the Holocaust and Israel's establishment, and *Exodus,* is strained. Summarizing the impact of the Bergson group's pageants, Whitfield notes that "the grandiose hopes that their organizers nourished were unfulfilled"; this historian estimates that to some unquantifiable degree, the pageants instilled in "American Jewish audiences a sense of transatlantic solidarity."[36] This sense, however, lacked foundation in an easily understandable, inspiring story. Uris's hundreds of pages presented Israel as the triumphant product of a definable historical process. Its heroic atmosphere of consummation is unlike the lingering despair and political doubts that gripped productions staged by the Bergson group;[37] and, more importantly, *Exodus*'s impact reached a mass scale that, perhaps tragically, had no precedent in the work of Hillel Kook and Ben Hecht.

The explosive support, and almost reverential attitude, that *Exodus* stirred after its 1958 publication cannot be fully understood unless we take into account residual feelings of bitter exasperation about the fate of Zionist messages in this early, pre-Israel period. People in the 1950s were coming to understand the extent of the crime committed by Nazis largely as a result of their control of a devilishly sophisticated publicity apparatus, and the dissemination of anti-Semitic propaganda. In retrospect, it was obvious that any progress notched by Zionist publicists in the interwar period had paled in comparison to the public relations blitzkrieg perpetrated by the Nazis—and the result of this differential was genocide. The time had at last come for the Jews to have their turn and to send their political messages to a belatedly receptive world.

Exodus should be contextualized as a bright, powerful contrast to gray, negligible publicity efforts undertaken by the world Zionist movement before 1948. However, in terms of background context, Zionist public relations (*hasbara*) is only half the story. *Exodus* must also be seen as the triumphant antidote to the public silence of American Jews regarding Israel during the 1950s. Something fundamental changed among American Jews as a result of Uris's book. One heavy layer of inhibition about being "too Jewish" was peeled away, and an articulated sense of connection with the state of Israel forever thereafter became part of the ethnic identity of the American Jew.

Impediments to pro-Israel expression in 1950s America were diverse and complicated. The sheer novelty of what some Jews had done in Eretz Israel, by resurrecting a model of Jewish sovereignty after two millennia, took time to get used to, not just among American Jews. Probably as stifling as anything else in the Cold War 1950s was the issue of political loyalty. Suspicions about treacherous American Jewish support for the Communist Soviet Union was stirred in this period by a few well-publicized incidents, such as the Rosenberg trial;[38] for American Jews, the early Cold War era's strict ethos of patriotic loyalty set psychological limits. Apart from Cold War politics, a number of overlapping factors—the vicissitudes of oil politics, State Department "Arabists" who believed that U.S. interests precluded any pro-Israel tilt in the nation's foreign policy in the Middle

East, and more—circumscribed the playing field for American Jews on Israel issues in the 1950s.[39]

In a circular way, we might observe that precisely because no Leon Uris had yet surfaced in mass culture to elucidate what subsequently appeared as obvious links between the Holocaust tragedy and the rationale of Jewish statehood in Israel, good-hearted American leaders and commentators who knew about the concentration camps and the meaning of Nazism were not prepared in this decade to endorse affirmative policy initiatives on Israel's behalf. President Eisenhower, who witnessed the human ruin left at Buchenwald but whose administration refrained from developing close relations with the Jewish state, is a case in point. Eisenhower operated in a political-cultural environment where even Jewish communities remained mum about Israel's efforts to revitalize Jewish life after the Holocaust. As Peter Grose observes, in the 1950s Eisenhower addressed Jewish audiences without even mentioning the state of Israel.[40]

Little in the 1950s Washington establishment portended a proactive disposition of support for a special relationship with the Jewish state. The title of Peter Hahn's well-informed study about American foreign policy toward the Middle East in the pre-*Exodus* era captures how a standoffish policy elite reluctantly dealt with Israel's ongoing security crisis—Hahn called his study of U.S. foreign policy toward the Arab-Israeli conflict, 1945–61, "Caught in the Middle East." The absence of proactive concern for Israel in the U.S. government was a key factor inhibiting American Jewish expression in the 1950s.

This was, in effect, organized inhibition. Throughout the first decade of Israel's existence, American Jewry failed to organize a substantive instrument for publicity work and lobbying on behalf of the new Jewish state. Isaiah Kenen, a Canadian-born journalist, handled this lobbying as a "one man office."[41] Originally called the American Zionist Committee for Public Affairs, Kenen changed this office's name to the American Israel Public Affairs Committee (AIPAC) in 1959, months after the publication of *Exodus*.[42]

After Israel's establishment, the American Zionist movement paradoxically lost momentum. The de facto existence of the Jewish state accentuated essential differences in the way Zionism had long been conceived in the United States as compared to other Diaspora countries. The basic problem could no longer be glossed: If Zionists in America did not want to sponsor waves of Aliyah immigration to the newly established Jewish state, why were they still calling themselves Zionists? Israel's charismatic prime minister, David Ben-Gurion, manifestly refused to acknowledge that there might be answers to that question. Now and then in the decade, American Jewish leaders pulled out their hair when the Israeli premier stated what he really thought, which was that after 1948 any self-respecting Zionist (or, for that matter, any Jew in America) really ought to pack his or her bags and settle in Israel.[43] Mostly, however, Ben-Gurion simply ignored organized Zionist groups in America and instead dealt practically with American Jewish groups and organizations that avoided ideological pronouncements about Zionism while generously providing donations for the mass absorption in Israel of Jewish immigrants from Asian and African countries, and for Israel's security needs.[44]

This arrangement worked well in that it ensured the flow of badly needed capital to Israel and also fostered quiet bonds of solidarity between Israel and American Jews. In private homes, and in discrete disbursement of philanthropic funds, American Jews expressed their love of Israel throughout this decade, even if they lacked the mechanisms and self-confidence needed to express this bond in public. When formulated aloud, the terms of this 1950s accommodation with Israel manifestly failed to inspire masses of American Jews.

In 1950, Ben-Gurion hammered out an understanding with American Jewish Committee president Jacob Blaustein that was supposed to set the tone in relations between the two groups of Jews, Israelis and American Jews, for years to come.[45] One notable clause in the portentously labeled "Ben-Gurion–Blaustein agreement" involved an Israeli promise to refrain from Aliyah proselytizing and any other activity that might compromise the American citizenship status of American Jews. When Ben-Gurion endorsed a document that stated that American Jews "owe no political allegiance to Israel," American Jewish organization leaders breathed a sigh of relief. However, distinguished contemporary commentators, such as Columbia University historian Salo Baron, were on target when they observed that the Blaustein–Ben-Gurion exchange meant little apart from how American Jewish and Israeli individuals and groups decided to implement it.[46]

As it turned out, the only professional group to be excited by the Blaustein–Ben-Gurion agreement has been historians, and its interest is retrospective. In the 1950s, nobody's Jewish aunt Minnie had a clue as to what had been written out between Israel's prime minister and the American Jewish Committee president. That is to say, there was in this period no articulated formula for a supportive relationship with Israel that captured the hearts and minds of American Jews.

The eclipse of organized Zionism in America in the 1950s did not necessarily entail a drop-off of the activities it had carried out before Israeli statehood in 1948. Those activities were picked up by synagogues and groups that had never had any use for "Zionist" nomenclature. The problem was that highly articulate leaders in the American Jewish community who were deeply passionate about Israel, and who had long-standing connections with the world Zionist movement, found themselves lost in the shuffle after 1948. These leaders became embittered as American Jewish organizations bypassed formal Zionist networks when they quietly but substantively supported Israel. Due to this dynamic, a leadership gap on the Israel issue yawned in America throughout the 1950s.[47]

Persuasive, strong-willed individuals whose words and actions had tremendous impact in favor of the Jewish statehood drive in the 1940s spent the ensuing decade, after Israel's establishment, out of the spotlight. The most notable no-show in the 1950s was Cleveland Reform rabbi Abba Hillel Silver, whose galvanizing oratory and lobbying for the Zionist cause at crucial wartime gatherings, such as the 1943 American Jewish Conference, constituted turning points in the acceptance of Zionist formulas in America and in some ways prefigured what Uris accomplished with *Exodus*. The Israeli historian Zohar Segev has recently uncovered an interesting roster of Israel-related initiatives and experiments with which Rabbi Silver became associated in the 1950s,[48] yet in popular perception Abba Hillel Silver receded from Zionist affairs the moment the miracle of Jewish statehood was accomplished. The withdrawal of this highly imposing Zionist figure from Cleveland symbolized something that happened to America's Jewish community as a whole in the 1950s.[49]

Scholars have long associated American Jewish reticence about Israel with suburbanization processes in the 1950s. One account of Jews in suburbia, published a few months after *Exodus*'s 1958 release, implied that in their new American suburban prosperity Jews were somehow uncomfortable about Israel in the 1950s. "Most suburban Jews have a friendly, though at times uneasy, feeling about the State of Israel," this study diplomatically observed.[50] Better known is evidence of apathy about Israel in 1950s suburban Chicago compiled by the groundbreaking social scientist Marshall Sklare, with

Joseph Greenblum, in the "Lakeville" study. This research included an influential survey, which ranked items listed by respondents who were asked about what it means to be a "Good Jew."[51] The Lakeville survey famously ranked Israel low on a list (14th, out of 22) of topics that were important to suburban American Jews in the 1950s. Just 21 percent of these Chicago suburb Jewish respondents ranked support for Israel as essential "to be considered a good Jew," and Israel was ranked behind a long roster of American-based desiderata ("Work for Equality of Negroes," "Help the Underprivileged Improve their Lot," etc.).[52]

The catch is that a careful reading of *all* of Lakeville's evidence does not support this study's reputation for having proven monochromatic apathy toward Israel among American Jews in the 1950s. In fact, a full-length chapter in the volume, "The Lakeville Jew and Israel," is rife with data overlooked by scholars that do not corroborate assumptions about 1950s apathy toward Israel in American Jewish suburban households.[53] There are reasons to wonder about the methodology of Lakeville's "Good Jew" survey. In fact, when Sklare returned to "Lakeville" a few months after the Six Days' War, a period when American Jewish passions for Israel were soaring sky high, his survey once again yielded findings about apathy toward Israel among Jews in suburban Chicago. This curious result left Sklare expressing puzzlement about the efficacy of his survey techniques on this Israel topic.[54]

Scholars and commentators have assumed that stupefying effects of suburban material culture—a landscape where, as the young Philip Roth sardonically remarked in his 1959 *Goodbye, Columbus,*[55] backyard oaks could more properly be called "sporting goods trees" whose limbs were filled with "two irons, a golf ball, a tennis can . . . and a first baseman's glove and what was apparently a riding crop"—contributed to American Jewish quiet or apathy about Israel in the 1950s. However, Diaspora Jews have retained feelings of impassioned attachment for Eretz Israel in environments infinitely more hostile and emotionally confining than the American suburbs, so no obvious explanation substantiates hypotheses about how the postwar exodus of second- and third-generation city Jews to the greener neighborhoods of Long Island, Westchester County, and elsewhere stifled enthusiasm for Israel. In fact, suburbanized American Jews in subsequent decades learned how to say or do quite a lot on behalf Israel. Pro-Israel lobbying became an unprecedented, effective event in American ethnic history *after* Jewish communities became firmly settled in suburban locales.

One scholar has described unsubstantiated ideas about stifling effects of Jewish postwar suburbanization as "elegiac" discourse.[56] Suburban Jews in the 1950s worried about the loss of something essential in their identities, suggests Riv-Ellen Prell, because an ethnic sense of community wrought by life in the circumscribed space of urban neighborhoods was suddenly gone. Being Jewish could no longer boil down to the simple fact of being in an urban neighborhood space that had dozens of synagogues, kosher butchers, and other Jewish institutions. To compensate for this loss of a spatial sense of identity, Prell explains, Jews in the suburbs developed a "logic of affiliation"—to reaffirm their identities as Jews, they became members of a rich array of religious, social, and leisure institutions and groups. This affiliation trend masked deep-rooted anxieties about complex patterns of social exclusion in the suburbs and about the ultimate aims of the Jews' efforts (whether they were joining clubs and organizations to be with Jews, or to parade an American way of life, was never clear). Suburban Jews in the 1950s, Prell shows, talked about a paradox. Superficially, they felt *more* Jewish in that they belonged to so many Jewish groups, and yet they simultaneously felt *less* Jewish because their affiliation experiences seemed to lack authenticity. Unease deriving from this "paradox" was articulated in the elegiac mode; whatever seemed authentic belonged to the past.[57] Arguably, the *Exodus* phenomenon can be understood in terms generated by this recent research. By the end of the 1950s, suburban Jews developed a new, vicarious form of affiliation; because Jewishness seemed inauthentic in suburban space, they sought membership in a far-off land whose moral credibility was rooted in a sacred Jewish past.

The suburbanization process triggered ambivalent identity impulses, and its participants expressed alternating feelings as Jews or as Americans by narrowing or increasing the emotional distance to various ethnic markers in their new environments. As Karen Brodkin and Eric Goldstein have observed,[58] Jews expended considerable emotional energy in twentieth-century efforts to join America's white establishment. Doing so meant making various problematic claims of cultural, or *ethnic* (a term that gained currency after World War II) superiority to blacks. Leaving tough city neighborhoods behind them, Jews embraced polished, suburban, Protestant-like manners, though sometimes, as in Norman Podhoretz's painfully candid 1963

Commentary essay, "My Negro Problem—And Ours,"[59] they confessed to vicarious admiration of traits of masculine vigor that they
associated with urban black culture. Becoming white suburbanites,
Jews dealt with an array of gender and ethnic anxieties. As Brodkin
emphasizes in her study, stereotypical myths of the Jewish mother,
and subsequently of the Jewish American Princess, reflected feelings
of confusion, resentment, and self-loathing as some Jews tried am-
bivalently to suppress their Jewish ethnicity; alternatively, fantasies
of *shikza* trophy wives appealed to some Jews as "visible and se-
ductive symbols of their masculinity and of their success in entering
the white mainstream."[60] The thrust of this argument about Jewish
"whiteness" in the 1950s is that the inwardly taxing suburbanization
process left Jews with insufficient emotional energy to relate to the
complicated topic of the new Jewish state.

At the risk of truism, it may be suggested that the noncommuni-
cativeness of suburbanized American Jews about Israel in the 1950s
should be seen as precisely that, namely, a communications issue.
The transition from dense Jewish urban neighborhoods to the more
sparse pastures of suburbia raised new communications challenges.
Gone was the milieu, brilliantly evoked in memoir literature such as
Alfred Kazin's 1951 *Walker in the City,* in which a neighborhood
resident was flooded with Jewish smells, sounds, sights, and ideas the
moment he or she stepped onto the city street.[61] Within this setting of
constant, intimate contact among Jewish residents of the city neighborhood in the first half of the twentieth century, first- and second-
generation Jews had deployed Yiddish- or English-language means
of communication (media, performance venues) in which they could
express enthusiasm or reservation about new developments in the
Jewish world. In the 1950s suburbs, these old city neighborhood dynamics of fluid daily contacts among Jews and accessibly circulating
means of communication were either scaled down or missing alto-
gether.[62] The implications of this communications challenge, particularly in relation to a topic like Israel that came wrapped with various
psycho-political anxieties about loyalty and sociological speculation
about attitudes in Gentile America, were significant.

The convergence of these 1950s political, psychological, and sociological inhibitions regarding Israel can be illustrated by the futility
of two American Jewish, pre-*Exodus* attempts to articulate pro-Israel action programs or vision, one taken from the realm of literature
and the other from theology.

"I have a childhood memory of my grandmother holding up her copy of *Exodus* and asking plaintively, 'what did he put in there that I didn't have in my book,'" writes Jeremy Popkin,[63] the grandson of the author of a forgotten but interesting novel, *Quiet Street*.[64] Published three years after Israel's founding, Zelda Popkin's *Quiet Street* was the first American novel about Israel's 1948 War of Independence. While it contains a few Uris-like scenes of war heroism, *Quiet Street* is a restrained study of the everyday struggles and emotional ordeals of several residents of Jerusalem's attractive Rehavia neighborhood during the siege on the city, from February through June 1948, and it diverges qualitatively from the militant spirit of *Exodus*.

Popkin, a tough-minded, independent character, began writing novels in midlife, after having run a public relations firm with her husband.[65] By October 1948, when she set out for Israel (where a sister lived as an immigrant) to undertake research for her Independence War novel, Popkin had completed six detective novels; a best seller called *The Journey Home* (framed around the 1943 "Congressional Limited" train wreck); and one of the early Holocaust novels, titled *Small Victory* (1947). A widow who relied on income from her writing, Popkin sought commercial success with *Quiet Street*; after the book came out, the former PR professional worked the publicity system, capitalizing on quirks of fate (*Quiet Street* made national news when then Chicago Cubs manager Frankie Frisch tossed a copy at an umpire during a dispute) and some favorable reviews. In May 1952, the book won the Jewish Book Council's "Samuel Daroff Fiction Award." Still, the book did not sell well, and, in keeping with the recollection of the author's grandson, the novel's failure naturally elicits comparisons to the astounding popularity of Uris's epic.

Quiet Street is plagued by clumsy transliterations of Hebrew expressions, ethnocentric depictions of Rehavia settings as extensions of Boston suburbs, and a deep ambivalence about women's activities in the postwar world that leads to completely polarized presentations of female roles during wartime as either a daughter tossing Molotov cocktails to derail Egyptian tanks or a mother getting by and keeping house in besieged Jerusalem. Nonetheless, much in the book's depiction of Israel's 1948 circumstances feels real. The author convincingly details the Jerusalem residents' petty resentments, dilemmas, and coping strategies (in some ways, *Quiet Street* recalls a series of compelling novels written by the Israeli author Hanoch Bartov that set the courageous decisions of young heroes to enlist in the 1948

struggle against a coldly realistic reconstruction of partisan bickering, uprooted religiosity, and economic hardship in one town neighborhood).[66]

Designated for American Jewish and non-Jewish readers, Popkin's brand of moral realism was several steps ahead of the game.
Jews in America in the 1950s were very much beholden to conceptualizations of Cold War patriotism and melting pot integration. For
them, and their Christian counterparts, the image of Jews elsewhere
unified in a fight for recognition as an independent, sovereign national entity was still very *foreign*. Readers required considerable
instruction as to why Jews would want to redefine themselves as a
separate political entity in a sea of Arab enmity.

In contrast to *Exodus,* Popkin lost track of the basic issue. For
it to be accessible outside of Israel a 1948 narrative had to be about
the hows and whys of Jews becoming a national group with its own
state, that is, something they had not been in America, Germany,
France, or anywhere else in modern times. Popkin took this transformation for granted and set about to write a book about how this
nation of Israeli Jews—citizens who belonged to unprecedented ju-
ridical, political, and ideological categories—contained persons who
worried about exceedingly "normal" considerations, not least of all
their children's well-being.

Unlike *Exodus, Quiet Street*'s list of protagonists includes American Jews. Its central character is Edith Hirsch, an immigrant from
Boston who has lived in Jerusalem for twenty years. Her settlement in
Mandatory Palestine is described perfunctorily as a matter of Zionist
pedigree (Edith's grandfather, the narrator reports, was a good friend
of Theodor Herzl's). Edith has two children, a boisterous ten-year-
old boy and an eighteen-year-old daughter, Dinah, who is settled in a
Spartan, dangerously vulnerable kibbutz, Gan Darom, in the Negev
desert. Her husband Jacob, a Russian Jew, also lived for a period in
Boston, where he studied obstetrics. Doctor Jacob Hirsch copes with
a series of harrowing experiences—including riding in the medical
convoy to the Hadassah Hospital that was brutally ambushed en
route to Mount Scopus—by working around the clock and nursing a
sardonic, self-effacing sense of humor. Edith does not work; she devotes her hours to scouring for food in besieged Jerusalem, avoiding
sniper fire in her shopping forays, and worrying about her daughter
on the isolated kibbutz. Among other low points, she is reduced to

begging British soldiers for dog food for the family pet and then uses the canned meat to feed her husband and son.

The central dilemma in the novel is this mother's worry. Does Edith have the moral right to risk sacrificing her children in the struggle to create a Jewish state? Popkin's grandson, who studied her notes for *Quiet Street,* records that the author was impressed by Israel's single-minded determination to win independence. This culture of "Ain Brairah," or "No Choice," was the Jews' "secret weapon" in the 1948 struggle, Popkin jotted in one of her spiral notebooks as she composed thoughts for the novel.[67] Eventually, she settled upon the conflict between this Zionist cultural standard of "No Choice" and an American sensibility of pragmatic individualism as the main problem in her book. "If I lose my child and gain a State, is it worth the great price," the mother asks, her worries exacerbated after the fall of the Jewish Kfar Etzion bloc gravely endangers Dinah's Negev kibbutz. This is not a question posed in the zealous, take-no-prisoners temperament of *Exodus.*

In *Quiet Street,* Popkin identified key issues related to Israel's founding, but she could not seem to analyze the Jewish state as part of a historical process. The peak moment in Popkin's book illustrates the failure of her approach. Residents of the Rehavia street gather in the Hirsch's home to listen to the wireless's broadcast of Ben-Gurion's reading of Israel's declaration of independence. As the residents celebrate the proclamation, one neighbor, the wise, compassionate Judge Winkleman, abruptly asks an uncomfortable question: "I wonder, if any of us had been asked, any of us who today are jubilant, which will you choose, six million dead or a State? Would anyone have wished for this State at *that* price?"

This is not in itself an unethical question, and its posing reflects a genuine sense of remorse about how millions of would-be benefactors of the state were viciously murdered before its establishment. The problem, of course, is that Popkin has formulated the issue in a fashion that inverts the way Jews understood their historic story to be unfolding. According to the narrative popularized by Uris and upheld unflinchingly by world Jewry, Israel's establishment was a historic necessity *because* six million Jews had been murdered. Other narratives might hinge upon different causal sequences—one could agree with Henry Winkelman's implication that had not such a large number of Jews been murdered, Zionist claims would not have won crucial support in the international arena, and thus Israel could not have been established. But that is not the causal sequence of import on the triumphant Jewish narrative that would be cherished by many millions of *Exodus* readers and viewers.

In Popkin's book, a Holocaust survivor responds curtly to the judge's blunt query. "Stop," the survivor interrupts. "You cannot ask that. My whole family was of the six million who died." Although vociferous, this objection does not bring the matter to a close, because the reader knows so little about the history of the neighbor who raises it. Popkin offers the reader nothing beyond the following telegraphic biography early in the book: "Rosenweig, a nervous, twitchy man who taught school and had the blue-green concentration camp brand on his arm, and new plastic teeth, replacing those knocked from his jaws by a guard at Dachau." Popkin's reserved treatment of this survivor's biography is a case in point: she gathered raw materials for the "big story," but she didn't know how to put them together.

Jewish, and other, readers were not looking for a 1948 narrative like Popkin's, which inserted a Holocaust survivor's life story in a free-floating discussion about various civil and ethical implications of Israel's founding. Instead, as Uris discovered, they were looking for a narrative that would show how such a survivor's life story and Israel's were, in moral fact, one.

This literary example of *Quiet Street* is apposite, because it reminds us that *Exodus*'s publicity triumph was far from inevitable. Had, like Zelda Popkin, Leon Uris chosen the wrong narrative strategy for his novel, *Exodus* would never have captivated hundreds of thousands of Jews and non-Jews. Yet a still more revealing example is to be found outside of the realm of literature because it features an American Jewish figure whose ability to combine ideological insights with practical community initiatives was probably unmatched in this postwar period.

Mordecai Kaplan, a rabbi ordained by the Jewish Theological Seminary and founder of the small but influential Reconstructionist movement in American Judaism, stood out in the postwar reality for a few reasons. He was a long-standing Zionist who had for some time devoted serious thought to creative ways of reconciling characteristic American Jewish attitudes and Zionist principles (as his biographer mentions, this Zionist enthusiasm permeated strongly among other members of the Kaplan family).[68] He was also highly respected for having crafted concrete institutional structures to promote his abstract ideas about Judaism as a many-sided civilization. In particular, Kaplan's "synagogue center" model—a multifaceted complex combining religious, social, and educational functions known affectionately in American Jewish vernacular as the "schul with the pool" set-up—was adapted with a keen eye to the challenges posed by the dispersal of second- or third-generation acculturating Jews in the American suburbs.[69] Logically, nobody in the 1950s should have had more to say than Mordecai Kaplan about the fostering of new, creative links between Israel and prospering, suburban American Jews.

In the mid-1950s, Kaplan, a prolific writer, released a programmatic book, *A New Zionism,* whose agenda was to guide American Jews toward a newly affirmative relationship with Israel.[70] Kaplan tackled the most complicated existential issues raised by the establishment of a Jewish state. In light of the Holocaust and Israeli statehood, Kaplan identified two reasons why long-standing Zionist principles needed to be revised. A "new Zionism" was needed because Jewish unity could no longer be expressed in conventional nationalist terms of common ancestry, blood ties, and kinship. "That," Kaplan wrote bluntly, "is too reminiscent of Nazism." In addition, Kaplan knew that American Jews could not fully accept the way Israelis conceptualized the Jewish nation. Jews in the United States saw themselves as members of the American nation, and so they looked for innovative terms to express their sense of unity with overseas Jews, including Israelis. After considerable semantic and ideological wrangling in this text, Kaplan believed he had found the term: "Not nationhood, but peoplehood would be the objective of the New Zionism," he proclaimed. Implicit in this maneuvering in favor of depoliticized definitions was a realistic grasp of American Jewish psychology, and of the special anxieties about loyalty bred by the Cold War environment.

Aware that redefining their bond with citizens of the Jewish state as one of *peoplehood* was not exactly going to spur hundreds of thousands of American Jews into assertive, coast-to-coast pro-Israel activity, Kaplan unfurled a multiplank plan for organized action in this book, *A New Zionism.* Indeed, under the rubric of Jewish peoplehood, Kaplan ambitiously spelled out a dizzyingly detailed agenda. His New Zionism in the 1950s went well beyond functions specifically tied to Israel. In fact, as he referred loosely and metaphorically to Israel and Zionism, Kaplan really had in mind a full-blown ethnic revival. He spoke about the American Jewish community compiling a registry of vital statistics, inducing every Jew to affiliate in a local or national Jewish organization, budgeting all needs of Jewish life, newly streamlining coordination of Jewish educational and religious activities, fostering the creative activity of Jews, helping Jews who met economic difficulties caused by discrimination, and collaborating with non-Jewish civil movements for the welfare of the general population.

That was a mouthful. Mordecai Kaplan's 1955 overreaching programmatic statement about Zionism was symptomatic of a decade-long logjam in American Jewry's relation toward Israel. It was as though even the most ideologically savvy, organizationally experienced voices in the American Jewish community had so much to say about Israel that they ended up saying nothing at all.

In 1958, some sixty years after the formula of the Jewish state was initially floated by Herzl, and ten years after that formula had become a reality established under extraordinarily dramatic circumstances, the inability of the Zionist movement to publicize its efforts persuasively was no anomaly, but rather a diplomatically costly and spiritually demoralizing routine. For American Jewry—a resourceful and, in the 1950s, newly dominant Diaspora community—it was beginning to seem as though talented, articulated groups and leaders had something enlightening to say about every subject under the sun, other than the most remarkable and inspiring Jewish occurrence of the preceding 2,000 years.

In his suburban Encino, California home, Leon Uris ignored the proposals to redefine Zionism in terms of statistical registries, educational bureaus, arm-twisting organizational recruitment, sound-bites about peoplehood, and all the other sophistic, sand-castle measures proposed in a manifesto such as Kaplan's. He came up with an all-in-one means of overcoming short daily distances of apathetic prosperity in the suburbs and long existential erosion of identity caused by generations of acculturation in Christian society. Leon Uris told a story about Jewish history.

2) *Exodus* and Jewish History

SO WHAT WAS THAT JEWISH HISTORY story about? What did the author (and his editors) intend by packing so much Jewish history into a mass-marketed book of fiction—since when are best sellers designed to provide history lessons? Why was the public so receptive to the "Jewish side of the story," to Israel's narrative of events surrounding its founding during the 1948 war? In what ways did Leon Uris remain committed to the facts or spirit of the Jewish story he told? To what extent was *Exodus*'s chronicling of major events in modern Jewish history faithful to actual occurrences, and what purposes were served when the novel took liberties with the facts? What, in sum, does the way Jewish history is told in *Exodus* say about Jewish identity needs after the Holocaust, about the way Gentiles wanted, or could be persuaded, to view Jewish life, and about the way mass culture restructures complicated historical realities in line with preexisting character stereotypes and storylines, and profit considerations?

Drawing upon the internal evidence of Uris's text, unpublished correspondence, and draft writings in the author's archive, and on findings of scholarly research relating to key real-life events that are fictionalized in *Exodus,* this chapter argues that *Exodus*'s status as a master text in post-Holocaust Jewish culture derives from its selective but engaged and informed treatment of Jewish history. Conceivably, Uris could also have sold many thousands of copies by leaving out much of the history and heating up the Kitty-Ari romance, but then *Exodus* would hardly merit retroactive attention—which is to say that biographical issues of authorial attention, commitment, and personal background have to be taken into account in an evaluation of *Exodus*'s historical impact. Surprisingly, these issues have been ignored. Only one full-length volume about Leon Uris, whose best-selling fiction addressed subjects other than Israel and the Holocaust, has been published, and it contains very little biographical analysis; and the same inattention to biography detracts from the few serious scholarly articles that have been devoted to *Exodus*.[1]

Beyond biographical considerations, the chapter argues that while *Exodus*'s popular, pro-Israel narrative exhibited fidelity to the facts of historical occurrences, its driving concern was to develop and defend a particular vision of Jewish empowerment. This vision kept some Jewish subgroups (for instance, Haganah fighters) in close focus while relegating to the background other subgroups, sometimes in ways that would prove to be practically and ethically untenable in the long run. Mass marketing the 1950s Israeli vision of Jewish history, *Exodus* sold a posttrauma narrative that, for decades, allowed Jews and Christians to overcome stereotypical images of Jewish weakness and embrace astonishing and inspiring new images of Jewish strength. The *Exodus* narrative, however, could not hold over time, partly as a result of issues to be analyzed in other chapters of this book. Here, in a chapter devoted to Jewish history and *Exodus*, our argument is that Uris's narrative, while indisputably empowering for decades after its publication, was *transitional* because Jews and others would eventually come to doubt whether Uris's images of superhuman Israeli strength and utter Jewish vulnerability in the Diaspora truly overcome age-old stereotypical thinking about Jewish history.

In form, Uris's *Exodus* audaciously evokes the Pentateuch format, as though it is the Bible of modern Israel. Action in the book spans ha'apalah efforts in Cyprus, in late 1946, to transport Holocaust survivors to Palestine in defiance of Mandatory policy restricting Jewish immigration to the end of the Arab-Israeli war more than two years later. The final words of the novel's continuous narrative, which are attributed to its premier political figure, Barak Ben Canaan, relate telegraphically to the main political problem left lingering by Israel's triumph. "The Arabs created the Palestine refugee problem themselves," writes Uris through his mouthpiece, dispensing the other side's story in a few short words. The long novel focuses on the Jewish side's story, and the consecutive narrative concludes at the end of Book Four with an exalted feeling of triumph. With the capture of Elath (Eilat) in March 1949, at the end of the War of Independence, two thousand years of humiliating persecution draw to a close: "And so—the star of David, down for two thousands years, shone from Elath to Metulla, never to be lowered again." Uris adds a postscript, Book Five, which stretches beyond the narrative's chronological frame, and touches upon events and trends in Israel after the 1948 Independence War. These include mass airlifts of Sephardic Jewish immigrants from Asian and African countries and security threats in border areas posed by *fedayeen* terror incursions.

True to its exodus imagery, the novel ends with a Passover seder, the annual spring gathering when Jewish families relive the escape from bondage in Egypt. Conducted at the Ben Canaan Galilee home at the fictional moshav Yad El, the seder, a symbol of Jewish continuity, is disrupted by the tragic news of the terror murder of an immigrant Holocaust survivor, Karen Clement Hansen, at her Negev kibbutz. Since Karen's recovery is the specific concern of the novel's heroine, an American Protestant widow named Kitty Fremont, her death symbolizes ongoing hardship in Jewish life. This unhappy ending, however, comes after hundreds of pages that cast Jewish settlement in Israel as a corrective to the humiliations and persecution Jews faced for two millennia outside of their ancestral homeland, and so few readers would regard *Exodus* as a negative book. Instead, it is a celebration in which forces unleashed by the world wars lead to the fulfillment of a sacred ancient promise.

Uris built his case for Israel upon an exhaustive review of Jewish history in the modern period. Book Two of *Exodus,* "The Land is Mine," is devoted almost entirely to history and presents capsule descriptions of anti-Jewish persecution in Czarist Russia's Pale of Settlement, the rise of modern anti-Semitic movements in Central and Western Europe and their workings in notorious events such as France's end-of-the-nineteenth-century Dreyfus Affair, Herzl and the birth of organized Zionism, Zionist Aliyah waves of immigration to Eretz Israel before and after World War I, Big Power diplomacy and Arab politics during and after World War I, and Labor Zionist innovations and institutions, such as the communal settlement movement. Uris, however, did not pack all of history telling into this richly detailed second book of *Exodus*. Virtually from the novel's start, its fictional characters and events weave through flashback narrations or digressive background accounts of actual historical processes and events.

Less than sixty pages into the paperback edition, Uris provides a detailed exposition of events of the Holocaust, told from the point of view of an assimilated German Jewish household (Karen Clement's family). This section contains graphic, extremely disturbing information about Nazi policies and actions in conquered areas and then in concentration camps. The reader, in other words, has barely snuggled into an armchair to read about the Ari Ben Canaan orchestrated escape of three hundred young Jewish detainees in Cyprus before he or she is confronted with blood-curdling anecdotes about an SS *Haupsturmfuehrer* who liked watching infants die in barrels of freezing water, and the shooting of 33,000 Jews at Babi Yar to the approval of cheering Ukrainians.

Even within this first book of the novel, crucial historical events are presented from varying Jewish points of view. Thus, to underscore the enormity of the Holocaust crime, Uris details Dov Landau's Polish Jewish family, showing that Karen's prominent, assimilated father and Dov's modest, Jewish-oriented father "had absolutely nothing in common except that they were Jews." Despite vast differences of socioeconomic status, self-perception, and attitudes toward Jewish tradition and culture, the Nazis maliciously destroy both Dov's and Karen's families.

By engagingly hitching reams of factually verifiable information about Jew hatred to the easy-to-follow, highly dramatic plot of *Exodus,* the high school drop out Leon Uris instantly became mass culture's most influential explicator of the Jewish past and present. Through the first half of the twentieth century in Jewish America (or elsewhere in the Diaspora) nothing resembled the sweeping ambitions and mass results of this exercise in the dissemination of information about Jewish history.

More than offering a mere quantitative presentation of facts about the Jews, *Exodus* exerted strong influence upon normative choices reached in the postwar world regarding the use of this information. *Exodus* presented the Holocaust as a topic that could not be ignored in discussions of the history of World War II and its aftermath. Well-known testimonials about personal or communal experiences during the Holocaust found mass dissemination roughly at the same time as *Exodus*'s publication—published in 1947, *The Diary of Anne Frank* passed from stage production to the silver screen in 1959; *The Wall*, John Hersey's gripping account of the Warsaw ghetto resistance, was published in 1950; and a committed publisher produced an English translation of Elie Wiesel's *Night* in 1960. However, in contrast to seminal personal testimonies or focused accounts of one specific Holocaust topic, Uris's novel historicized the Holocaust, presenting the Jewish tragedy in Europe as the outcome of one chain of events and as the precursor of a new drama in the Middle East. For an educated, informed reader in 1958, dealing with a sustained argument about the Holocaust might not have been a novel experience; yet a situation in which hundreds of thousands of readers turned the pages of a gripping novel that conceptualized the Holocaust as part of one continuous story and that relied heavily upon Zionist analyses regarding the causes of the tragedy, and appropriate responses to it, was groundbreaking. Half a century later, mass culture has not finished processing all that was directly and bluntly conveyed and quietly implied by the perceptual revolution Uris triggered with his book.

Uris solidified the link between the Holocaust and Israeli statehood in a narrative where the Jewish tragedy in Europe becomes part of the past history and personal identity of all the fighters who struggled to establish the Jewish state. With the novel's two young heroes, Dov Landau and Karen Clement Hansen, this connection is readily evident—one takes part in the Warsaw ghetto uprising against the Nazis, the other survives the Holocaust by being put under the guardianship of a kindly Gentile couple in Denmark; then both become symbols of ha'apalah rescue, the Independence War struggle, and early Israeli state-building. While the Holocaust-era biographies of Dov and Karen are singularly and extensively detailed in the book, virtually all of Uris's characters have an apprehensible personal link with the Holocaust. For instance, on the eve of the Nazi genocide, the ubiquitous Ari Ben Canaan appears in Berlin on assignment with the Mossad L'Aliyah Bet and facilitates the last-minute escape of several German Jews (including Karen). And the half-Jewish British brigadier Bruce Sutherland, who moves in the novel from Cyprus to Safed, where he acts as a consultant to Haganah operations in the Galilee while remaining troubled by his nonfulfillment of his mother's final request for a Jewish burial, reportedly provided testimony at the Nuremberg war crime trials after having served as commander of troops that liberated Bergen-Belsen.

Uris does not allow the reader to compartmentalize any aspect of the Holocaust. Everything is swept up, avenged, and redeemed in the dramatic story of Israel's founding. An incapacitated Holocaust survivor such as the tragic Professor Clement cannot be seen in the absence of his daughter, a refugee immigrant to Israel and idealistic pioneer on a Negev kibbutz; it is impossible to digest the reported news of Karen's death in a fedayeen terror attack without recognizing that her fiancé, Dov Landau, a partisan in the Warsaw ghetto uprising and an Auschwitz survivor, will find a way to avenge it.

Causal links between Holocaust burdens and sorrows and Israel's statehood struggle are so inextricable that one subject simply cannot be contemplated in the absence of another. Rather than imposing something "heavy" upon the heroic story of Israel's founding, this linkage probably had the opposite effect. *Exodus* lightened 1950s anxieties about the Holocaust, thereby ushering the subject's entry, for better or worse, into popular culture discussion. *Exodus* was, as Uris proclaimed, "the story of the greatest miracle of our times," and it cast Jews in the role of triumphant heroes. Persuading insecure or uncertain readers about the powerful character of Jews in Israel, Uris's story made it easier for everyone to discuss intelligently the preceding tragedy in which Jews seemed to be cast in the role of history's ultimate losers.

Exodus is thus simultaneously permeated with an unrelenting awareness of Jewish tragedy and an equally unremitting faith in the Jews' ability to reverse historical fate in the triumphant state of Israel. Uris was as obsessed with the horror of the Holocaust as he was inspired by the victorious spirit of the Jewish state's founding, and generally of life in the democratic West after World War II. The key to *Exodus*'s power was the way its author balanced conflicting modes of tragedy and triumph in one narrative; examination of Uris's own life and values promises to shed light upon the character of this balancing act.

In 1989, the sixty-five-year-old best-selling American author Leon Uris traveled abroad on a Jewish mission sponsored by the B'nai Brith organization in the expectation of a "new Exodus" of Soviet Jews to Israel. In a speech delivered in Riga, Uris spoke from the heart when he proclaimed that "the day I became a Jew for life was the day we started to learn about the Holocaust." He explained, "I felt that I had to fulfill a promise I had made to myself, that I would try to do something in literature about the Holocaust, and to sort of pay my debt to the Jewish people."[2]

What was Uris's "debt to the Jewish people"? What sort of Jew was he, really? How did the Holocaust become so central in *Exodus* (as well as the novel's successor, *Mila 18*)? What emotions and normative beliefs controlled Uris's thinking and writing about the Holocaust? The answers to these questions can be culled with some precision from Uris's personal papers, life circumstances, and activities in the years leading up to the drafting of *Exodus*.

Leon Uris was born in Baltimore on August 3, 1924. Both his parents came from traditional Jewish families, but in his later life Uris traced his Jewish roots almost exclusively on his father's side, apparently on account of his volatile and problematic relationship with his mother, Anna Blumberg, and also because of a colorful Zionist pioneering episode in the life of his father, William Uris.

His father was born in Novogrudok, White Russia, in 1896,[3] and for a short period attended Rabbi Reines's Yeshiva in Lida, an important institution devised for pious young men by the founder of the religious Zionist Mizrachi movement. William's yeshiva days were cut short because his father, a *shochet* (ritual slaughterer) was only able and willing to pay two rubles a week to support the studies of another son, Eliezer, who was considered a more promising religious scholar. When World War I erupted, William's family was settled on the Polish border, in Wolkowysk in the Grodno province. William evaded service in the Czar's army and ended up working on the railroads after the Germans occupied his home area; when the armistice came, he was saving up funds for departure for Palestine on the Third Aliyah wave of immigration, a step that William's father, himself a Zionist, supported, and that the new Polish government was not likely to oppose.

En route to British-controlled Palestine, in the new era of Balfour Declaration policy in support of a Jewish national home, William posed for a portrait in Wolkowysk as part of a pioneering group of self-declared Zionist *halutz* pioneers. In Eretz Israel, he spent several months in 1920–21 as a Third Aliyah pioneer, working on a Labor Battalion road crew outside of Haifa and as a watchman at the Petah Tikva colony. A dreamy idealist prone to doctrinaire Marxism and critical of pragmatic adaptations of socialism that were being instituted by the Labor Zionist Poale Zion movement, William proved unable to assimilate the rough and ready spirit of the halutz

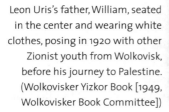

Leon Uris's father, William, seated in the center and wearing white clothes, posing in 1920 with other Zionist youth from Wolkovisk, before his journey to Palestine. (Wolkovisker Yizkor Book [1949, Wolkovisker Book Committee])

communes. He was too argumentative and impractical to last as a pioneer in Palestine—or, for that matter, to succeed as a small tradesman in America, where he arrived in search of family relations, and opportunity, after he left Eretz Israel in 1921.

With merciless insight, Leon Uris depicted his father's character and circumstances in a late autobiographical novel called *Mitla Pass* (1988).[4] Leon derided his father as a *shtetl Jew,* as a lifelong drifter whose aptitude for lively disputation about moot ideologies and beliefs rendered him unfit for success in worlds outside of the Pale of Settlement. This characterization of his father left its impress in Uris's fiction, where there is an unflinching preference for action, not words, and even an admirable character, such as *Exodus*'s Barak Ben Canaan, the father of the novel's superheroic protagonist Ari and a composite of various Labor Zionist icons, is indicted for wasting too many words in defense of the Jewish state at various international summits about the Arab-Jewish crisis in late Mandatory Palestine. Action is what Uris wanted in all of his novels' positive characters, partly because it was so preciously lacking in his father's biography.

William, whose family name switched from Yerusalimsky to Uris at Ellis Island, drifted from Pittsburgh, where he had relatives, to Philadelphia, Cleveland, and Baltimore. In the early days, mostly he sold subscriptions to the Yiddish Communist paper the *Freiheit,* and recruited for the Communist Party. Later he worked as a paperhanger, which was not a lucrative pursuit, particularly during the Depression when wallpaper was out of reach in most homes in the urban milieus known to the radical organizer.

In 1923, the twenty-seven-year-old immigrant met Anna Blumberg, a divorcée who had a five-year-old daughter, Essie, and married her five days after their first contact. This betrothal was an impulsive and highly unsuccessful decision. Leon's birth in 1924 was its sole positive outcome.

Anna, born in Havre de Grace, Maryland, was a complicated, hard-to-please woman. In *Mitla Pass,* Uris's dark account of his mother's background differs qualitatively from the negative but not atypical characterizations of his father as a hapless *schlimazel* whose dreams of a perfect world for all distract him from serious introspection about his own many personal imperfections as well as from any form of practical achievement. Uris's thoughts about his own family history were influenced by the fact that his father had brothers of genuine intellect, learning, and character who survived the Holocaust and settled in Israel. For all his father's faults, William's family had, in the Jewish world, stature and character. In contrast, Leon saw his mother's family as a study in Jewish pathology; apart from several searing pages in *Mitla Pass*[5] (which were published late in his life, in contravention of Uris's numerous previous declarations about his distaste for psycho-autobiographical writing), he basically fled from it, and her, all his adult life.

Indeed, in 1958–59, when *Exodus* was turning into a multimillion seller, Uris famously pronounced that he wrote his hard-hitting novel about Israel's military triumph because he was tired of American Jewish literati writing about nothing but how much they hated their parents.[6] For the most part, he shaped his writing career in line with this announcement; from the biographical standpoint, however, Uris's writing agenda can be misleading. That Uris found creative relief by writing action fantasies rather than psychological family dramas did not mean there was a shortage of the latter in his childhood.

The mother image Uris rendered in his fictional memoir *Mitla Pass* is repulsive. The character modeled after Anna Blumberg appears as a self-centered woman who adheres to the forms of her traditional upbringing and religion without grasping their true spirit, who subjects a succession of husbands to various sexual torments and then abandons them at moments of dire humanitarian need (one of the husbands deserted by this mother figure is a World War I veteran with a severe respiratory ailment), and who is too psychologically imbalanced to notice that she spoils her own parvenu agenda of making it materially in America due to her inability to make minor changes in traditional Jewish observances that hold no meaning for her.[7]

In this biting, autobiographical novel, *Mitla Pass,* Uris's attempt to extenuate the disastrous behavioral patterns he attributes to his own mother is lame and unconvincing. The author inserts in *Mitla Pass* some loose references to patterns of brute sexual behavior that are supposedly passed on from generation to generation in repressive traditional Jewish societies and ultimately poison the outlook of the book's mother figure, who is the daughter of a miserable, passive-aggressive Orthodox tailor who emigrates from Queenstown, Ireland to Havre de Grace, Maryland. In his fiction, Uris used such perfunctory references to transgenerational sexual frustration as an analytic key to the understanding of cultures he considered to be backward and violent, from the contemporary Middle East to Europe in the Nazi era. The appearance of this theme of inherited sexual repression and behavioral brutality in an autobiographical, coming to America novel is therefore disarming.

In terms of understanding where Leon Uris and *Exodus* came from, the scant information we have about his mother, none of it flattering, points to a few overlapping conclusions. Uris's lifelong recoil from his mother's background and personality prevented him from exploring ideas of "return" in intimate, personal terms, as a search to recover or reinterpret emotions and values of his own childhood. And apart from such psycho-biographical speculation, Uris's scathing, embittered portrayal of his mother's world sets him apart objectively from many other American Jewish writers. Whether as irony or measured fact, success-story conceptualizations of Jewish immigrants coming to America could never be a factor in his fiction. For Leon, his family's story, particularly on his mother's side, was so bad that he did not want to think seriously about it. The author of *Exodus* lived in permanent exile from the idea of America as a Jewish success story—that is, he kept his distance from the dominant topic of American Jewish writing.[8] He would look elsewhere in the Jewish world for a utopian model of immigrant success.

Pregnant, Anna left William in Cleveland and returned to her mother's apartment in Baltimore to have their child. William was not in Baltimore when his son was born; it is not clear whether the boy was named Leon in tribute to Trotsky, in deference to his father's radical politics. The parents' union dissolved forever when Leon was just five or six. He stayed with his mother, who drifted to Norfolk, and he attended J. E. B. Stuart grammar school in that city. When his divorce was settled, William lost touch with his son for fifteen months. Miserable, he stepped up his work for the Communist Party, migrated to Philadelphia, and found another wife, Anna Rabinovitz, with whom he uncharacteristically found decades of stability. Years went by, and Leon and Essie returned with their mother to Baltimore, where he attended Garrison Junior High School. On weekends, his mother pinned a baggage pin on him and sent him by train to visit his father in Philadelphia; this shuffling routine continued until Leon was fourteen.[9]

At that age, the teenager began to compile a record for truancy and failure in various school subjects. Nobody doubted his intelligence or believed that he was antisocial. In Philadelphia, where fifteen-year-old Leon asked to be enrolled in Bartram High School, the father recalled that the house was often "gay with joy and laughter from youngsters" brought over by Leon. His son, an "avid reader of books and plays," was "loved and admired for his intellect, his perception and as a raconteur." Still, even in his father's appreciative recollection, there were worrisome signs. Leon was, his father attested, "restless, and somewhat unruly, very emotional." He added some "F" grades to his repertoire of adolescent rebellion. After he became a famous writer, Uris loved to cut a figure of self-made success by disclosing in publicity materials that he had flunked English at Bartram—the claim troubled officials, who combed the school's archives and announced that Leon failed physics, not English. High school, at any event, stimulated little interest.[10]

On occasion, as in the 1970 novel *QB VII* (based on Uris's involvement in a Holocaust libel case),[11] a benevolent-spirited teacher or editor appears in Uris's writing, but his penchant for meticulous research in the preparation of historical novels stemmed from self-motivation, not from training provided by a mentor. Perhaps it, too, reflected the psychological residue of a difficult upbringing. Uris loved to teach himself, and millions of readers, about Jewish History and Irish History and other topics because he assumed that little was really learned in school.

One element, at least, in his upbringing appears to have stirred highly charged, ambivalent responses during Leon's teenage years, rather than apathetic withdrawal. Up to the outbreak of World War II, he felt torn emotionally between his father's Communist activism, and the liberal humanitarianism of FDR's New Deal. As a well-known, patriotically American writer, Uris preferred not to reminisce about this boyhood dilemma so long as world politics remained locked in Cold War categories. With Glasnost in place and the end of the Cold War in sight, Uris at last spoke candidly about the politics of his youth. In his 1989 Riga lecture, an emotional Uris spoke about the political atmosphere he imbibed in his father's home.[12] In the 1930s, Uris recalled, the Communists were the only group that struggled unhesitatingly for the empowerment of underprivileged groups, particularly blacks. On the one hand, Uris was surrounded by radical idealists who crusaded for international justice, such as two young men who signed up for the Abraham Lincoln Brigade in the Spanish Civil War (in *QB VII*, Uris admiringly fictionalized their experience). On the other hand, FDR was "like a father to me," and also Stalin's purges and the Soviet-Nazi pact incited "tremendous disenchantment" in the American Communist movement. The succession of impressions and events in the 1930s bred ambivalence. Fifty years later, the ambiguities still echoed. In the same Riga reminiscence, Uris declared simultaneously that "we were very certain we were doing the right thing as young Communists" and also that "being an American I never totally embraced Communism."[13]

Pearl Harbor resolved the political ambiguities, erased the alienated truancy of the lonely teenager, and ultimately mandated the ethical and political orientations of Uris's writing. The eruption of World War I had set his father on an indefinite life course. William evaded the Czar's call-up; and in several senses, he did not know where he stood during and after the Great War. For Leon, Pearl Harbor had exactly the opposite effect. Forever thereafter, military valor would be the answer to his own individual predicaments and to every group problem Uris took seriously. For our purposes, it is important to demonstrate how the problems of Uris's youth, and his solution to them by enlistment in the U.S. Marine Corps after Pearl Harbor, governed much of his thinking and writing about the Holocaust and Jewish history in *Exodus*.

In January 1942, the underage Leon abruptly demanded that his father sign a Marine Corps application. When William refused, the determined seventeen-year-old traveled from Philadelphia to Baltimore to obtain his mother's consent. She, too, refused. Leon, however, persisted, flashing Navy and Marine applications and ultimately leaving his parents no choice.[14]

Uris trained in San Diego and was shipped off for the first island-hopping offensives in the Pacific via New Zealand and Hawaii. In his first novel, the 1953 best seller *Battle Cry,* Uris provides a vivid, albeit idealized, account of his enlistment and training as a radio operator in the U.S. Marines.[15]

Generally, Uris made his mark as a popular writer at a propitious moment. The book business had been part of America's mass culture since 1939, when paperback marketing began in earnest (the first best seller in this paperback revolution was Dale Carnegie's *How to Win Friends and Influence People;* paperback sales began to soar in the 1940s when publishers discovered how to distribute their wares via newspaper and magazine stands).[16] In 1951, paperback sales reached 214 million in the United States, an astronomic leap from the 1939 sales figure, 3 million. In 1953, the year of Uris's debut as a writer, insiders commented favorably on the dynamism and diversity of the

Uris selling books for his first novel, *Battle Cry.* (Harry Ransom Humanities Research Center, the University of Texas at Austin)

paperback industry, which was dominated by seven firms (the *New York Times Book Review* editor David Dempsey described the market as a "highly competitive mélange of serious literature and trash, of self-help and pseudo-science, of sex and inspiration").[17] America's most popular novelist in this postwar period was Erskine Caldwell (after its publication by Penguin in 1946, Caldwell's *God's Little Acre* sold 3.5 million copies; by the early 1960s, sales of Caldwell's books reached 64 million). A political leftist from Georgia, Caldwell wrote in a distinctively American naturalist style; indisputably, his strongest skill was as storyteller and his merits continue to be debated.[18] This same talent for threading events together in a page-turning tale is what attracted publishers to Uris's *Battle Cry*. In fact, the fight to win the paperback rights for Uris's first novel became an event in American book publishing. Pocket Books was the frontrunner for the paperback rights, but Oscar Dystel of Bantam Books put together a persuasive bid of $25,000 and a film plan with Warner Brothers. Owing to overdistribution of low-selling books, Bantam Books was at the time struggling financially, and the Uris deal was considered a godsend. "The place went wild" when Uris signed with Bantam, Dystel recalled. "That was the beginning of the turnaround at Bantam."[19] Beyond Uris's evident skills as a storyteller, *Battle Cry* had, for publishers, one compelling feature. Readers in this period were drawn mesmerizingly to war stories. During World War II, America's most popular novels were religious epics, but starting in 1948 with Norman Mailer's *The Naked and the Dead* and Irwin Shaw's *The Young Lions*, war fiction was publishing gold.[20]

In its opening sequences, *Battle Cry's* kaleidoscopic narrative presents the adventures and viewpoints of a number of marines (the latter part of the book is narrated largely in the first person by a good-hearted sergeant named Mac). Uris's own real-life experience is reflected in the novel as a mix of the attitudes and activities of a few characters, including an athletic, eager achiever from Baltimore named Danny Forester whose enlistment and subsequent romantic entanglements temporarily befuddle his family and a tough intellectual named Marion, who diligently keeps notes of his training and combat experiences for future writings while finding effective ways to rein the antics of the bad-attitude incorrigibles in the unit. None of these autobiographical prototypes are Jewish. Uris's depiction of the hard-drinking shenanigans of these green marines as they head off to the brutal warfare of the Pacific retains a feel of authenticity, even if it did not challenge conventions of patriotic war writing. More than anything, this novel of life in the Marine Corps projects an inner search for authority, constructive discipline, and practical fellowship, which were poignantly lacking in Uris's childhood homes.

This pressing personal need for order and fellowship kept all of the characterizations in *Battle Cry* within strict bounds. The author allows the reader glimpses of the self-destructive binges of marines on furlough and the self-interest of officers for whom the sacrifice of fighting men in battle means glory and personal promotion. Also, as in the example of a Mexican American bemoaning redneck prejudice in his native Texas town, passing echoes of the rough ethnic undertone of prewar American society can be heard in Uris's narrative. However, none of these dynamics challenge the novel's overriding understanding of the marine experience as a just fight waged by men who came to genuinely care for one another.

In addition to the delineation of marine camaraderie, the author of *Battle Cry* had a second purpose, and he molded it in his novel in such an outlandishly unconnected and hyperbolic fashion that few of his critics or readers have seen fit to comment on it. The topic, however, warrants attention here, as a biographical turnstile and also as a telling suggestion that in the making of *Exodus,* the state of Israel itself figured ultimately as a *means* to a supreme end of empowerment pursued urgently by Leon Uris. In the Marshall and Gilbert islands, Uris took up arms against the Japanese; but emotionally the battle he waged was against demeaning perceptions of Jewish weakness embedded in American society and its armed forces as well as against the lethal form of anti-Semitism that generated the Nazi genocide in Europe.

Within the covers of *Battle Cry,* the Japanese are a faceless enemy, and they are forgotten the instant the reader reaches its final words. In contrast, lingering forever as the enemy in Uris's writing is the stereotype of the vulnerable, cringing Jew. Just as much as he was revisiting his father's Third Aliyah experience and imaginatively remedying its disappointing conclusion, when he wrote *Exodus,* Uris authored the most influential Jewish book of the postwar era in order to rectify stereotypes and realities of Jewish weakness that perturbed him throughout basic training in the Marine Corps, and that also resulted in unimaginable catastrophe in Europe's death camps. The full frontal assault Uris waged in *Exodus* against stereotypes of weak, defenseless Jews is foreshadowed in the final pages of *Battle Cry,* Uris's debut novel about World War II that is not remembered for having said anything about the Jewish people.

Two Jewish war heroes suddenly enter *Battle Cry*'s Marine Corps landscape, in the final third of the five-hundred-page book. One, Jake Levin, is a homely, medium-sized radio operator. A drafted man thrust into a unit of volunteers, Levin comes across at first as an eager wannabe who does double duty on guard shifts and who trains out in the cold until chilblains virtually cripple him. "I ain't no pop off. I was trying to be one of the guys," Levin explains. In turn, Mac, the sergeant-narrator, is equally obvious. "Levin," he asks, "why are you trying so hard? Is it because you are a Jew?" With one of the unit's bigots, a Texan named Speedy Gray, ranting in the background about yellow Jews, Mac's question does not need to be answered. In battle, however, Levin demonstrates his mettle. In fact, in Uris's rendering of his marine unit's climactic moment of combat, the turning point at Red Beach One at Garapan occurs when this Brooklyn Jew sacrifices his life by racing for a blinker gun and signals to the crew of an amphibious "Alligator" tractor. This heroic blood sacrifice turns the tide of the battle and also eliminates anti-Semitism in the unit. Speedy, the Texas redneck, attends to Levin's funeral arrangements in solemn respect, making sure that a Star of David, not a cross, is placed on his coffin.

As the historian Deborah Dash Moore has shown, Jewish service in the armed forces during World War II contributed in perceptible ways to the overcoming of prejudice and to enhanced integration in American society.[21] Levin's portrait is therefore based on a reality, but it is nevertheless disarming. Handling other ethnic characters in his novel, Uris patiently explored an array of topics in home environments; with Levin, in contrast, a few rapid-fire, secondhand remarks about Brooklyn sufficed. That is because Uris conceptualized the Jew in armed combat not as a complex character but rather as a concentrated rebuttal to anti-Semitic stereotypes. From the Marine Corps at Guadalcanal and Tarawa in *Battle Cry,* to the Haganah at Safed and Latrun in *Exodus,* to the Jewish fighters of the Warsaw ghetto uprising in *Mila 18,* Uris waged the same war, standing anti-Semitic stereotypes on their head and depicting two-dimensional pop-up pictures of Jewish war heroes to be pasted over unbearably humiliating and sorrowful images of Jewish weakness.

This device of stereotype reversal comes out yet more sharply in the figure of *Battle Cry*'s second Jewish marine, Max Shapiro. Uris's first super-Jew, this marine raider is the Pacific theater ancestor of *Exodus* hero Ari Ben Canaan.

The short, bespectacled Shapiro has the look and the name of a ghetto Jew and the miraculous bravery of an Israeli *Exodus* hero. In Micronesia, at the ferocious battle of Tarawa, Shapiro turns the tide for the Marines by devising a ploy that pulls the Japanese into a trap. His battle grit is legendary and inspirational in the special "Fox" commando squad, which Shapiro commands. Uris deliberately contrasts this Jewish commander's no-nonsense battle instincts with the cowardice of his deputy, a WASP named Bryce, a college professor whose erudition produces no practical benefit. During lulls in the fighting, the Jewish commander takes part in the high jinks marine mischief of beer guzzling and creative procurement of valued equipment, whereas the brainy Protestant Bryce remains aloof and unpopular. When the fighting resumes at Tarawa, Shapiro's courage appears as a "holy image or something inviolable." He ambles fearlessly about the trees, pointing out Japanese snipers for his men to cut down.

Uris's hyperbolic description of Shapiro merits quotation, since it demonstrates how his own U.S. military experience was heavily, even oppressively, invested with concern about overcoming anti-Semitic stereotypes about soft-bellied Jews:

> The men in the CP gazed in awe. Max Shapiro was moving as unconcernedly through the hailstorm of lead as if he were taking a Sunday stroll through a park. . . . The Captain [Shapiro] was acting like he was a holy image or something inviolable. His appearance was like magic and put iron into the embattled boys he led. The legend of Two Gun Shapiro was no idle slop-shute story; it was quite true. He walked from rock to rock and tree to tree slapping his boys on the back as if he was coaching a football game.[22]

Uris recalled stormy quarrels with his editors at G. P. Putnam about drafts of *Battle Cry,* but it appears that his publisher overlooked this hyped-up depiction of super-Jew, Max Shapiro, in Micronesia. In the book's main draft, just a few of the young author's far-fetched words about Shapiro were red penciled.[23]

Did Uris imagine super-Jews saving America's war in the Pacific because in his time in the Marines he experienced a lack of respect for East Coast city Jews? Were brave Jake Levin and Max Shapiro figments of psychic compensation? For years, this possibility touched a sensitive nerve, and Uris shunned public discussion about it. *Battle Cry* was marketed aggressively as the first book ever to be sold with a money-back guarantee; and since it was pitched, truthfully, as a patriotic war story written by a proud marine veteran, Uris was not positioned to expound about any ethnic hard knocks he had taken in the U.S. armed forces.

The impolitic interpretation appealed to members of Uris's family circle, however. *Battle Cry*, which became a motion picture in 1955 (Uris wrote the screenplay solo, which was an unusual feather in the cap for a first-time novelist), stirred interest in Israel, where Uris had several close relatives on his father's side. In early 1956, a Hebrew translation of the novel, published by Masada Press, topped the fiction best-seller list in Israel, and (as will be discussed later) a few months into the year, its handsome Jewish American author trekked far and wide in the country, collating research materials for what became *Exodus*. Uris was somebody to talk about, and his relatives did that.

Uris's father had three brothers and a sister in the country, each in possession of his or her own gripping war story about escape from destruction and personal or group renewal. The most learned relative was Leon's uncle Eliezer, who survived the Holocaust with his wife and sons, and who would in the early 1960s publish a number of significant Hebrew memoirs about the Holocaust.[24] Without directly acknowledging that he was writing about his nephew (the uncle only dropped veiled hints about his connection to his subject by occasionally identifying *Battle Cry*'s author as Uris-Yerushalmi), Dr. Eliezer Yerushalmi published in the *Ma'ariv* newspaper (April 20, 1956) a review of *Battle Cry*.[25] Opening with an anecdote about Uris mixing it up with three tough Irish Americans on a train, as the group headed west on a train to boot camp, the article accentuated rough ethnic mixing in the U.S. armed forces.

Yerushalmi wrote that his nephew's *Battle Cry* "could not legitimately ignore one problem that troubles any Jew who served in the armies of states from the West and the East, and that is anti-Semitism." In periods of war, Yerushalmi claimed, latent anti-Semitism "sheds its cloak and appears with all its dark lusts and . . . zoological hatred." The author of *Battle Cry*, wrote Uris's Israeli uncle, notes in passing that the disease of anti-Semitism punctured Marine Corps camaraderie; but Uris was unable to resist saccharine Hollywood pressures and capped his brief portrayal of Jews in the marines with a "happy ending" that "disrupts the unity and spirit of the novel," wrote Yerushalmi.[26]

This interpretation holding that he had concealed Jew baiting in the Marines riled Uris. Petulantly, he complained to his father about his uncle. "Eliezer wrote an absolutely ridiculous article here full of baloney," Uris wrote to his father from Israel on May 13, 1956. "There will be some words."[27] Yerushalmi had hit a raw nerve, and Uris's defensiveness was disingenuous. Ironically, the first aggrieved group Leon Uris overlooked in his writing about war was not the Palestinians, but rather American Jews. He was not prepared to come forth candidly about hard knocks taken by Jewish GIs during World War II.

Late in his life, Uris confessed that the Marine Corps in 1942 was not exactly a welcoming home for a city Jew. In 1989, en route to the Soviet Union, Uris spoke in thoughtfully measured terms about the quality of his marine experience, from the Jewish standpoint. "In my battalion of 800 men there were half a dozen Jews, or less," recalled Uris. "While I didn't suffer any physical abuse from anti-Semitism, I met boys from all over America, farmers, cowboys, men who had come from thousands of miles away, who had typical, ignorant anti-Semitic views." Anti-Semitism incited nothing sinister in Uris's own military experience, and yet "it was something that was very uncomfortable."[28] The Marine Corps was not exactly the constructively integrating crucible of action depicted by his fictional memoir, *Battle Cry.* Leon Uris would have to keep searching for a story that would, at least imaginatively, take him to a home he never had as a child.

In 1946–47, just as he was settling into civilian life in the San Francisco Bay Area after his discharge from the Marines, Uris received a draft manuscript, written in broken English and tentatively titled *Hellenic Interlude,* produced by another one of his paternal uncles, Aaron Yerushalmi.[29] Aaron's story shocked and thrilled his family. During World War II, Aaron, sometimes called Harry, enlisted in the British army along with 30,000 other Jews from the Yishuv, and he advanced to the rank of sergeant in the Palestine Brigade. After his unit was sent to Crete, Aaron was captured by the Nazis; he escaped, was recaptured, and finally freed himself from a blood-curdling ordeal when he landed in Italy with the Palestine Brigade. Aaron and his family wanted this story told, and Leon agreed to represent and possibly repackage it. By June 1947, Uris was peddling a synopsis of *Hellenic Interlude* to various possible sponsors. Leon polished his uncle's English in this synopsis, but he faithfully recorded Aaron's details and judgments. The June 4, 1947, negative response of the Jewish Book Guild of America was typical—the guild said the outline was "interesting and dramatic," but not fit for publication.[30]

The manuscript Uris received a few months after his return to civilian life provided a close-to-home example of personal courage in the confrontation with Nazism, and it also offered testimony from a family member about the reach of the Nazis' criminal genocide. As importantly, Uris's failure to publish his uncle Aaron's tale as a story about Jewish survival was a significant dress rehearsal for *Exodus,* since it forced him to think more creatively and systematically about the presentation of one ethnic group's grievances, experiences, and dreams in mass culture.

His uncle's 1947 manuscript was haunted by lugubrious awareness of the extent of the Nazi crime.[31] The synopsis contained horrifying descriptions of how Nazi captors separated Jewish prisoners from other soldiers who had been captured at Corinth and transported them to a special camp. ("Ovoroff was the Greek concentration camp. It had a few advantages. They used a firing squad instead of ovens and gas chambers.") Aaron wrote about how guards beat prisoners senseless in the camp, took groups of eighty or ninety inmates to a yard and chased and beat them for several hours and periodically entered cells and selected a quota of Jews for instant execution. Later in the story, Aaron and a few comrades from the Palestine Brigade are transported to Stalag XVIII in a small village called Wolfsberg. Yerushalmi's text stresses Nazi anti-Semitic propagandizing and selective predations against Jews. The Nazi guards, the manuscript noted, "published a paper and put books into our library to twist their slimy theories. They showed us pictures of Jews raping German women. They tried to weed the Jews out of the compound for a special torture camp."

Uris was unable to find a publisher for Aaron's manuscript. His uncle was an unknown writer and, as importantly, the text contained material infused with awareness about the Holocaust of European Jewry that was not readily absorbable in mass markets of the late 1940s and early 1950s. (Aaron Yerushalmi published his memoir in Hebrew in 1957.[32]) Then, after his Marine Corps novel sold over two million copies, Uris rode the coattails of *Battle Cry*'s success and reworked his uncle Aaron's war story for publication under his own name. After *Battle Cry* publisher G. P. Putnam rejected the new version, called *The Angry Hills*, Uris secured a contract with Random House. *The Angry Hills* carried an author's blurb up front disclosing that the story was loosely based on the wartime experiences of, and a manuscript written by, Uris's uncle, a veteran of the Palestine Brigade.[33]

In retrospect, the blurb looks like a formality. *The Angry Hills* sanitized and mostly erased his uncle's story. The only things that remained were the Greek setting and episodes of courageous escape from Nazi pursuers. Whereas the fundamental concept of Aaron's original story was valiant Jewish survival in defiance of the global ambition of the Nazis' genocidal anti-Semitism, Uris repackaged the narrative as an American action thriller and sprinkled in a few trimmings about the indestructibility of the democratic idea.

In a tentative, unconvincing way Uris imagined himself to be writing installments of an American epic about World War II. *The Angry Hills* (published in 1955) has a few loose connectors to *Battle Cry*—for instance, its protagonist, an American widower from San Francisco named Michael Morrison, is a struggling writer whose minor novel, called *Home Is the Hunter,* recapitulates words recorded in the diary of *Battle Cry*'s literary marine, Marion. The fast-paced *Angry Hills,* however, was not written on a grand scale. Morrison unintentionally becomes, in newly Nazi-occupied Greece, a courier of valuable information for British intelligence, and the story conveys little more than the improvisations of this clever and brave amateur spy as he eludes ruthless Nazi pursuers. The moral of the story, elucidated at its end by a worldly Greek wheeler-dealer to an outwitted Nazi officer, is the invincibility of ordinary, freedom-loving Americans (along with the incorruptible peasants from the angry hills of Greek resistance): "Oh, yes, the world is filled with bumbling amateurs like Mr. Morrison. They are given to sentiment, they wrangle with their consciences, but somehow the Michaels . . . end up on the path of righteousness."

That message played relatively well with the public in the mid-1950s. At most, *Angry Hills* received lukewarm praise, such as a mid-October 1955 *New York Post* review that noted that "there is nothing really wrong with Uris' thriller" except that established masters of espionage yarns, such as Manning Coles, "do it so much better." Other reviews correctly predicted that *The Angry Hills* would never attain the sales popularity of *Battle Cry*.[34] Uris was mostly disappointed with the book's reception, though by the end of the decade he took solace when interest in the story in the United Kingdom led to the production of a film (starring Robert Mitchum as Michael Morrison, with Theodore Bikel in a supporting role). Incidentally, the unexpected and delayed modest measure of success of Uris's sanitized version of *Hellenic Interlude* caused Aaron Yerushalmi to wonder whether he had gotten his share. That feeling soured relations between nephew and uncle—in 1975, almost thirty years after Leon hustled the text as his uncle's literary representative, Uris grumpily informed his father that he had received a season's greeting card from his uncle Aaron, "that darling man who managed not to mention a thing about all the millions I owe him for *The Angry Hills*."[35]

Such family unpleasantness would not be worth mentioning were it not connected to the psychology underlying Uris's writing about the Holocaust. While any interpretation of the fact's meaning can only be speculative, it has to mean something that the writer who popularized Israel's image as the Jews' political and ethical redemption after the Holocaust had periodically uneasy relations with two uncles and an aunt in Israel (his father's siblings) who were survivors. The two uncles, Eliezer and Aaron Yerushalmi, also wrote at length about the Holocaust; their works had none of the popular impact of the Holocaust writing produced by their American nephew who spent World War II in the U.S. Marine Corps. In Aaron's case, Uris was unable to sell an English version of Aaron's story and subsequently bowdlerized it in *Angry Hills*, whereas with regard to Eliezer, who published an important diary of his experiences in Shavli, a Lithuanian ghetto, the case can be made that the nephew's dramatized writing about the Holocaust is a mirror image of his uncle's gruelingly unembellished documentation.[36] The third relative, his father's sister Esther, survived a concentration camp and settled in Eretz Israel but apparently became mentally unstable. In spring 1956, on his research visit to Israel, Uris paid one visit to his aunt Esther but was "startled" by her "weird character" and decided to "avoid her."[37] (In *Exodus*, Uris appears to have imaginatively reworked feelings generated by this reunion with a psychologically damaged survivor in the scene where teenage immigrant Karen Clement-Hansen tracks down her father, formerly a distinguished professor, in Mandatory Palestine, but finds that his ordeal in the camps has left him completely incommunicative.)

Uris's handling of his uncle's manuscript was not seamless, but he appears to have taken something more than the bare setting of time and place from it. Elements in its spirit of resistance inspired him. The image of Greek peasants as freedom fighters opposing the Nazis in "angry hills" where democratic ideals first flourished encouraged Uris to think about World War II in creatively new ways. His sense of the meaning of victory was broadening. World War II meant more than the defeat of the Nazi menace as the flip side to the triumph of the great Allied powers. The victory could bring new worlds into being, unite the past to present, and allow peoples to rediscover themselves.

When Uris describes the circumstances and motivations of Morrison, the writer-hero of *The Angry Hills,* it almost seems as though he is previewing his own impulse to write about the resurrection of the Greeks' ancient counterparts, the Jews: "As he came from the hills an urge to write again overwhelmed him—to write about wonderful, beautiful people he never knew existed. People who faced crushing tragedy not with defeatism, but with hope."

As a novelist, Leon Uris compiled a divergent track record on Jewish issues before he set out to write the *Exodus* story about the establishment of the state of Israel. The plot episodes of *Battle Cry* furnished Uris with no logical reason to depict superman Jews as the saviors of American island hopping in the Pacific; yet in his first novel, Uris invented Jewish war heroism of a sort that could never have existed. For his second novel, Uris had in his hands unimpeachable evidence of small-scale, but genuine, Jewish war heroism in defiance of the Nazi menace; yet in this case Uris proved unable to document and publish a real-life Exodus story of one individual's, his uncle's, escape to freedom. The vicissitudes of book publishing helped produce this contrast, but generally Uris's inconsistent handling of the same issue, Jewish power or Jewish weakness, reflects the intense pressure upon his identity and writing that was exerted after the war by revelations of the Nazi crime.

Such, then, was Uris's existential journey en route to the writing of *Exodus.* By the mid-1950s, he had a deep need to write about empowered, courageous Jews, but he lacked both a setting and a convincing way of writing about Jewish soldiers. *Exodus* emerged out of its author's decade-long experimentation with models of Jewish redemption and recovery. Thanks to arduous research, a knack for action storytelling, and some good fortune, Uris succeeded monumentally where these early, forgotten efforts failed. He told a story that urged millions of readers to discard Holocaust-era images of Jews as defenseless, cowering victims and to see them instead as heroic masters of their own fate.

These empowered images, however, applied only to one group of Jews, the victorious Israelis. Uris's *Exodus* identified Jewish strength with Israelis, and did little to challenge anti-Semitic stereotypes regarding Jewish vulnerability in the Diaspora. The novel popularized the pitiless, "sheep to the slaughter" orientations that informed Israeli thinking about the Holocaust in the 1950s. The idea, which drew upon the long-standing Zionist ideology of the "negation of the Diaspora," held that Jews were incapable of defending themselves against Nazi violence because centuries of Diaspora humiliation and persecution kept them weak.[38] Inherent in this view was a merciless retroactive accusation holding that European Jews had made the wrong choice when they rejected Zionism and chose not to immigrate to Eretz Israel before genocidal Nazism rose to power and annihilated them. Describing this stance upheld by the core group of native-born Israelis toward Holocaust survivors, sociologist Oz Almog writes that "feelings of compassion and empathy for the survivors were accompanied by an 'I told you so' attitude."[39] Having little in his own personal background to urge love and compassion for Diaspora Jewish life, Uris identified with these Israeli orientations. He was drawn to Israelis as Jews who had risen to the challenge of the World War II and defined themselves anew via military triumph, just as he himself had done as a U.S. Marine.

In a revealing letter written to his father in March 1958, on the eve of *Exodus*'s publication, Uris explained that he had read *The Diary of Anne Frank,* had seen its stage production, and was "tremendously shaken up by it." Despite his "feelings of compassion" for the story's victims, Uris recoiled viscerally from *The Diary of Anne Frank*. "I do not like to see Jews hiding in attics, and feel there is something far more decent about dying in dignity which is, of course, the choice that every Jew had," he declared.[40] Uris added in his letter that he preferred the story of the Warsaw ghetto uprising (which he would not long thereafter turn into the topic of his *Exodus* follow-up, *Mila 18*).

Presenting the Holocaust as the supreme test of Jewish endurance and honor, *Exodus*'s narrative rewarded only those Jews who engaged Guadalcanal-type acts of heroic resistance against the Nazis. The old ghetto Jews who related passively to their tormentors had no license to live in Uris's imaginative world. Condemning the Frank family, Uris expressed this view with blunt remorselessness. He wrote to this father about how he "resented the fact that this family subjected to this type of life showed no anger toward the Nazis. I hope this type of Jew has ceased to exist forever."[41]

In *Exodus*, Uris used fact-filled flashback scenes and somewhat oblique indictments to express his own resentment toward Holocaust victims who did not take part in acts of military defiance against the Nazis. Readers of these flashback sequences stayed focused on plot development, and so they probably never grasped the implications of problematic suggestions holding that Hitler's victims deserved their fates because they were not Zionists. In one scene, recollected in the aftermath of *Kristallnacht* in Germany, Ari Ben Canaan suddenly appears and angrily berates local Jews in response to Professor Clement's request for exit visas for his own family. Ari's tirade casts Hitler's targets as victims of their own political mistakes and fawning assimilation. Speaking to Karen's father as a Zionist immigration emissary, Ari explains: "For five years we have pleaded, we have begged you to leave Germany. Now even if you can get out the British won't let you enter Palestine. 'We are Germans . . . they won't hurt us,' you said."

The forty-two days of resistance in the Warsaw uprising, recounted in *Exodus* in flashback sequences detailing the biography of young hero Dov Landau, served as Uris's heroic standard, and he remained fascinated and inspired throughout his life by this story of how a small group of desperate Jews held off the Nazis for a spell of time longer than the brief intervals that elapsed before the Nazi blitzkrieg conquered entire European countries. Dov's evolving circumstances and character in *Exodus* are a microcosm of Uris's outlook on the Holocaust. The youth's psychic-emotional problems are inevitable outcomes of the war, since Uris understood the Nazi crime as having damaged absolutely everything in Europe, but his recovery in Eretz Israel is preordained by his heroism in Warsaw. Cleverly,

Uris hinges the youth's survival at Auschwitz, as well as the fate of the *Exodus* ship rescue operation, upon Dov's expertise in forging documents; the message is that nothing authentic could sprout in Europe, and that skills involving the distortion of the historical record would obviously appeal to, or beguile, Nazi marauders in Europe and oil-maddened British oppressors in the Middle East.

In *Exodus,* revenge is the natural handmaiden of settlement in Eretz Israel in the recovery of Jews from acts of outrageous persecution. The crucial factor in Dov's recovery is his activity with the Jewish underground, called the Maccabees in *Exodus,* but obviously modeled on the right-wing Irgun.[42] While the Irgun promotes contemporary political objectives of terrorizing the British into yielding concessions on immigration and land issues and ultimately surrendering political control of Palestine, its actions in *Exodus* unmistakably quench revenge impulses. One example of the Maccabees' work is the reprisal killing of vulgarly anti-Semitic British Major Fred Caldwell, who had earlier brought about the savage murder of a Maccabee prisoner by dumping the Jewish boy in front of an enraged Arab mob in Nablus. Flung atop the Old City of Jerusalem's Dung Gate, Caldwell's dead body has upon it the Maccabee-written inscription, "an eye for an eye." That biblical revenge motto is the title of *Exodus*'s Book Three, which is filled with examples of collaborative reprisals conducted by the left-wing Palmach and the right-wing Maccabees, culminating in the shrewdly executed revenge assassination of a British military commander, General Sir Arnold Haven-Hurst, who had earlier ordered lethal strikes against the Yishuv's political leadership and who is caught and shot with his pants down during a tryst with an Arab woman in Jerusalem's Baka quarter.

The description of Dov at the end of the novel constitutes *Exodus*'s most cogent statement of Uris's belief that the Jews' use of terror and violence to intimidate and deter their enemies and to redress wrongs perpetrated by those foes is a natural occurrence in their rebirth as a political nation: "He [Dov] had completely burst out of his former darkness. Now he was warm and filled with humor and showed uncommon understanding for those people who suffered. Still rather slight in stature, with sensitive features, Dov had become a handsome young man. He and Karen were deeply in love." As the novel ends, Dov's place of residence is up in the air; an expert in water science with a degree from the Weizmann Institute, he is considering continuing his studies at MIT.

That seems like a long commute for a character who a few years earlier starts out as an angrily dysfunctional survivor, screaming and hurling objects in a Displaced Person (DP) camp in Cyprus. After chronicling the disastrous Holocaust experiences of the Landau family in Poland in excruciatingly dense, believable detail, Uris appears to leapfrog impatiently over details of Dov's rehabilitation at the end of the War of Independence. He sees no need to explain how an MIT graduate degree can be a worthy dividend for Dov's bravery during the War of Independence fight. As a character prototype, Dov represents abstract principles of Jewish continuity and survival: do-or-die resistance at moments of truth such as the Warsaw uprising and correcting injustice. The narrative stirs a fighting spirit supportive of those principles; details about final results they might yield in the real world are irrelevant, and the narrative's most abiding commitment is to the description of acts of Jewish heroism and historic redress rather than the presentation of a persuasive case for permanent Jewish settlement in Eretz Israel.

We should be more precise: *Exodus* is about Jewish empowerment, and its ultimate commitment is to Jewish history. True, Uris's contention that ghetto fighters and other militantly active Nazi resistors were the true Jewish heroes of the Holocaust is debatably interpretive. (For example, continuing discussion and renaming of the annual Holocaust memorial day in Israel, currently known as Remembrance Day for the Holocaust and Heroism [*Yom HaZikharon laShoah ve-laGvura*] shows how heatedly contested, and influential, *Exodus*'s point of view about the Holocaust has been in Israeli culture.[43]) However, that the *Exodus* narrative is argumentative does not necessarily mean that its author's concern with Jewish history is purely instrumental, as though he uses facts from the historical record selectively just to score specific political or moral points. It is more accurate to say that Uris, his Israeli subjects, and (eventually) millions of readers and movie viewers had one consistent way of conceptualizing Jewish tragedies and triumphs. *Nothing* in the narrative is selective; Uris had only one way of grasping history and telling Israel's story,

Admittedly, that grasp was often very loose. In *Exodus*, key story episodes often bear only nominal resemblance to "real life" events. Surely the most notable example of this loose grasp of history is the case of the *Exodus* ship, in which the main connection between the novel's story of the three hundred Holocaust orphans and the real-

The real-life *Exodus* ship. (Frank Shershel, Israel government press office)

life ship appears to be the name "Exodus" itself. Confusingly, in the novel, many of the events of the real *Exodus* ship are interpolated in a flashback sequence relating Dov Landau's history, and are attributed to a different, imaginary hapa'alah ship, called by Uris *The Promised Land*.

It is thus technically impossible to measure the historical fidelity of Uris's novel via a blow-by-blow comparison of whether the novel's treatment of this or that battle or episode matches a real-life counterpart. Instead, in order to assess rightly the character of Uris's commitment to Jewish history it is helpful to consider the broad constellation of circumstances relating to a particular, dramatic symbol or event of Israel's statehood struggle, such as the *Exodus* ship incident. For lack of a better word, did the *spirit* of actual events accord with the emotions and understandings Uris stirred in *Exodus*? Is his history correctly proportioned—did he give the right emphasis to groups and individuals who had the most impact upon the unfolding of phases and processes in Israel's statehood campaign? Does his fiction reliably represent the internal moral logic and broad sociological realities of crucial circumstances related to Israel's founding?

These are interesting, but broad, questions, and they are best addressed by specific example rather than abstract, detached discussion. "Historical fiction" remains an impossibly oxymoronic term until we look closely at how a creative writer handles specific events. Therefore, let us turn now to a comparative assessment of the "real" *Exodus* ship episode and the relevant points of interpretation in Uris's fictional narrative.

At 3:05 a.m., July 18, 1947, seamen from the British Royal Navy boarded a steamer they called the *President Warfield*, but which is known to history as the *Exodus*.[44] The vessel, originally used for pleasure cruises on the Chesapeake Bay, was intercepted beyond the territorial waters of Mandatory Palestine, a fact the British architects of Operation Mae West, the *Exodus* capture, subsequently refused to acknowledge. The British intent was to stop the vessel before it could run up the shore in Haifa Bay and unload some 4,500 Jewish Displaced Persons, Holocaust refugees, in Palestine. Under the British refoulement policy, the DPs, designated as illegal immigrants, were to be removed to British ships and transported back to their country of departure, France.

British seamen and Jewish DPs skirmished fiercely aboard the *Exodus* for two hours. One gruesome moment came early, when the *Exodus*'s second officer, an American named Bill Bernstein, was clubbed to death by British soldiers who stormed the ship's wheelhouse. For a spell, this violent assault by six British soldiers on the vessel's helm was pointless because the *Exodus* crew managed to transfer control to a reserve steering wheel manned at the back of the ship by its captain, Ike Aronowicz. The British capture plan envisioned two hundred soldiers commandeering the *Exodus* after just a few minutes, but after two hours of fighting, only forty British seamen managed to scramble aboard the *Exodus*. With British destroyers in pursuit, the DP boat zigzagged wildly; Jewish fighters on the *Exodus* hurled American-made emergency flares, oil, and canned food items at their British assailants.

The Jewish refugees swung ropes and clubs and threw food and flares and smoke bombs, but they did not fire guns because their handlers from the Yishuv believed that the use of live weapon fire would backfire. Yigal Allon, the commander of the legendary Palmach strike force, and probably the Jewish nationalist fighter who most closely resembles Ari Ben Canaan, the fictional hero of Uris's *Exodus,* believed that Jewish refugees who sailed for Eretz Israel but were stopped at sea by the British ought to display "firm and prolonged opposition" but also remain unarmed.[45] For their part, the British seamen fired bullets, and Jewish casualties mounted. Besides Bernstein, two other *Exodus* fighters were killed, and two hundred Jews were injured, seventy of them seriously. This was a rough scene. The British were relieved when the Jewish resistance came to a halt sometime after 5:00 a.m.

Since the *Exodus* became a famous symbol of unyielding determination to recreate the Jewish people in the new state of Israel, the surrender decision subsequently became a source of discomfit to commentators. The *Exodus* fighters, however, had no choice but to desist. Only three medical personnel were on hand to attend to the dozens of seriously injured fighters. Their ship having been rammed by British battleships, some *Exodus* crewmembers believed (incorrectly, as it turned out) that the steamer was about to sink. Journalist Ruth Gruber, who was in Palestine on assignment from the *New York Herald Tribune* to cover United Nations Special Committee on Palestine (UNSCOP) proceedings, and who raced up to Haifa from Jerusalem when she heard radio reports about the battle aboard the refugee ship, memorably photographed the damaged ship. Her equally vivid written description left little doubt about why the Jewish fighters aboard *Exodus* had to desist. "The ship looked like a matchbox that had been splintered by a nutcracker," wrote Gruber.[46]

Yet the physical damage was not the sole consideration motivating the *Exodus* surrender decision. Crucially, players in this real-life drama (not unlike the ones in Uris's fictional ha'apalah struggle) were aware that its results would ultimately be judged in political, not military, terms. The image of Jewish resistance aboard a ship like the *Exodus* was more important than any tangible battle result, and so it was imperative that the DPs struggle against the British on July 18, 1947, but there was no need for them to fight to the death aboard a floating Masada.

Since the British deducted one immigration authorization certificate for every Jew who illegally entered the country via DP smuggling ha'apalah operations, episodes like the *Exodus* were not about the numbers game. Until the state of Israel was created in May 1948, the British could doctor the tangible results of any specific immigration struggle such as the *Exodus* standoff any way they wanted. Yet on the public relations battlefield, a key front in the rapidly escalating dispute about the future of Palestine, the image of Holocaust survivors fighting against one of the West's most august symbols of power, the British Royal Navy, to rebuild their lives in the ancestral Jewish homeland was invaluable. The political/public relations calculations were no less persuasive than immediate medical needs or the threat of flooding on deck; the *Exodus* fighters could afford capture after having put up a good fight. What could be a more poignant symbol of injustice in the postwar world than Holocaust survivors being barred from Palestine and being redirected back to France, and then, horrifically (due largely to the obtuse statesmanship of British foreign minister Ernest Bevin), to Germany?

Following the tussle in waters outside of Haifa, *Exodus* passengers valiantly refused over a three-week period to disembark from three British ships upon which they had been herded in Haifa, and which docked at Port-de-Bouc in southern France. Their plight caught some limited notice in the Yishuv. Jewish residents of late Mandatory Palestine staged a few, somewhat listless, strikes in support of the *Exodus*'s DPs' refusal to get off the boats in France. Media interest in the Yishuv was not particularly keen, according to historian Aviva Halamish.[47] Only one Yishuv newspaper had a correspondent on the spot at Port-de-Bouc, and the other Hebrew papers relied on wire reports. The Yishuv's attention was riveted by other stories, such as the UNSCOP deliberations or anti-British reprisals conducted by zealous right-wing Zionist militias.

Who really fought the *Exodus* battle? For millions of *Exodus* novel aficionados around the globe, the narrative of Israel's founding, starting with the ha'apalah struggles in Cyprus detention camps, became tied almost exclusively to a new type of Jew, the heroic, Israel-born sabra, personified in Uris's story by the steely Ari Ben Canaan. However, in the real-life *Exodus* ship drama, just a handful of Haganah-deployed, native-born sabras, or youths who had been socialized in the Yishuv,[48] campaigned with the passengers during various stages of the ordeal. En route to Haifa, thirty-six Americans sailed on the *Exodus*.[49] History recorded the name of slain second officer Bill Bernstein. As a medical student when the war broke out, he had been eligible for a World War II deferment but climbed up in the U.S. Navy as an ensign.[50] Nine American Jews aboard the *Exodus* had long-standing Zionist backgrounds, Halamish records. Gruber explains that the Americans "were by no means all Zionists, but they had all determined to help the Jews."[51] The few Israelis aboard the steamer did not fully trust these American volunteers, and records of the journey reflect American grumbling about being kept in the dark about key decisions. Still, American Jews were a significant presence in the symbolically fraught *Exodus* voyage, and their contribution was credibly noted by a key Israeli player in the drama, Captain Ike Aronowicz, who testified that the American volunteers "were no less determined than the people of the Palmach." As the crew prepared for the journey, the Americans, Captain Ike confessed, "were far better trained professionally than we [Yishuv men] ourselves were in those days."[52]

In real life, then, American Jews played an active, courageous role in the *Exodus* struggle to bring thousands of Holocaust survivors to Israel. In the novel, however, they were left off the boat. This was because Leon Uris feared that a portrayal of American Jews deeply involved in the Jewish statehood struggle would be confusing and would possibly alienate readers who were worried about political loyalty issues during the Cold War. This creative principle was articulated by Uris well before *Exodus* reached readers. On a research trip to Israel in September 1956, Uris declared privately to his father that in the writing of his novel "I will completely avoid putting in an American Jew and his particular problem and relations to Israel."[53]

This example of Americans aboard the *Exodus* suggests that Uris's decisions as to which Jews (and non-Jews) were, or were not, to be passionately engaged with the events of Israel's founding in his novel were not always shaped by the complicated, and sometimes inconclusive, sociopolitical realities of the 1948 statehood struggle itself, but rather by the identity politics of his own later time.

The possibility that American Jews might have out-numbered, or out-muscled, the Israelis in the fight against the British aboard the *Exodus* is out of the orbit of Uris's fictional universe. This produced one of the great ironies of *Exodus*. In the real-life story, whose details were never widely known, American Jews played an important supporting role in the heroic drama. In the fictionalized story, whose images became known to millions, the American Jewish element was mostly edited out of existence. The supporting actor became the audience.

Uris's system revolved around the contrast between the cowering Jew of the Exile, and the new, tough Jew of Israel. This meant that the *Exodus* passengers needed to be children and teenagers, and not adults irreversibly rooted in the subdued patterns of Diaspora life.

In the novel, the main passengers on the ship are three hundred Holocaust orphans. Their heroism on the boat symbolically reinforces this idea that Jews have no source of heroic nourishment outside of the Land of Israel. The Jewish children stage a death-defying hunger strike—or, more precisely, the strike is staged for them by their Israeli handlers—and the youngsters, like the ship *Exodus* itself, turn into receptacles of a famished existence driven by forces more powerful than themselves.

In real life, the dynamics were rather different. The "real" *Exodus* was about the Jewish DPs, known as *sherit hapletah*, or "the surviving remnant." According to Halamish,[54] the 4,500 passengers were a reliable cross section of residents of DP camps in 1947. The refugees came from many lands—Poland, Russia, Lithuania, Czechoslovakia, Hungary, Romania. Some survived in areas of Nazi occupation, having lived through the war in forests or among underground partisans, or in the hell of concentration camps; others came from areas not conquered by the Nazis, particularly Asian parts of the Soviet Union. One tally recorded 1,842 adult males, 1,632 adult females, and 955 youths—needless to say, these real-life demographics contrast sharply with Uris's image of a boatload of orphans.

The fight against the British in the shipboard drama outside of Haifa was led by the ma'apalim. The Royal Navy sailors reported that the most vigorous antagonists were refugee youths, aged sixteen to eighteen; most of the Jewish casualties of the clash were from this age group, though even younger Jewish DPs fought and were injured. This real-life scene was shorter and messier, though no less excruciating, than the hunger strike staged in Uris's fictionalized version.

After the violent altercation at sea, outside of Haifa, the crucial moment in the real-life *Exodus* saga occurred after the DPs were transported back to France aboard the three British vessels. The Jewish refugees refused to get off the boats, and their persistence compelled Bevin and the British to search for an alternative haven. The perversity of their choice, Germany, created a humanitarian and public relations fiasco and played right into the Zionists' hands.

Several factors contributed to the fateful moment in France when the DPs steadfastly refused to disembark from the three British ships (*Ocean Vigour, Empire Rival, Runnymede Park*) at Port-de-Bouc. These included the earlier British refoulement decision to depart from the practice of sending ma'apalim to overcrowded detention camps in Cyprus; the behavior of the French, whose compliance with British requests went no further than halfway, and who refused to remove forcibly the DPs ("human beings must feel ashamed when they see any injustice," one French official explained to Ruth Gruber[55]); the partially successful effort of some Israeli Haganah men to relay "stay aboard" messages to the DPs; and occasionally, intimidation tactics were used by more militant DPs against equivocating refugees who were tempted by the French shoreline. In the end, however, it was the DPs themselves who resolved to stay in the "floating Auschwitz," the three British ships, and endure three weeks of torment at the French port. Hence, the ultimate moral measure of the real *Exodus*'s journey is to be found in the hearts and minds of these DPs.

Exodus is "about" what the vast majority of these 4,500 in the surviving remnant decided to do. Because that is the case, the bottom line of the real-life story of *Exodus* does not differ in essence from the message inculcated to millions of readers and film viewers in Uris's fictionalized story. What everyone understands about *Exodus* from the novel or film is *really true*: the Jews in the story wanted to remake their lives in the Land of Israel, which they conceptualized, spiritually or metaphorically, as their home.

That is an important, sweeping claim, and in this comparative analysis of the "real life" and fictionalized events of *Exodus*, it behooves us to pause briefly and consider how recent scholarship relates to the general issue of DP settlement motivation in the period Leon Uris wrote about. Has historical scholarship corroborated his assumptions about ma'apalim determination to reach the shores of Eretz Israel?

In fact, generalizations about settlement inclinations among this DP surviving remnant population can be inaccurate. The political pressures surrounding the ha'apalah issue should be set in demographic perspective; because the demographics were vital, various players in the drama had an interest in influencing surveys and reports regarding the settlement preferences of the Holocaust refugees.[56]

In demographic terms relevant to the Zionist statehood struggle, the DP population in Europe was not small. From 1945 to 1951 some 333,000 Jewish DPs passed through refugee camps in Germany, Austria, and Italy. On the eve of statehood, the Yishuv's population numbered about 600,000. Besieged by a mass of Arab hostility, the

Yishuv understandably viewed this DP population as a valuable pool of civilian and military manpower. Yishuv activists therefore had reasons to induce Zionist feelings among survivors in European DP camps, and the ideological lobbying of Yishuv emissaries in these camps influenced the expressed settlement inclinations of survivors.

Before this Zionist lobbying was effectively organized, just as the World War II fighting ended, a majority of weary, battered survivors seemed intent upon returning to their lost European homes. One survey conducted in early May 1945 among 2,190 survivors at Dachau indicated that two-thirds of the refugees wanted to go home, and inclinations among the remaining third were split between Eretz Israel and the United States.[57]

In a research study that critically examines various assumptions about the Zionist outlook of postwar DPs, Yosef Grodzinsky points out that at the end "less than half of the Jewish DPs became citizens of the state of Israel, much to the chagrin of the Zionist leadership."[58]

That may be so, but in the critical period leading up to episodes such as the *Exodus* ship journey, surveys and observers pointed to an upsurge of DP desire to immigrate to Eretz Israel. As early as October 1945, Joint Distribution Committee (JDC) officials who surveyed 5,000 DPs in the Landsberg camp found that 63 percent wanted to settle in Palestine. Judge Earl Harrison, whose commission surveyed DP camp conditions in the summer of 1945 in order to formulate recommendations to President Truman, stated emphatically that "Palestine is clearly the first choice" among members of the surviving remnant. Later surveys, some conducted by United Nations Relief and Work Agency (UNRWA) officials, found that as many as 98 percent of DP respondents listed a preference to settle in Mandatory Palestine.[59]

Everyone knew that numbers like 98 percent were inflated, to some extent. Grodzinsky quotes the off-the-cuff analysis of one Zionist official, who was delighted by a survey result of near total DP unanimity in favor of Eretz Israel immigration: "We never prayed for such results, and we knew that they didn't reflect the reality. When we asked one Jew, whose plans to immigrate to the US were known to us, why he answered 'Eretz Israel' on the survey, he said simply: 'my journey to America is a private matter, whereas Jews need Eretz Israel.'"[60] Also, throughout the entire saga of DP resettlement, there was always a suggestive correlation between increased numbers of Yishuv emissaries (twenty in December 1945; 150 in 1947) in the DP camps, and the rise in numbers of survey respondents who attested to Eretz Israel as their preferred choice for settlement.

These figures and factors, however, do not substantively detract from the long-held understanding that the logic of immigration to Eretz Israel became increasingly powerful among a critical mass of the surviving remnant, just as the Jewish DP situation reached a boiling point in summer 1947. At that time, Jewish DPs constituted about 25 percent of Europe's recorded refugee population, a significant increase from the figure two years earlier. On all accounts, these DPs lived in squalid misery in European camps. Under the circumstances of the period, their attraction toward a country defined as the Jewish homeland was understandable in emotional terms (particularly since the Zionists had worked hard to cultivate a sense among the refugees of Eretz Israel as their home).

The *Exodus* DPs refused to disembark at Port-de-Bouc for reasons that can legitimately be explicated in Zionist vocabulary—in other words, Jewish nationalist motivation is as real a component of the story as anything else. Halamish, the author of an extended, no-nonsense history of the *Exodus* journey, concludes that it would be wrong to "lampoon the [motivating] power" of the Zionist tenet of "no choice." The DPs on the three British boats believed that they had "no choice" but to persist in the struggle to reach Eretz Israel. Halamish writes:

> And let us not denigrate the power of "no choice." Where could they have gone? The same reasons which had made Palestine the preferred destination for Jewish displaced persons after the war, were several times more valid with regard to the *Exodus* immigrants after what they had gone through. If they were still able to think in terms of "home," then Palestine was their home. It was there that they could meet up with relatives and people from their home towns, people with a common background and similar ambitions.[61]

Nationalist resolve, the yearning to resettle in Eretz Israel, is a constant running through the *Exodus* story, in its real life and its fictionalized versions. Uris, of course, took liberties in his story. Very little in the book and film depictions of the DP ship episode accords with the actual facts of the case (indeed, in the most basic sense it is reasonable to conclude that Uris's *Exodus* is not about *Exodus*).

Nonetheless, the book has a reality principle, and, paradoxically, this principle derives from the intensely subjective realm of what people, as individuals and as a collective, want. The DPs on the British boats wanted Eretz Israel. Had they reached for berets and café au lait and assimilated in France on the basis of the British postwar policy of treating Jewish DPs as nationals of one European country or another, Uris's fictionalized version would have had no credibility. *Exodus* could not have happened in Haifa or Hollywood.

The real-life *Exodus* was about what the DPs did on the boat, but it was not really remembered that way. By ignoring the DPs heroic deeds, by downgrading the DPs as politically dependent juveniles, or (as in the case of the Dov Landau character) by deferring their political development to a later stage of action in Israel during the War of Independence, Uris was not alone. As *Exodus* moved from the real-time events of summer 1947 to the realm of nationalist myth, the DPs were excised from the center of the story. At the bitter end of the *Exodus* expedition, just as the British boats finished unloading the DPs in camps in Europe, the various Zionist parties and organizations began to joust with one another, attempting to put their own Ari Ben Canaan sabra types at the helm and to take as much credit for the dramatic story of Jewish resilience as they could. Adulatory books published in Israel lavished praise upon a few heroes in the story who came from Yishuv movements and kept the spotlight from the 4,500 DPs on the boat.

In large part, this retelling of the *Exodus* story reflected the central contention of Zionist historiography. The premise, defended in various ways by influential, Israel-based historians, holds that power and redemption in modern Jewish history comes from Eretz Israel. Historians of modern Jewish affairs have put the spotlight on the Yishuv and have kept the Diaspora in the shadows, explains the scholar of the real-life *Exodus,* aptly describing the trend.[62] By diminishing the activism of American Jews and Holocaust survivors in his fictionalized *Exodus,* Uris did nothing to contest this outlook. In fact, he popularized it. With telling ingenuity, he managed to make the Zionist idea of the "negation of the Diaspora" wildly popular among Diaspora Jews themselves.

In Uris's narrative, Holocaust survivors like Dov Landau recreate themselves through heroic deeds in Israel, far away from the context of the European genocide. Had Uris delved too deeply into what his characters' real-life counterparts actually did on the *Exodus* and the three British transport ships he would have rigged his story with difficult or unanswerable questions. The refusal of the DPs to disembark in France enacted the belief that Jewish life is doomed anywhere outside of Eretz Israel. Did this imply a retrospective condemnation of slain Holocaust victims who chose to remain in Poland and Germany? More to the point, how was a moralistic writer supposed to relate to the denouement of the *Exodus* story, given that the real-life DPs relented after the boats reached Hamburg on September 8 and disembarked from the British ships with no more than moderate displays of opposition? This decision to disembark departed from zealous, Masada martyrdom norms that dictate collective suicide in instances when the fundamental aims of a Jewish national group are unrealizable.

The real-life decision to disembark paid practical dividends. The *Exodus* DPs were sent to camps in Germany; before not too long, many managed to slip away and find their way to Eretz Israel. At the time of Israel's establishment on May 15, 1948, half of the *Exodus* ma'apalim already resided in the new Jewish state.[63] The last of the *Exodus* DPs departed for Israel in September 1948, just a year after the three British boats arrived in Hamburg. At this juncture, some 15,000 DPs still remained confined in Cyprus, and many of them had been involved in ha'apalah struggles to reach Israel that were waged in periods preceding the *Exodus*'s departure from France in July 1947.

In the abstract, it might be unfeeling to conclude that a Holocaust survivor was smart to agree to spend another few months, or a year, in a DP camp in Europe. However, given the realities of September 1947, and in light of developments that ensued after that date, the *Exodus* DPs indisputably reached the right decision when they disembarked in Germany. The somewhat prosaic conclusion of the actual *Exodus* story points to the interaction of self-interest and self-sacrifice in the story of Jewish renewal after the Holocaust. As Uris determined to tell the story, however, *Exodus* was not about Jewish prudence and practicality.

Uris was not a Zionist philosopher or party politician, but his narrative shared a serious flaw of the Jewish nationalist vision during the first years of Israeli statehood—that is, ideological rigidity that prevented the Israelis from viewing Diaspora Jews as active historical agents endowed with positive powers of everyday persistence and prudence and capable of carrying out heroic deeds that contributed to Jewish continuity and survival outside of the Land of Israel. His vision frozen by this dogmatism, Uris found it virtually impossible to describe positive acts of Holocaust victims undertaken both in real time and outside of the Land of Israel. Apart from the example of ghetto uprisings, which he examined in *Mila 18,* Holocaust Jews could not be seen as active participants in history.

Thus, in Leon Uris's fictionalized world—a cultural realm that quickly became far more influential and "real" than the actual story of the former Chesapeake Bay pleasure steamer and its Jewish passengers—*Exodus* is emphatically not about the DPs on the boat. They do not have their own place in history.

In popular culture, it bears mentioning, 1950s Israeli conceptualizations of Jewish Holocaust victims as sheep to the slaughter and as depersonalized vessels handled by heroic Palmach fighters in episodes such as *Exodus* was not uncontested. For reasons to be elaborated later in this book, the *Exodus* film's presentation of key aspects of Israel's founding story was qualitatively unlike that of Leon Uris's novel. We will argue that while Otto Preminger's film *Exodus* further popularized the basic ideas and images of Uris's novel, it also contained the seeds of the future "unmaking" of the conventional Zionist narrative of Israel's founding. Since our discussion here of the "real" events of Israel's founding struggle and the *Exodus* narrative is focused on the *Exodus* ship episode, we should pause for a moment to see how the film describes the boat's adventures in Cyprus. This comparison of the film, the novel, and the real *Exodus* ship story provides insight about how popular culture struggled to come to terms with the complexity of dilemmas faced by Hitler's victims and to uphold normatively as active resistance all forms of behavior undertaken by Jews in the name of survival and the protection of their loved ones.

The filmmaker Otto Preminger, who (as we will see) wrested control of the film script of *Exodus* from Uris in an acrimonious process, approached the subject of Israel's founding from an assimilated Jewish standpoint unlike that of the Baltimore-born author. Preminger, born in 1905, hailed from a family of Eastern European Jews, but he always claimed Vienna as his birthplace. He was raised by successful, assimilated parents. Through World War I, his father Markus, an able lawyer, avidly prosecuted nationalist and political subversives in defense of the Austrian Empire, and he subsequently made a small fortune in private practice. Preminger's father was a strong-willed man of character. Even though he was lax in his Jewish observances, Markus refused tempting promotion offers that were conditioned upon his conversion to Catholicism (and he managed to avoid paying a price for such refusals to convert).[64]

In Vienna, the Preminger family confronted anti-Semitism almost any way it turned, but this proximity did not really alarm the family. The Premingers' last apartment in Vienna was situated on a street named after the city's anti-Semitic mayor, Karl Lueger, yet that did not bother members of the family. Dismissing Lueger's Jew-baiting as mere politics, Otto Preminger's brother Ingo, who later served as Leon Uris's agent, recalled that "it was well known that, privately, Lueger did not hate Jews."[65]

Otto Preminger's life changed because of the rise of the Nazi menace on the continent. However, he was not exactly a Holocaust refugee. When he arrived in America in the autumn of 1935, Preminger was a famous theater director who had (his most recent biographer records) departed Austria "on his own terms and by his own choice," and who was accorded "a hero's farewell."[66]

Such life experiences encouraged Preminger to recast attitudes and images that Uris had incorporated in *Exodus*. For instance, while he was acutely conscious of the Holocaust's tragic dimensions, Preminger grasped elements of human inanity in anti-Semitism; totally unlike Uris, he sometimes evinced irony or even humor about the subject. More importantly, since he really had no reason to be bitter about his life in Europe prior to Hitler's rise, Preminger was unlikely to embrace the Zionist attitude of unyielding criticism of Jewish Diaspora life that laced through Uris's text. Nowhere is this more in evidence than in the film's handling of the *Exodus* ship episode.

The film significantly alters Uris's Zionist paternalist zealotry whereby the all-powerful sabra, Ari Ben Canaan, orchestrates a hunger strike among all-compliant Diaspora children. In the movie, after Ari grabs a megaphone to begin plotting a plan of action with the six hundred DPs brought to the *Exodus* after brief internment in Cyprus (in the film, the *Exodus* passengers are veterans of a recent, failed ma'apilim journey aboard another ship, the *Star of David*), he is abruptly interrupted by an old but feisty, cap-wearing and bearded refugee. With humor, wisdom, and persistence, this survivor of the European Holocaust demands action. As the camera bounces back

Unlike the *Exodus* novel, Holocaust survivors in the film play an active role in the Jewish struggle for redemption. Here DPs on the *Exodus* ship negotiate tactics with the sabra hero, Ari Ben Canaan. (*Exodus* film)

and forth between the sabra Haganah operative and the DP, the issue of who is giving orders to whom is unclear. Ari seems soft-spoken and needs a megaphone to project monotonous orders, whereas the ma'apil booms out heroic messages in his own folksy timbre. Subsequently, Ari defends the hunger strike as a publicity maneuver, whereas this brave DP delves into Jewish experience to find rationale for the extreme action. Jewish tradition sounds wiser than Palmach activism.

Cerebral and endearingly stubborn, this *Exodus* DP previews changes in the way world Jewry perceived the Holocaust tragedy. The film's orientation points to rethinking about the Holocaust based on a nostalgic sense of what was lost rather than inchoate avoidance of the subject or nonsophisticated ways of imagining the victims' plights. The shtetl Jew was increasingly seen as being wise and noble for preserving Jewish tradition rather than being fated for destruction as a result of poor choices. With *The Diary of Anne Frank* (whose movie version came out in 1959), and *Fiddler on the Roof* (whose original Broadway production was staged in 1964), the *Exodus* film was part of a transition in popular culture by which the Jewish past, with all its predicaments, foibles, humorous warmth and endurance, was being seen by millions in newly evolving ways, and these orientations differed significantly from the Zionist "Denial of the Diaspora" ideology that governed Uris's impassioned but monochromatic narrative.

In Preminger's film, Jewish mothers become diehard fighters on the boat. As the hunger strike enters its 92nd hour, Ari succumbs to the pragmatic advice of the ship's medic, the elderly Dr. Odenheim, and orders that children be removed from the *Exodus* and fed on shore. Hungry and exhausted, the doctor himself passes away, but his recommendation is overruled by insistent Old World mothers. The *Exodus* film script's directions leave little doubt about how the heroic spotlight in this phase of the film shifts from the dashing Palmach fighters to the Holocaust survivors, who are symbols of indestructible Jewish spirit:

> Sarah Frenkel is a large-boned, work-seasoned woman in her early forties. She has been witness to horror, and nothing will ever frighten her again. A boy of three and a girl of five cling to each of her hands. Miriam Hirschberg is perhaps twenty. She is petite, terribly thin, with enormous eyes and a complexion, which has become almost translucent, and curiously luminous. In her arms she tenderly carries a six months old infant.[67]

These two mothers hold their young babies in front of Ari's face and remind him that they have no place to grow up outside of Eretz Israel. Personifying Jewish will and experience, the mothers are this scene's source of authority. Ari's "Hagannah order" for their children to desist from the hunger strike is roundly dismissed; and this exchange entirely reverses the moral world of Leon Uris, in which combat courage and military authority, and not the accumulated experience of the Jewish shtetl, bring about historic restitution and Jewish statehood. The following snippet from the *Exodus* film script could never have been written in a Leon Uris novel:

> ARI: "I'm sorry, Mrs. Frenkel. The children must go back. You can go with them if you wish. It's a Hagannah order."
> MRS. FRENKEL (this is too much): "Hagannah, Schmagannah! You're an important man, Ari Ben Canaan, but you know nothing!"[68]

In the *Exodus* ship sequences, Preminger uses Eva Marie Saint's Madonna-like presence to express, even sanctify, an inclusive vision of Israel's founding struggle. When the two Jewish mothers enter Ari's

Zionists used hunger strikes and other zealous tactics in the postwar immigration struggle against the British, and the *Exodus* narrative sought Christian approval for these do-or-die efforts. Here, the American Protestant, Kitty Fremont (Eva Marie Saint) is framed as a Madonna symbol, as she listens to Ben Canaan and DP mothers plot a hunger-strike protest to foil the British. (Exodus film)

cabin to persuade him to include children in the hunger strike, Kitty Fremont, played by Eva Marie Saint in the movie, peers sympathetically through a window, from on deck. Her irenic Madonna pose symbolizes the Christian world's understanding of the power and passion that is driving the Jews back to their land.

The scene is contrived to present the zealotry of mothers who would sacrifice their children in the Eretz Israel immigration campaign as an entirely natural response to the circumstances that led up to the 1948 war. Kitty, for her part, has lost a child due to an unnatural and unnecessary journey to Palestine—early in the film, she reveals to General Sutherland that a year earlier she had a miscarriage in a Jerusalem hospital, where she traveled after notification of the death of her photojournalist husband. Borrowing Uris's blunt idiom, the film applies unnatural natal references to various objects and symbols: "can this abortion make it to Palestine," Ari asks ship captain Hank, the first time he sees the *Exodus*. The idea is that only the Zionist passion for return to Eretz Israel, to consummate the rebirth of the Jewish people, prevents symbolic miscarriages of justice and history. When the film's plot twists are woven together with the audience's prior knowledge of the *Exodus* ship legend and understanding of Israel's establishment as an against-all-odds triumph, the scene that features Kitty framed as Madonna emerges as a kind of seaborne Zionist nativity scene. The passion and courage of the

Hagannah men, the Holocaust survivor ma'apilim, and Christian supporters plant the seed for the miraculous delivery of the Jewish state.

The differences between Uris's Israel-centered analysis and Preminger's inclusive vision are significant, and they reflect dissimilarities of biographical background and creative intention as well as different stages in the making and unmaking of Israel's founding narrative. Ultimately, however, the *Exodus* ship incident was about neither its real-life facts, nor Uris's Palmach heroes, nor Preminger's concert of brave Israelis and DPs and sympathetic Americans. The *Exodus* incident, in its real and fictionalized guises, was about politics.

Throughout the real-life saga of the *Exodus,* the Zionist leadership grasped its political implications. "From the very start," writes Tom Segev, the *Exodus* ship affair "was intended as a public-relations tool for the Zionist movement."[69] For instance, throughout the *Exodus* ship affair Palmach chief Yigal Allon displayed a keen awareness of its political and public relations utility. Allon cabled Palmach comrades in Europe, saying "it's inconceivable that Jews can be expelled from Eretz Israel without their doing the utmost to resist deportation." Much like the fictional Ari Ben Canaan, Allon understood that while Jews would need to fight to win political independence, the value of this particular battle over *Exodus* was not to be measured in terms of what actually happened on the boat. Its worth was the way waves lapped from the ship in public consciousness. Resistance to the British, Allon explained in his June 21, 1947, cable,

> should make the process of deportation as difficult as possible, since this, anyway, is one of the less pleasant tasks an oppressive administration has to fulfill. Now and then resistance has to rekindle the support of our people in the Diaspora, who might be able to help us and to awaken the conscience of those nations of the world who have not yet lost theirs.[70]

In the battle for public perception, one of the Zionists' strongest cards was the ship's name. A brilliant, and highly deliberate, designation chosen by Moshe Sneh, the head of Mossad le-Aliyah Bet (the organization that spearheaded the illegal Jewish immigration to Palestine),[71] the name "Exodus" reinforced a contemporary understanding that the Jewish campaign for survival and rebirth had universal implications. As it happened, just one other of dozens of ha'apalah ships had a name (*The Four Freedoms*) that was immediately comprehensible to non-Jews.[72] In the annals of illegal Zionist immigration to Eretz Israel, the name *Exodus* was uniquely rooted in biblical ground recognizable to Christians and Jews alike. The name powerfully associated the age-old Jewish struggle for freedom with the uplifting sense of democratic triumph in the postwar world. "The name is a stroke of genius," noted the highly communicative director of the Jewish Agency's Political Department, Moshe Shertok (Sharett). "This name by itself says more than anything which has ever been written about it [the boat's story]."[73]

Few parties connected to the *Exodus* affair questioned the morality of relating to the 4,500 DPs as instruments operated to promote political visions of Mandatory Palestine's future. Few wondered whether it was cynical to exploit the fate of Holocaust survivors for political purposes. In this important respect, fiction followed real life.

In Uris's fictional *Exodus*, Kitty Fremont remonstrates here and there about how Ari Ben Canaan is an "inhuman beast," after the Yishuv partisan orchestrates an eighty-five-hour hunger strike to stir world sympathy for the boat (which is, in the novel, quarantined in Cyprus). Overall, however, Ari's act is lauded in the book as consummate politics, and Kitty, his American admirer, comes to accept the necessity of his methods. Similarly, in the real-life *Exodus* episode, the political and public relations effects of the DP's plight took precedence over their actual suffering—virtually nobody among the Zionists or their supporters identified this tendency as cynicism. Chaim Weizmann stands as one exception. As the nomadic DPs approached Hamburg, Weizmann spoke sincerely to Zionist gatherings about the untold suffering of refugees who were being returned to the home of Hitler.[74] Weizmann's motives, however, were not entirely humanitarian (at the British Mandate's 11th hour, the architect of the Balfour Declaration was chary about the escalating conflict between Zionists and the British); and, at this late stage of his distinguished career as a Zionist leader, Weizmann met with British officials merely as a private citizen.

As long as the wanderings of the DPs generated useful sympathy for the Jewish state agenda, the Zionist leadership, headed by David Ben-Gurion, staved off efforts such as Weizmann's to find practical solutions for the DPs. The Jewish Agency, in Tom Segev's words, "had an interest in the sentimental and symbolic aspects of deportation to Germany."[75]

It could not have been otherwise. The Jewish Agency, functionally the government of prestate Israel, was a political institution, and the politics of the *Exodus* affair were inextricably tied to calculations about world public opinion. The intensity of the *Exodus* ha'apalah struggle was calibrated strictly in line with public responses. As soon as Ben-Gurion and other Zionist leaders judged that UNSCOP's officials had turned the corner and were formulating recommendations in favor of a Jewish state, they knew that the time had come to scale back the *Exodus* struggle.

As the DPs logged the last leg of their weary journey, traveling from France to Hamburg, Ben-Gurion was involved in Zionist meetings in Zurich. In one key discussion,[76] two field bosses, Shaul Meirov, head of Mossad Le Aliyah Bet, and Haim Hoffman, who headed the Jewish Agency delegation in Europe, lobbied for stiff DP resistance the moment the boats reached Hamburg. "Extreme action should be taken," they told Ben-Gurion, "so as to escalate the struggle and cause real clashes with the British." A third official, Daniel Levin, a Jewish Agency official in charge of the British-controlled region in Germany, demurred. "The *Exodus* ma'apilim have been through enough, and it is wrong for us to wage a struggle on their backs," he stated. In the end, Ben-Gurion chose the temperate course because the Zionist cause had no more diplomatic and political mileage to gain from the *Exodus* journey. More fistfights with the British at sea might have unnerved the UNSCOP members who were at that moment leaning toward support for the Jewish state formula.

As this Zurich meeting example indicates, the course of the *Exodus* was charted by calculations about international politics and public relations. One needle on the ship's compass was media, and the other was politics; this navigational fact points to the final, ironic point of convergence between the "real" *Exodus* and Uris's fictionalized account. As this analysis has suggested, Leon Uris was not really concerned about being faithful to the details of the actual *Exodus* episode. He took the boat's name and loosely followed the main frame of the real-life story about the attempt of Holocaust survivors to immigrate to Palestine against British law and British power. Uris's fictionalized account, however, captured the true spirit of the events and their main players. This convergence of fact and fiction is reflected by Uris's grasp of the public relations politics of Israel's founding. In his novel, exactly as in the real world, the *Exodus* vessel's final destination is public opinion.

Uris's most prescient comment on the perception politics of Israel's founding was to present a journalist, Mark Parker, as the first character who appears in his story. Everything that Ari Ben Canaan does with the *Exodus* ship is coordinated closely with this American correspondent, so that the cruel British detainment of a shipload of Holocaust orphans spins with maximal pro-Zionist effect in world media. Taking his cue from Ben Canaan, Parker scripts the whole story before it all happens—all he has to do is cable a prearranged sign, and the *Exodus* saga begins to spill over world media the second Ben Canaan and his Yishuv partisan buddies ditch their stolen British lorries and bring the young DPs on deck. As Uris constructs his tale, *Exodus* becomes a public symbol almost before the Jewish heroes do anything. Ben Canaan plays the journalist Parker like a fiddle, and Uris unapologetically depicts his version of *Exodus* as a pro-Zionist public relations stunt.

How important is the media in the politics of *Exodus*? Mark Parker, a minor character in the story, seems dwarfed by the ubiquitous, crafty and courageous Ari Ben Canaan. Yet Ari's work on the *Exodus* caper would mean nothing without Parker's publicity. This relationship between the American journalist Parker and the new Israeli hero Ben Canaan represented Uris's cogent understanding that whoever had power over perception and public opinion would have power over Palestine. In ways the author might not have fully appreciated, this understanding subverted the imposing powers, the almost comic-book strengths, that he wanted to attribute to young Israeli fighters like Ben Canaan.

After *Exodus* became famous, Uris publicly admitted that Mark Parker's sudden disappearance after the novel's first book was an error in plot construction,[77] but this explanation appears to have been disingenuous. Uris could not deny that the real-life Israeli Ben Canaans depended upon the real-life American Parkers; nor could he have readily elaborated upon this point. In the narrative universe of *Exodus,* Ari Ben Canaan's reliance on Mark Parker is a contradiction in terms, and it reflects the ambiguities of Israel's developing reliance upon America in the postwar world. Ten years after its establishment, the embattled state of Israel needed *Exodus,* because its bid for stability continued to depend upon the largesse of public opinion.

Just as Ben Canaan would have not succeeded in his campaigns without Mark Parker, so too is it the case that neither Ben-Gurion nor successors in his office such as Golda Meir and Yitzhak Rabin would have fulfilled important planks in Israel's diplomatic agenda without the help of publicists such as Leon Uris.

A crucial point of tangency between the "real life" *Exodus* and Uris's fictionalized version is the author's semiconscious realization of this fact, which was always lurking beneath his earnestly felt celebration of Jewish empowerment in Israel and his convincingly articulated defense of Zionist claims. In fact, the way Israel's leadership expediently supported and appreciated Uris and *Exodus* uncannily parallels Ben Canaan's cagey dealings with the American journalist Mark Parker. The enduring creative mystery of *Exodus,* of its fictionalized presentations of Jewish history and Israel's founding, is to be found in this extremely complicated relationship between the author and his subject matter. In his novel, Uris wrote with emphatic certitude about the events and characters of Israel's statehood struggle— and yet, as hinted by the ambiguity of the relationship between Mark Parker and Ari Ben Canaan, it remains difficult to understand what Israel really meant to Uris, and what *Exodus* meant to Israel.

What was the author looking for when he chose the young Jewish state as a topic for his third novel, after succeeding with a best seller about his service in the U.S. Marines and experiencing mixed results with a second novel whose serious Jewish content was omitted? Did he really *believe* the contents of the story he was presenting, or did he perceive himself as a propagandist in the service of the Jewish state (or as a best-selling author in need of no real motives other than commercial profit)? As an assimilated Jew who had never had a Bar Mitzvah,[78] who was (as we will emphasize in the next chapter) intermarried, and who had already publicly celebrated his American patriotism with the popular *Battle Cry,* is it possible that Uris assembled *Exodus*'s information about Jewish history in a completely detached way, as a professional collector and analyzer of some other people's experiences? Or, assuming that such absolute detachment would have been existentially impossible, what really was Uris's perception of the connection between his American Jewish identity and the heroic Israeli story he related?

Uris's relationship to the "facts" of 1948, we have argued, was complicated. His narrative was undeniably punctuated by distortions and omissions, but it also effectively evoked the spirit of transformative events such as ha'apalah illegal immigration efforts. Intriguingly, Uris's narrative popularized partisan Zionist-Israeli conceptualizations of Jewish history, and its highly argumentative interpretations of pivotal events in this history won wide, nearly universal appeal. These findings, however, do not satisfactorily answer all dimensions of this chapter's fundamental question: why did Jewish history come to matter so much in *Exodus*?

This query, as with many other things connected to *Exodus*, has an important and heretofore neglected biographical dimension. Much like the sleight of hand in *Exodus* whereby credit for the success of Ari Ben Canaan's most daring exploit goes to an American journalist whose commitment to the Israeli statehood story is never really explained, we have always taken for granted various items in Uris's biography, be it his pre-*Exodus* life as a Marine Corps veteran who had worked on cowboy western screenplays, or his post-*Exodus* life as a popular novelist whose work often addressed non-Jewish topics, as exemplified by *Trinity*, a novel about Irish history that topped the best-seller charts at the time of the U.S. Bicentennial in 1976.[79] Rarely has anyone wondered about the relation of these biographical factoids to a book that brought hundreds of pages of Jewish history to the attention of hundreds of thousands of readers. What, really, was the nature of Leon Uris's commitment to the history of Israel's founding?

Exodus's monumental success has long provoked the suspicion that some cunning commercial or organizational genius beyond its author's own comprehension was the novel's real patron.[80] This suspicion is manifestly untrue. Throughout the book's making, Uris remained in control of what he wanted to do. Insofar as it is possible to direct the effects of a cultural product about a complicated topic that circulates in the millions, the correlation between the intents of Uris's activities when he gathered backers and resources for his book and the project's outcome a few years later is impressive. This success was not preternatural—there are a few other notable examples of authorial design redeemed in the wildly popular reception of a very political novel. In such cases, from Harriet Beecher Stowe to Leon Uris, existing political and commercial machinery clearly facilitated book sales, but the essential component of success was the ability of an impassioned writer to craft a story whose home was the heart of an era.

By the middle of the 1950s, Uris had the novel and screenplay of *Battle Cry* notched on his resume, and, in a major coup, he was contracted by producer Hal Wallis to write the screenplay of a new western. Wallis owned the rights to an article about events at Tombstone, Arizona, and he assigned Uris to write it up for a film. Under orders from Wallis, Uris wrote the screenplay for a memorable western, *Gunfight at the O.K. Corral.*

The proximity of the 1957 release of this well-known cowboy movie to the 1958 publication of Uris's famous historical novel about Israel generated amusing overlapping details. For instance, after mulling over possible surnames for his Protestant American heroine of the *Exodus* story, Uris finally named her after a street, Fremont, located in the area of the famous gunfight at Tombstone. However, the movie's connection to the making of *Exodus* appears tenuous. It suffices to note *Gunfight*'s place on the upward trajectory of Uris's professional career. Uris himself frequently spoke of his research and writing of *Exodus* as a make-or-break moment in his career, and his recollection brims with emotional authenticity. In sheer professional terms, however, Uris's self-description lacks evidence. He was solidly positioned as a writer before *Exodus,* and his major novel about Israel did not lift Uris out of obscurity.

For reasons he never thought necessary to revisit and record, by the end of 1955 Uris prepared himself emotionally and professionally to write a big book about the establishment of the Jewish state. To that end, he put himself on a crash course. "It is hard to become a Jew in just three weeks, but I'm trying," Uris wrote to his father.[81] "I guess I've read 50 books in the past few weeks," he explained to William. (Typically, the moment his father heard this, he sent his son a list of more books to read.)

Uris handled his professional arrangements for this career-making book with clever acumen. His agent Malcolm Stuart helped him in this initial stage, and Uris later thanked him profusely in a prefatory note to *Exodus*. Mostly, however, Uris was propelled by his own will. His proposed product reached all the necessary doorsteps, and Uris stayed in the stairwells until he got the answers he wanted. Within weeks, in January 1956, he put together a good package.

Although it has been supposed otherwise, Uris's idea was to write a novel and use a film deal as leverage for the novel's success. Given his professional background at the time, this goal was natural and sensible. He had never concealed his hopes to "make a million" from writing,[82] but in this period cash advances and guarantees had instrumental value as well. As he explained to his father, he was not going to set out to Israel until he had the means to "dedicate a year to the project, [doing] research and writing" in the country. It "takes a lot of money to travel and keep a family," Uris noted in an early 1956 letter to his father. He cited the commercial rationale of the arrangements he was cobbling: the "reason we want a studio commitment first is because it puts me in a position to demand more from a publisher."[83]

When Uris peddled his story proposal, well-placed executives in the film and book businesses, some of them Jewish, were deal facilitators but not deal makers. For years speculation has held that Uris was a hired hand of film studio executives who were, for political or financial reasons, interested in producing a major motion picture out of Israel's founding story. This interpretation has centered on Dore Schary, a liberal-minded, innovative figure of note in film history who was sometimes known in the industry as a "professional Jew," and who was at the time in his fifth (and final) year as president of the Metro-Goldwyn-Mayer studio. "In Hollywood the champions of Israel were thick on the ground," writes one exponent of this theory. "Dore Schary had the power and the means to lay the foundation stone. He called in Leon Uris . . . You must write a dramatic novel about the birth of Israel [Schary told Uris]!"[84]

Such interpretations, however, were fanned retrospectively by Otto Preminger supporters, and they are colored by hard feelings generated by the tempestuous feuding between the filmmaker and Uris after their ill-fated collaborative effort on the script of the celluloid version of *Exodus*. In actual fact, Schary's role in the making of *Exodus* was important but modest. He agreed to the book-film package the writer proposed, but nothing more than that.[85]

A week after Uris signed his joint deal with MGM and Random House, he summed up his relation to Dore Schary in a private letter. Uris admired Schary as a liberal Stevenson Democrat who had backbone (Schary was a well-known critic of McCarthy's witch hunts), and he appreciated the MGM head's support—that was the entirety of their relationship. Uris wrote: "I met Dore Schary, head of Metro, and he is a real mensch. He told me that when a man with my ability comes to a studio with an idea, it is the studio's duty to back him. He makes many mistakes and has many enemies, but he is the only one in town running a studio that has ideals. Also, he is a Democrat."[86] Not MGM, nor any other satellite in the star system, made *Exodus.* From the moment of Israel's establishment, Uris had been passionately, even militantly, engaged with its story. In the summer of 1948, at the height of Israel's War of Independence, Uris exclaimed to his half-sister Essie, "You can bet your bottom dollar if I weren't married I'd be over there shooting Arabs!"[87] Uris looked for a context to substantiate images of Jewish revitalization and strength that nestled inchoately in his mind but had never found convincing expression in his writing. For reasons appreciably connected to his own unhappy family history, he searched for a community and context where Jewish life had meaning. These were the motives that propelled Uris to offices like Schary's, and that helped make *Exodus.*

What came out of those offices was a handsome deal. Under the terms of his January 25, 1956, contract with Random House, Uris received $42,500 for his proposed book, then tentatively titled *The Big Dream,* to be paid in installments (half after two years of work, the remainder at final stages of publication). This book contract provided bonus incentives in the event that Uris's work came to be serialized in various popular journals or selected for book-of-the-month frameworks; if realized, the bonuses would almost double Uris's preroyalty profit from the book.[88] Concurrently, a screenplay contract with MGM guaranteed Uris another $25,000.[89] Somewhat to Uris's chagrin, this advance was also to be paid on a delayed installment schedule. Ingo Preminger, the brother of the well-known independent film producer, represented Uris in dealings with MGM.

In his early thirties, the Marine Corps veteran smoked, had a history of asthma, and also indulged (if Uris's later writings about this period are to be believed) hard-drinking habits and an active, varied late night schedule. With his Israel book contract signed, Uris quit smoking and worked himself into shape, playing sets of tennis in the morning and getting his weight down to 160 pounds.

Also, in February/March 1956, after signing on the book-movie deal's bottom line, he made another circuit of preparation, this time to let Israeli authorities know he was coming. Israel's Foreign Office promised to put a capable man at Uris's disposal and also to provide unlimited entry to sites in the country and a car.

In early March 1956 Uris declaimed his creative intents in a revealing private letter. "Let this be known," he announced:

I am not writing this book for the Jews or the Zionists. I am writing this book for the American people in hopes I can present it in such a way that Israel gets what she needs badly—understanding. I am writing this book to bring a major film company into Israel which will produce a motion picture that will present this story to a billion people around the world on film. I have a big task. I cannot write a book for all men. I write for Leon Uris and I hope most men like it.[90]

After having grown up in radically secular circumstances where his radical father worried that the Communist Party would take reprisals were the slightest vestige of Jewish ritual to infiltrate the home,[91] Uris had to learn the ABCs of Israel's circumstances almost from scratch. His notes from this period include baldly elementary facts and reminders. "Passover prayers include the words 'Next Year in Jerusalem,'" Uris cited in his notebooks, along with "Bakshish is the Arab word for bribe."[92] Soon enough, however, his crash course went beyond the basics. By his own count, Uris read three hundred books before and during his field research in Israel. Many of the titles can be found in his private papers; they combine standard overviews of Jewish nationalism and Israel's founding written by prominent Zionists or philo-Semites along with a large number of relatively technical treatises and materials, not all on military topics.[93]

Uris combed the books of Isaiah and Jeremiah for passages about return to Eretz Israel. He obtained, or compiled himself, detailed, bullet-line summaries of major developments and topics that would be featured in his book. One was a "Summary of Outstanding Actions of the Jewish Underground." Another was a summary of the ha'apalah illegal immigration of Holocaust survivors to Mandatory Palestine. One line entry in this summary, devoted to the *Exodus* ship, conveyed laconically: "July 18 1947—Name of Ship: President Warfield; passengers 4493, 3 Jews killed, several injured when Royal Navy boarded ship to Haifa; Most Jews . . . transferred on British transports and taken to Hamburg." Particularly detailed was Uris's "Research Material on Concentration Camps." This list cited the progression of Nazi mass murder methods, culminating in Zyklon B, and also the extermination routine in the camps ("washing station, imitation showers, stripping, soap of stone . . . periodic clearing by Sonderkommandos"). This list emphasized that "every atrocity known to man" was perpetrated in the concentration camps and gave some examples ("torture, castration, 17000 operations without anesthetics"); later (as we shall see), one of these details, culled from Joseph Tenenbaum's study, *Underground: The Story of a People,* embroiled Uris in a dramatic libel suit in London.[94]

From the start, Uris adopted an inclusive attitude toward the Jewish community, the Yishuv, in prestate Palestine. Uris understood that extended analysis of pre-1948 ideological schisms between the left-wing, dominant Labor Zionist camp (represented, in the military sphere, by the Palmach) and the right-wing Revisionist Zionist movement (with its underground affiliate, the Irgun) would be arcane to most American readers.

Uris's creative reasoning was transparent and convincing: if you were trying to frame together an inspiring account of America's founding, it would be foolish to elaborate on picayune minutiae of ideological rivalry between Federalists and Republicans. Also, in this case, as in many of Uris's creative decisions in the writing of *Exodus,* there was a discernible psychological component. He had been raised by a father who perorated obsessively about positions upheld thirty-five years before by David Ben-Gurion during a strike at the Shulman-Levenstein candy store in Jaffa and other such forgotten disputes between Labor Zionists and other Zionist groups. Uris believed that his father had gotten nowhere in the pioneer days of Mandatory Palestine precisely because he had stumbled pointlessly over esoteric ideology. Uris was determined to hurdle past the pratfalls of the shtetl Jews while he prepared his book on Israel.

For this reason, on March 31 Uris defiantly rejected his father's request that he ignore the Irgun in his research.[95] "To avoid or dodge an issue as big as Irgun and its part in the War of Liberation would be shirking my duty as a writer," Uris explained. He wanted his narrative to rise above internecine Zionist rivalry, even if doing so would be at the expense of punctilious historical accuracy. Uris explained to his father: "As a novelist, I must hear all sides of the story; and I may use the right to distort a little to dramatize a point."

In April 1956, Uris started field research in the Jewish state. Settled in the Accadia Hotel, outside of Tel Aviv, Uris was a visitor of note in Israel. Remarking that Uris's story *Battle Cry* ranked as Warner Brothers studio's biggest box-office draw ever, the *Jerusalem Post* profiled Uris as a celebrity. Uris's projected third novel would feature a cross section of Israeli pioneers, *Post* correspondent Zvi Halmer noted, and was sure to "interest the whole English reading public, not just Zionists."[96]

This newspaperman was not alone in noting that Uris had a "knack of making friends quickly." The Hebrew woman's style magazine, *L'Isha* profiled Uris as a glamour playboy. The American Jew was a talented and well-known writer, this popular journal wrote, and he was also not reluctant to let people know it; yet "even if he [Uris] could be a little arrogant," it was "hard to get angry" with such a handsome young man who cut a "bronzed, vigorous masculine" figure.[97]

The highlight in the visit's first days was Uris's participation in Israel's eighth Independence Day celebrations. An Israel Defense Forces (IDF) military parade thrilled him. In Haifa, as 250,000 proud celebrants packed into the night, Uris couldn't stop taking pictures. "These are magnificent people, a kind of Jew you and I have never seen before," he wrote, flush with emotion, to his father. Even in this private correspondence, Uris's writing on Israel uniquely combined earnest ethnic pride and propagandistic social realism. "As I watched these tall, strong Hebrew warriors parade, I felt that Mr. Nasser had better have an army of 50 million beggars to win. Israel cannot be defeated," Uris proclaimed to his father.[98]

"Dad I swear the good Lord sent me to Israel to write this book for my people. This magnificent land is indescribable. I hope to be able to capture its people in fiction," Uris added in another private letter, several weeks after his arrival in Israel.[99] Crisscrossing the country (he later claimed to have traversed 12,000 miles in the country while conducting research), he followed a whirlwind routine. Arranging interviews and gathering materials, he relied on his Foreign Ministry aide, Ilan Hartuv;[100] half a century later, Uris's productive professional relationship with this Foreign Ministry official, who later attained the rank of ambassador, seems tinged with suggestive irony. Uris was in Israel to collect facts for a book that would show the world how a new type of Jew had risen heroically from tragedy and used the sword courageously to control his own destiny. Twenty years later, Hartuv himself became a living symbol of these themes, as one of the hostages rescued in the daring IDF *Matkal* commando rescue operation at Uganda's Entebbe Airport (Hartuv's elderly mother, British Israeli Dora Bloch, was left behind at a hospital and later murdered by Idi Amin's soldiers).[101]

The writer and his Foreign Minister sidekick made the rounds of kibbutzim, from the Galilee to the Negev, and Uris took notes about the experiences and outlooks of sabra offspring of legendary figures in the halutz pioneering movement, such as Yitzhak Tabenkin. In Jerusalem, he interviewed Teddy Kollek, who was then the chief staffer in Ben-Gurion's office; Chaim Herzog, a prime mover in the IDF's Military Intelligence branch; Moshe Pearlman, another Ben-Gurion aide; and writer Haim Gouri. At Abu Gush, outside of Jerusalem, Hartuv and Uris conversed with Arab notables, and they also met local Arab and Druze leaders in the Galilee.[102] Uris recorded many of these interviews on what he later claimed was three miles of tape. Insignificant and sometimes odd inaccuracies in the text of *Exodus* bear the impress of orally transmitted information. This appears to be most true with respect to false facts in Uris's extended discussion of the Holocaust—for example, *Exodus*'s description of Adolf Eichmann ("he had been born in Palestine and spoke fluent Hebrew").

Other stops in his 1956 tour thrilled the Marine Corps veteran. Taking advantage of special clearances provided to him by Israeli authorities, Uris accompanied Israel Defense Forces patrols at the farthest reaches of the land. On one patrol, with sixteen paratroopers, including his first cousin, uncle Aaron's son, Yossi Yerushalmi, Uris traversed "ravines and wadis and wilds" in the Negev; on desert floors, temperatures reached an incredible 127 degrees. The fact that Jewish soldiers were in control of such forbidding country fired his imagination.[103]

The appreciation and vicarious identification that materialized on the Negev paratrooper patrol followed Uris everywhere. It is on his face in a snapshot, apparently taken during this Negev patrol, in which a machine-gun-bearing Uris leans on an IDF jeep—the photo was used in *Exodus* publicity campaigns.[104] The paratrooper group was later dropped at the Suez Canal in the 1956 Sinai War. In his 1988 novel *Mitla Pass,* Uris imagined himself parachuting down to Suez with these paratroopers as an observer-participant during the same war.

IDF soldiers impressed Uris in every way. Uris had been mulling over the concept of a Jewish Marine Corps for years, since his experimentation in *Battle Cry*—it will be recalled that the Jewish strongmen he created in this first novel appeared more as theoretical demonstrations than as human beings. In Israel, Uris was convinced that he was seeing the genuine article. Sabra fighters were (in the au-

Uris in military garb, touring in the Negev desert with an IDF paratrooper unit while compiling research notes for *Exodus*. The photo was used in publicity materials for the novel. (Harry Ransom Humanities Research Center, the University of Texas at Austin)

thor's words) the "real Israel," and when Uris identified with them he was consciously rebelling against his father's "shtetl" intellectualism. He never tired of beating the war drums in his private letters. "The real Israel is one you do not comprehend," he informed his father:

> It is a nation of young marines, Sabras, the Hebrew war-rior of Giora and the Macabees [*sic*] and Bar Kochba. This is Israel, the fighter who spits in the eye of the Arab hordes and dares him. This young Israel shrugs its shoulders at the Talmudic foolishness of the old folks. If you think that this spirit was gained here by the old scholars, you are mistaken. Israel was won by the gun and it will be saved by the gun.[105]

The author locked onto this gun-barrel theory of Jewish redemption by summer 1956. In this period, he began to speak bluntly about what his new book would be about. Its hero, tentatively named Avi Ben Canaan, "a fighting Jew who won't take shit from anybody, who fears nobody," would be "a breath of spring air for the American people."[106]

However immodest, Uris was articulating an enabling sense of creative confidence when he wrote to his editor in September 1956 about how the "hand of God has something to do with this book."[107] He had "never seen objectives and characters so clearly before." Comfortably settled in a Herzliya home after the arrival of his wife and children, the plan of the book consolidated in his mind. With telling candor, he unveiled it to his editor.

The rationale and promise of his book-in-the-making, he explained, had to be put in context. Israel had remained "one of the most conspicuous holes in fiction" for appreciable reasons. For one thing, the "vastness and complication" of Jewish history intimidated writers. Also, the "heavy slant of pro-Zionism" in existing works about Israel confused or deterred non-Jewish readers. Therefore, Uris announced, his "first and major goal" would be to "create a work for the American people, outside of the Jewish people." A device in the attainment of that American end would be the depiction of a "heroine who is a mid-Western Christian girl who knows Jews from a hole in the ground."[108]

Uris also discussed with his editor what probably turned out to be *Exodus*'s most effective device. The author was determined to frame his narrative as "just another page in the story that started 4000 years ago with Genesis." Framing his narrative as a continuation of the biblical story would draw in the "Mid-West Lutheran and the Southern Baptist." His heroes would be the "modern Moses, David and Barak." He would not allow his readers "escape from the Biblical parallels," Uris pledged.[109]

That being the case, he searched for an appropriately biblical title for his book-in-the-making. For several weeks in the summer of 1956 Uris tried out "The Land is Mine," from Leviticus 25:23, but he subsequently dropped it when confidants advised that it sounded "too Zionistic"[110] (the phrase resurfaced as the name of *Exodus*'s Book Two, and, more importantly, as the cotitle of Pat Boone's "Exodus Song," in lyrics written for Ernest Gold's Academy Award–winning score for the *Exodus* film). Thereafter, Uris debated various book title options for months. Throughout the High Holy Day season in Israel, in autumn 1956, he consulted with Yigal Yadin, the former IDF commander who had recently earned his doctorate in archaeology for research on the Dead Sea Scrolls. Uris trusted Yadin, "a great authority on the Bible," but no obvious title choice emerged.[111] Several months later, in February/March 1957, Uris toyed with the phrase "Awake in Glory," taken from the 57th Psalm of David. However, that title got negative feedback as being "too literate."[112]

Frustrated, in mid-March Uris decided that less would be more. "The new title will simply be Exodus," he announced to friends and family. "I hope you like it."[113] A month later he pitched this new title to William Bradbury, managing editor of Doubleday and Company, which had recently acquired rights to Uris's manuscript from Random House. "Let's call it Exodus," Uris wrote to Bradbury, urging him to ignore the fact that about a dozen other works, "mostly British plays," bore the title. Uris sounded resolved.[114] He explained to his father (on April 25) that the name "Exodus," much like the phrase "Battle Cry," was instantly recognizable. "The word Exodus is known by every man, woman and child."[115] With this title choice, Uris closed the circle in his decision to tell the story of Israel's founding as though it were a supplement to the biblical narrative. "Nothing nicer could happen" to his book, Uris privately conceded, "than to mistake it for a Bible connection." After all, in 1955, the "Bible sold six million copies."[116]

In the fall of 1956, Uris's plan was to spend several months with his family in a pleasant Herzliya neighborhood, by the sea. He arranged membership in the local country club, and he and his wife Betty made friends easily with South African and American diplomatic personnel in the area around their temporary home. "The children are really getting indoctrinated in Jewish ways," Uris happily wrote to his father in late September. His family had just eaten some meals in a Sukkah during the Jewish Feast of Tabernacles holiday. Things were going well.[117]

Suddenly, the eruption of the Suez-Sinai War in late October 1956 destroyed the Uris family's overseas idyll, and also accelerated the making of *Exodus*. The war confirmed all of Uris's observations and thoughts about the emergence of Jewish power in Israel. Hours of harrowing experience for the writer and his family affected him in a number of ways, but mainly Israel's 1956 war triumph was, for him, a message clincher.

The origins of the 1956 Sinai War are to be found in Israeli anxieties about a "second round" of confrontation with the Arab states that date back to the failed Lausanne peace conference of 1949.[118] For years, Israel had been plagued by fedayeen terror attacks launched across its unstable border with Egypt. Although the motivations of border infiltrations have been disputed by historians,[119] as early as 1953 Israel's military leadership appears to have decided in favor of initiating a war against Egypt to eliminate terror attacks and forestall a potentially catastrophic second round of all-out conflict with the Arab world.[120] In years before autumn 1956, the bellicose rhetoric of Egyptian president Gamel Abdel Nasser reinforced the consensus among IDF planners in favor of preemptive war; the belief was that Israel was too small and fragile to absorb a blow from Egypt and then sustain an effective counteroffensive. Various moves taken by Nasser pushed Israeli military-political leaders irreversibly toward the preemptive war option. Historian Mordechai Bar-On, who was at the time IDF chief of staff Moshe Dayan's private secretary, emphasizes Egypt's arms deal with Czechoslovakia, which was announced in September 1955, as the crucial turning point. "The Egypt-Czech arms deal changed the prevailing situation overnight," writes Bar-On. The deal promised Nasser an arsenal that would "be three times larger than what Israel had or could expect to acquire in the near future."[121] Other studies have claimed that this Egypt-Czech accord actually marked the end of one phase of a continuing process leading to war,[122] but all research concurs that the security concerns that brought Israel to war are to be distinguished from the aims and circumstances of Israel's partners in the 1956 Sinai campaign. When the crisis about the Suez Canal erupted in late July 1956, as a result of Nasser's announcement of the canal's nationalization, England and France maneuvered on the basis of their own strategic interests; as it dealt with the Suez crisis, France kept one eye on its conflict in Algeria, where an anticolonial revolt had erupted in November 1954 and had escalated into a full-scale war by summer 1956 (in contrast to the situation in France, Britain's leadership, and its public, proved to be divided about the events preceding and following the Sinai War). Israel wanted the 1956 war, but it waited for the two major European powers to sanction it; "the time of war was determined in Paris and London," writes Motti Golani.[123] The war's rationale and implementation was never really challenged in Israel. Shimon Peres, then defense minister director-general, spoke for many when he declared: "There was no sense of conspiracy; it was a decision taken to defend ourselves before our enemy rose up to slay us."[124] The results of the Sinai War remain open to debate. Bar-On notes that Israel was forced to withdraw from territories it gained in the fighting, the Sinai peninsula and the Gaza Strip, without receiving substantive international assurances about its security interests; however, he adds, the IDF victory provided Israel a decade of "relative tranquility" in which it directed "its resources and energies to economic and social goals."[125] Certainly, Israel's leadership and public remained convinced after the war that the country had acted on the basis of a clear moral right.[126]

On Saturday/Sunday, October 27/28, Uris watched young Israeli neighbors abruptly leave their homes for predetermined IDF assembly points. He contacted Colonel Dave Peterson, military attaché at the U.S. embassy, and was informed on Monday that Americans were being advised to clear out of the country.[127] It was the beginning of Operation Kadesh, for the conquest of Sinai; a paratrooper battalion, led by Lieutenant Colonel Rafael Eitan, was dropping down around Jebel Heitan on the peninsula.

Uris stalled. The next afternoon he conferred with Betty; in an ingenious formulation dispatched by cable to the *Philadelphia Inquirer,* the bare-knuckled war writer explained that the parents decided on an evacuation plan for the sake of their children's grandparents. In other words, Uris would stay, but the four others were putting on their running shoes.

This decision precipitated a frantic sequence, all in the darkness of a wartime blackout. By candlelight, Betty and Leon dumped the family's belongings into his old Marine Corps sea bags, while ten-year-old Karen found some paint to cover up the car's headlights. The Lydda airdrome not being easy to find in daytime, Uris (in his words) "prayed to whatever saints came to mind" that he would find the terminal with covered headlights in a blackout. When, at last, they nervously entered the terminal, they found a situation that "looked like a Chinese refugee scene of the 1930s." The kids dozed and cried. At one stage Betty "broke a little" and asked her husband to join the departure, but, Uris replied, a "writer had to stay on the job." Before dawn on Wednesday morning the family greeted the arrival of U.S. Air Force Globemaster Boxcars with enormous relief. Uris's heart swelled with American patriotic pride as he watched the military planes coming to the rescue of his possibly imperiled family, looking like a sheriff leading tough, honest cowboys down a hill. When the "crew of cocky, clean American lads" stepped out of one Globemaster, "I knew that my tax dough was well spent, and that my wife and kids were safe."[128] Not too long after the war, Uris reconnoitered with his family in Europe, and by 1957 the Uris clan was resettled in California.

The combination of his family's stirring pick-up by U.S. military planes and the IDF's rapid-fire conquest of the Sinai Peninsula reinforced Uris's sense of moral continuity between post–World War II American power and the triumphant battles of the young Jewish state. In Uris's stint as a military correspondent during the short Sinai Campaign he managed to cable off just two or three dispatches to a few foreign newspapers. Corroborating everything he had researched for seven months, Uris witnessed an incredible spectacle of Israeli power and Egyptian ruin in the Sinai. For years, the 1956 Sinai Campaign remained in his memory as an image of Israeli invincibility—this, of course, was more than a decade before other American Jewish literati became immersed in the same image as a result of a still more spectacular Israeli victory, during the 1967 Six Days' War.[129]

Uris's writing in the 1956 Sinai dispatches wedded bellicose World War II–era slang to his theory about the value of finding biblical connectors in any mention of Israeli reality.[130] "From Nitzana to Ismalia, the Israelis struck with the velocity of a baseball bat hitting a raw egg," Uris cabled to a London news agency, in hard-hitting cadence. "Even in these days of souped-up warfare, the Israeli cyclone must have set some sort of record." Uris described how he set out, "with a backside full of penicillin, to the "choking sand-blown mass known as the Sinai." The war's result was astounding. In one hundred hours, Israel had "completely obliterated" Nasser's forces, and "occupied a territory three times its own size." He rode along a highway strewn with "wreckage of tanks and vehicles of every description." Most haunting were shoes left behind by panic-stricken Egyptian soldiers, who reckoned that it would be easier to flee through sand barefoot. Elsewhere, as in a dispatch to the *San Francisco Examiner*, Uris dramatized his copy with biblical allusions. The Sinai campaign became an "exodus in reverse into Egypt." Just as rabbis from the tribes had gathered to address Joshua's warriors during the crossing of the River Jordan into the Promised Land, nine rabbis had stood before Israel's "tough little army" as it embarked upon a "campaign of retribution" in Operation Kadesh.

When viewed from a long-term biographical viewpoint, Uris's emotional experience reporting on the IDF's rapid-fire conquest in the Sinai contains hints about the limits of his conceptual playing field as the author's relationship with Israel evolved over the decades. America's setbacks in Vietnam and Israel's struggles in the 1973 Yom Kippur War and the 1982 Lebanon War did not eradicate his bedrock beliefs about the moral alignment of military forces in the world after World War II, but suggestions of eroded optimism can nonetheless be garnered from his final novel about Jewish issues, his 1988 volume *Mitla Pass*.[131] In this late novel, Uris's 1956 perception of American power coming, cowboylike, to the aid of innocents in distress in Israel has vanished. In *Mitla*, the hero-author manages to evacuate his wife and children during the 1956 Suez crisis, but only after he parries extortionist demands from a U.S. diplomatic-military spook. Also, as an implicit symbol of disillusionment, Uris selected the site of the IDF's sole tragic fiasco in the 1956 Sinai campaign, Mitla Pass, as ground zero for the action and narrative flashbacks and digressions in his 1988 novel.

These, however, were no more than tentative symbols of eroded faith in Israeli power. During the final decades of the twentieth century, Uris remained unwilling or unable to assess systematically whether his old, Exodus-era, images of Israeli heroism had stood the test of time. What remained unchanged in his writing about Israel and the Middle East was a punishing view of Israel's enemies. In spirit, the high-blown and pitiless phrases that capped Uris's 1956 reports on the Sinai campaign—"And the wind blows over the Sinai, and the shifting sands swirl and cover Nasser's soldiers, who died running with their shoes off"—resonate in Uris's later writings about the Arab world.[132]

After his return to California, Uris labored on the final stages in the composition of *Exodus* throughout most of 1957. One passing, sour note in this period was a dispute with Random House, and its legendary cofounder Bennett Cerf, about the disbursement of advance payments. Cerf was a formidable personality who managed a diverse stable of literary talent, from Faulkner and Capote to Dr. Seuss; but Uris, who worked up a new contract with Doubleday and left Random House, does not seem to have been fazed by this episode.[133] He was in this period grinding away on *Exodus,* making sure that the book would be finished and released by the second half of 1958, in sync with Israel's tenth anniversary. "There will be a real coast to coast wing ding," he explained to Doubleday's managing editor, William Bradbury. In order to capitalize on the tenth celebrations, spring/summer 1948 "would be a damned good target to bead on in."[134]

At the end of 1957, as Uris banged out the final words to *Exodus* on his typewriter, he purchased a new home in Encino, about two miles from his old one. Surrounded by two hundred trees, the 3,500 square foot home had three bedrooms, a large patio, a swimming pool, and a separate writing area.[135] Months before *Exodus*'s publication, the scent of citrus fruit and success was in the air.

Uris's early drafts sprawled over hundreds of pages, and he was forced midway through this productive year of 1957 to pare down and tighten up his story. The most nerve-wracking, and, in retrospect, significant element in this editorial process involved Uris's audacious intention to craft dozens of pages in *Exodus*'s Book Two as a modern Jewish history survey of the rise of anti-Semitism in the modern era and Jewish responses to this malice, culminating in the Yishuv's pioneering efforts in Mandatory Palestine. If best-seller fiction had ever seen anything like that before, neither Uris nor his Doubleday editors were aware of it.

Learning by doing throughout his project, Uris found it impossible to write his minihistory during one prolonged sitting. He would read about Jews in Czarist Russia, write about his fictionalized Rabinsky–Ben Canaan brothers (Ari's father and uncle), and then pick up several more books about Entente powers in the Middle East during World War I before getting back to his pioneering stories about the days of the Second and Third Aliyah immigration waves to the Yishuv. "I am at work on the second book, in effect a history of the return to Palestine from 1885 until World War II," Uris announced to his family in late April 1957. He reported that he had another "15 books to read before I start writing again." He was "fascinated" by the political intrigue at the time of the Ottoman Collapse at the end of World War I to the issuance of the British White Paper of 1939. Jewish responses to these dramatic events, the rise and fall of their hopes in British-controlled Palestine, constituted "electrifying and almost unbelievable reading." It was also complicated. "I only hope I can clarify it for the reader and simplify it without getting too involved."[136]

Whether or not this feat of simplification in a text packed with information about Jewish history could be pulled off worried Uris and his editors for months, really up to the minute *Exodus* went to galley proofs. Uris's literary idols, particularly John Steinbeck, had written popularly accessible books that followed family histories, stitched in biblical imagery, and depicted poignant social processes. However, facts about an ethno-national group's modern history—from, in this case, the Czar's mandatory conscription of the Jews in 1827 to the 1939 British White Paper's restriction on Zionist immigration and land purchases—were nowhere to be found in these literary precedents. Could a book be accessed by a mass, mixed audience and contain reams of information unknown to anyone but the Zionists and their engaged supporters and antagonists? Uris wondered. He was more sincere than supercilious when he noted privately: "This book is not written for a few people who indulge in high level thought planes, but for the masses to understand." Then he got to the point: "The intricacies of Judaism and Israel MUST be simplified for the average reader to understand."[137]

Eventually, Doubleday agreed. Through June 1958, days before final work on *Exodus*'s galleys commenced, Uris tapped into fast-talk talents he had honed for years in contacts with cultural impresarios, since his discharge from the Marine Corps, and his days trying to sell a relative's manuscript. The debates with his publisher about Book Two were ridden with tension. Bradbury periodically had cold feet about all its Jewish history; and, at the eleventh hour, he proposed that outside readers take a look at Book Two before Doubleday printed *Exodus*. On June 4, Uris declined, pulling out all the stops. This was D-Day for *Exodus*.

"Ultimately there are only two opinions worth a fiddler's fuck, and that's yours and mine," he implored in a note to Bradbury. He admitted that Book Two was slow, in contrast to the action-packed descriptions of three hundred Holocaust orphans staging a hunger strike aboard their stalled ship in Cyprus in Book One and the subsequent descriptions of the War of Independence. "The one and only question which we have to concern ourselves with is not the admitted slowness or the completely intentional effort to indoctrinate our reader with history, but whether *will we lose him or won't we*," Uris explained to Bradbury. Uris reported that he had consulted with agent Ingo Preminger and others, and nobody found the history sections to be a deal breaker in terms of the book's reception. At worst, Uris expected, "we may make him [the reader] yawn after the lightning action of Book One . . . but I am not convinced that we are going to lose a single reader."[138]

History remained in *Exodus*'s Book Two.

Another lesser but serious concern was whether the history and events in *Exodus* would receive a stamp of approval from Israelis. For Uris, this consideration had a personal aspect, since he had written his book out of obvious admiration of the Jewish state's founders and sabra defenders and had also forged a number of productive contacts in Israel's military-political establishment while doing his field research. For his publishers, it was business. As it marshaled resources for a major publicity campaign for *Exodus,* Doubleday had reason to worry about a scenario whereby word floated down from high quarters in Jerusalem that the book was unreliable while Uris was making the rounds of Hadassah banquets and book signings. This concern, however, was definitively disposed of by the time the book reached the printers.

More than has been known, Ben-Gurion gave firm backing to Uris's intention to popularize Israel's case. Months after *Exodus* became a best seller, world media circulated what appeared to be the bottom line about Ben-Gurion's response. Thus, the *Christian Science Monitor* in December 1958 relayed what was said to be the Israeli prime minister's response to *Exodus:* "I don't usually read novels. But I read that one. As a literary work, it isn't much. But as a piece of propaganda, it's the greatest thing ever written about Israel," Ben-Gurion reportedly said.[139] It sounded like hearsay.

In fact, Ben-Gurion watched Uris's progress very closely; whatever his aesthetic judgment about the writer, he had respect for Uris's communicative capabilities. For instance, while *Exodus*'s sales skyrocketed and Uris shuffled between California and the Jewish state while working feverishly on a follow-up that eventually became a gripping novel about the Jewish uprising in the Warsaw ghetto, *Mila 18* (1961),[140] Israel's prime minister came to view the American as a master chronicler in popular culture of the Jews' historic determination to survive as a people. On April 30, 1959, an obviously flattered Uris wrote a confidential letter to Doubleday, reporting that Ben-Gurion was urging him to write a trilogy, following the projected Warsaw uprising book with a historical novel about the last stand of Jewish rebels against Roman imperial forces, at Masada in 72–73 CE.[141]

In so doing, Ben-Gurion was essentially placing in the hands of an American Jew a uniquely potent symbol in Zionist-Israeli iconography. The story of Masada, derived from an account in Josephus Flavius, could not be found in Jewish traditional sources following the Exile from Eretz Israel; but, owing to landmark writings such as a 1920s Hebrew poem by Isaac Lamdan, the towering site above the Dead Sea had mesmerized Zionist activists as a symbol of everlasting Jewish will to survive. A few years *after* Ben-Gurion's proposal to Uris, during Yigal Yadin's 1963–65 monumental excavations, Masada effectively became, for decades, Israel's national symbol.[142] Uris appreciated that he was being handed a story with aura by Israel's foremost personality. Breathlessly, he explained in confidential letters to Doubleday that Masada was "virgin and a helluva story." For weeks, he toyed with Ben-Gurion's suggestion about a trilogy spanning 2,000 years, featuring the "three great stands of the Jews," against Rome at the Dead Sea, the Nazis in Warsaw, and in the War of Independence.[143] The trilogy, of course, never materialized, but the episode suffices as an example of the extent of Ben-Gurion's appreciation of Uris. The American Jew, for his part, rapturously dedicated a pictorial survey that he compiled with the Greek photographer Dimitrios Harissia, *Exodus Revisited* (1960), to Ben-Gurion.[144]

It is therefore clear in retrospect that Israeli officialdom was not going to stand in the way of *Exodus*, but at the time the prospect worried Uris and his editors. Their fears were allayed on July 22, 1958, in a letter sent from Prime Minister Ben-Gurion's office.[145] Providing what was in effect Israel's official response to *Exodus*, Moshe Pearlman, the prime minister's advisor on public affairs, excitedly praised Uris's "fine work," and mostly limited his critique to technical matters and errors. Uris, for instance, erroneously referred to Givat Hashlosha as the Hill of Five (instead of three) and to Jesus being transfixed (instead of transfigured) on Mount Tabor.

Pearlman's comments relating to Uris's handling of the divisions between right-wing and left-wing Zionist movements in the fight for Palestine went beyond technical editorial correction. Pearlman, a journalist by profession and the IDF's first spokesman,[146] objected that Uris's narrative was not sufficiently analytic about the moral debate between the Haganah and the right-wing Irgun militia regarding the use of force. Whereas at crucial junctures Haganah sponsored offensive counterattacks against Arabs, it limited its use of arms to strikes against Arab bands implicated in terror and shunned the killing of a stray Arab in reprisal for the murder of a Jew. The Irgun, in contrast, was not so discriminating, believing that if "an Arab were killed whenever a Jew was killed," such use of force would restrain the Arab terror groups.[147]

Sensitivities about the taxonomy and ideology of rival political and military groups in the Zionist movement were familiar to Uris. Nothing that Ben-Gurion's office could say would deter him from the generic, bipartisan gloss he put upon the Yishuv's struggle for national liberation, and he correctly guessed that Ben-Gurion and other leading Israeli politicians understood that long-standing disputes about roles played in the 1948 struggle by offshoots of the Labor Zionist and Revisionist Zionist movements lost their edge outside of Israel. Pearlman's comments, Uris assured Doubleday, are "strictly within bounds." With its Israeli stamp of approval, *Exodus* was about to hit the stage.

Uris's editors signed off on the book in a mood of quasi-religious ecstasy. After having logged innumerable hard hours preparing *Exodus* for publication, seasoned word crafters in Doubleday's editorial rooms spoke about the narrative's links between the 1948 events and the biblical world not as metaphor or cagey plot device but rather as though they had been planted in the soil of the Holy Land by God. Exodus had soul, not spin.

Bradbury privately confessed to an "odd feeling I have about *Exodus* that's mystical, spiritual, magical or something." Here was a hardened editor speaking earnestly about the divine logic of the plot of his company's upcoming book:

> Not only is the modern day story of the rebirth of Israel a fulfillment of the words of the ancient prophets and in itself mystical, but in the actual events described in the book, some pretty odd things happen. When a unit of the Haganah, during the Israeli-Arab war, overpowered by a superior, better-equipped Arab force was facing obvious annihilation, only to have a miraculous downpour turn the roads into mud and bog down the Arab mobile armament, all this in the *exact same spot* where thousands of years ago a force of ancient Hebrews led by Rebecca faced the same kind of annihilation from Canaanite legions.[148]

The expectation of big sales added to such enthusiasm, no doubt. Yet the irrepressibly energetic Uris had brought his publishers aboard; the making of *Exodus* was, his editors believed, a small miracle that uncannily reenacted Israel's amazing triumph in 1948. Uris had been touched by something.

Bradbury breathlessly tried to put it into words, writing to an associate on August 13, 1958: "To have listened to Uris in the early days talk about the feeling of fulfillment and destiny that led him to this story, and then to have seen how in the face of impossible odds everything broke right for him to be able to produce *Exodus,* to get to Israel precisely at the right time and to participate in the Sinai campaign. . . ." Doubleday's managing editor finished the thought with a preciously phrased profession of faith. Uris's passion turned even non-Jews into believers. "Believe me the whole thing is enough to make a Christian out of you," testified Bradbury.[149]

Uris and his publishers indulged hype when they talked about and promoted *Exodus*. "A miracle few could resist, the most dramatic event of the 20th century," declared the back cover, referring to the founding of the Jewish state with the subtlety of a circus hawker. Inside the covers, Uris wrote about Israel in slashing, take-no-prisoner prose. The hyped-up language suited the commercial culture of bestseller publishing, but not everything in *Exodus* was about business. A review of the author's own private correspondence and the letters of his own business associates and family members shows unmistakably how *Exodus* was prepared as a once-in-a-lifetime project, as testimony of faith in the historical processes that led to democracy's triumph in World War II, and to the redemption of an ancient promise to an ancient people.

Well before *Exodus* was published and climbed up the best-seller charts, Uris realized that the novel could mean, for him, big money. Undeniably, motives extraneous to Jewish issues (the thirst for fame and fortune, and perhaps also the psychological drive of a high school drop-out who is eager to prove intellectual command of a difficult subject) propelled Uris forward; his writing career after *Exodus* showed that his interest in Israel and Jewish issues was far from all consuming. Yet it is impossible not to be impressed by how personally engaged Uris became with the historical subject he turned into a best seller. As a metaphor for a journey toward a cherished dream, "exodus" was *his* own story.

For Uris, liberation at the end of the exodus journey meant feeling strong as a Jew. In his biography we can identify intangible but genuine dynamics that led him to this journey—the childhood feelings of embittered estrangement from which he fled when he enlisted as a marine after Pearl Harbor; a sense of outrage about the Holocaust that was deepened by Uris's encounter with Israeli relatives who survived the camps, and who had terrifying stories to tell; a desire to close the circle of a Zionist pioneering effort his father had attempted on the Third Aliyah; and (as the next chapter will emphasize) an impassioned need to associate Jewish experience with the inspiring sense of triumph Uris felt in postwar America. As he completed his novel, Uris had no doubt that the state of Israel was the answer to every question raised by these dynamics and desires. That answer, he believed, could be understood by anyone, so long as the questions surrounding Israel were assessed in terms of everything that had happened to Jews in modern times.

With such existential concerns dictating it, Uris's commitment to Jewish history well exceeded the financial, social, and professional benefits he could have expected to accrue by writing an exciting story about Israel's founding. In the end, nothing other than these existential needs compelled him to include in *Exodus* history-saturated elements such as its Book Two. His enthusiasm for the history he was telling became contagious. His publishers, and (as we shall see) his readers, became convinced about the link between *Exodus*'s narrative of Israel's founding, and Judeo-Christian destiny.

In Uris's mind, the link between his novel and the abstract questions of human identity and national being was supported by the reams of facts he researched and incorporated in *Exodus,* but it did not ultimately depend upon any of the historical details. Since the spirit of the book's evocation of Israel's founding was correct, it did not matter if *Exodus* was technically wrong about any specifics. By and large, the world agreed. As an example of Uris's orientation toward the facts and spirit of *Exodus*'s treatment of Jewish history, and of the public's approval of Uris's approach, it is appropriate to close this chapter with an example from the Holocaust, the history topic of utmost concern to the author.

In spring 1964, Uris willfully defended Holocaust atrocity claims made in *Exodus* in a libel action brought against him in a London court. Underlying Uris's involvement in this colorful trial was the defiant attitude he expressed in his Anne Frank letter to his father about the need to "show anger" in response to Nazi horror.

Being Leon Uris, he dramatized his own defense of *Exodus*'s disputed Holocaust claim. The author wrote a best-selling novel about the libel case, *QB VII* (1970),[150] that contained exaggerated characterizations and that occasionally refashioned somewhat blurry real-life circumstances in a Manichaean fictional frame. Nonetheless, *QB VII* described an actual, highly colorful episode in Uris's life (key courtroom passages of the novel draw virtually verbatim from the transcript of the libel trial), and the author's behavior throughout it not only personified the *Exodus* ethic of never backing down on Holocaust issues but also presaged future incidents in which Jewish figures refused to bow to pressures involving claims they made in writings about the Holocaust, such as the example of the 2000 libel suit pursued in a London court by Holocaust denier David Irving against the historian Deborah Lipstadt.[151]

In one passage about Auschwitz in *Exodus*, Uris wrote: "Here in Block X, Dr. Wirthe used women as guinea pigs and Dr. Schumann sterilized by castration and X ray and Caluberg removed ovaries and Dr. Dehring performed seventeen thousand 'experiments' in surgery without anaesthetic." The last figure mentioned in this description, Wladyslaw Alexander Dering (Uris misspelled his surname), sued Uris, claiming, correctly, that the figure of 17,000 operations without anesthetics had no factual basis.

Dering, a Polish nationalist, received his medical training at Warsaw University. As a prisoner of war, he was subjected to various indignities and physical abuses by the Nazis after the German conquest of Poland, before being put in charge of the operating theater in Auschwitz's Block 21. The plaintiff's side in the libel action submitted that Dering had been in charge of some 20,000 operations at Auschwitz, but only a small number of them, around 130, had been done without an anesthetic.[152]

After the war, Dering surfaced in England, working at a Polish General Hospital in Huntington. War crimes allegations followed him, and he spent nineteen months in a prison in Brixton before he successfully avoided extradition to Poland. Running away from the legacy of his past, the controversial physician obtained a post as a medical officer in the Colonial Service, in Somaliland. His research and medical labors there won recognition, and Dr. Dering returned

to England in 1960 with an Order of the British Empire (OBE). He
believed that his reputation in British society was sufficiently established to withstand counterattacks in a libel suit about his doings at
Auschwitz. Dering died shortly after the embarrassing failure of his
libel suit, and he may have gone to his grave believing that his behavior, under the hellish circumstances of Auschwitz, had been defamed
in fact and spirit in *Exodus*. If that was not the case, he committed
perjury on the stand at the April 1964 trial. Dering testified "I tried
to do my best" when asked whether he felt in retrospect that he had
done all he could for his "suffering fellow creatures at Auschwitz."[153]

When Dering's complaint was lodged, Uris was far from expertly
versed in the facts of Auschwitz's Block 21. His claim about Dering was taken from a credible source, the volume *Underground:
The Story of a People*, written by Joseph Tenenbaum and published
by the Philosophical Library in 1952.[154] Tenenbaum had rich, long-
standing experience in Jewish affairs—as a young Galician econo-
mist in 1918, he turned up in Paris as a delegate representing Eastern
European Jewry at the Peace Conference, and worked closely with
American Jewish leader Louis Marshall in the drafting of minority
rights proposals.[155] Uris borrowed most of the information (including the misspelled surname) in Tenenbaum's claims about Dering.
Tenenbaum's *Underground* recorded:

> Some "surgeons" to demonstrate their skills, operated with
> the speed of an electric razor. Many of these operations were
> performed without the use of an anesthetic. Dr. Dehring,
> Professor Clauberg's assistant and one of the surgeons of the
> camp, was later apprehended. He had performed a record
> number of 17,000 operations of which 16,500 were in the
> nature of pseudoscientific experiments. A Pole, he left Ger-
> many after the Nazi debacle and joined the Anders Army.
> He was assigned to the post of surgeon at the Polish Army
> hospital at Huntington, England, where he worked until his
> discovery.[156]

Upon investigation of the facts of Block 21, Uris decided not to be
cowed by Dering's complaint. Uris's team, led by Solicitor Solomon
Kaufman who dedicated two years of research to the case, engaged
a prodigious fact-finding operation, and its results discouraged the
author from granting the Polish physician a moral victory.

In *QB VII*, the fictionalized Uris, Abe Cady, decides to brave the libel suit after encountering several Auschwitz survivors, mostly Israelis but also one world-famous European musician, who were mutilated by castration operations perpetrated by the novel's version of Dering, as part of the Nazis' insane sterilization experiments. Uris's novel also conveys various hints about forms of assistance the author received as he decided to take up the cudgel in the libel suit: in the novel, leading lights of Britain's Jewry and other Diaspora communities provide him moral, and perhaps financial, support, and Israel's security services even pitch in, tracking down corroborative witnesses behind the iron curtain. Describing, among other things, a warmly supportive relationship between author and editor, *QB VII* contained undoubtedly accurate information that provides insight about the sources of Uris's strength in this episode. Still, separating fact from fiction in his riveting best seller is difficult—in a broad sense, doing so is unnecessary. Once he drew a conclusive moral impression about Dering's character and his behavior at Auschwitz, Uris could never have buckled by issuing an admission of substantive guilt. To have done so would have belied everything *Exodus* stood for.

By his own admission, Dering was involved in several malicious castration and ovariectomy procedures (the number of operations remained in dispute; by the plaintiff's own admission, "perhaps" some dozen procedures of testicle removal were conducted). In the trial, the Uris defense team, led by Lord Gerald Gardiner, later Lord Chancellor of England, devastated Dering's self-serving explanations, demonstrating how the plaintiff's claim that he would have been shot by the Nazis had he not cooperated with vicious sterilization experimentation had no clear basis in the circumstances of Auschwitz. Dering's contention that he had medical reason to remove testicles that had already been radiated by others was founded on spurious scientific foundations, as well as circular, morally malfeasant, reasoning, Uris's legal team established. Uris attended all of the trial hearings but never took the stand because neither he nor his publishers disputed the plaintiff's factual complaint about the error in the *Exodus* passage—Dering had not conducted 17,000 operations without anesthetic. That did not exonerate the physician; even after *Exodus*'s printers, Purnell & Sons Ltd., published a retraction, and paid Dering 500 pounds, Uris and his publisher refused to issue any statement bearing substantive contrition. The Auschwitz doctor, in Uris's view, did not deserve any trace of retrospective rehabilitation.

Many years after the episode, Uris summed up his position on the Dering suit. "The issue at stake was how far a man can go and still claim membership in the human race," the author explained. Dering was morally beyond the pale. "As a Jew and as an American, I had no choice but to fight," he stated.[157]

The jury deliberated for just 150 minutes before awarding Dering contemptuous damages of one halfpenny. Uris's triumph in the case furthered his career in many ways. Among other things, his *QB VII* version of the trial was dramatized in a popular, six-hour mini TV series that grabbed six Emmys (Anthony Hopkins played the nemesis of the Uris character in the drama). It was an engaging, multinational trial—proceedings were conducted in Greek, Polish, Hebrew, English, German, Czech, Russian, and Ladino—centered on enduring issues of human responsibility.[158] The trial was one of the most representative moments of a writing career that combined shrewd publicity instincts with compelling moral stamina. Its outcome vindicated *Exodus*'s spirit, though not all of its facts.

3) *Exodus* and the Americanization of Israel

FOR MANY DECADES, before the world wars, American Jews fashioned what the scholar Jonathan Sarna has described as the "Cult of Synthesis."[1] Often in an obsessive fashion, American Jews reinterpreted Jewish religion and cultural traditions to prove that they were causally or compatibly synthesized with identifiable building blocks of American democratic life. Postwar Jews in America had a new compulsion. Not Jewish tradition, but the new Jewish state needed to be seen as inherently democratic and suited to the salient values and norms of the American way of life. Fusing America and Israel, this was a different cult of synthesis. In this new, baby-boomer era of Jewish matchmaking, *Exodus* played a leading role.

Objectively, gaps between the two countries, Israel and the United States, were wide and forbidding. As Steven Cohen and Charles Liebman have observed, conceptualizations of nationalism, Jewish tradition, and state power versus individual liberty developed rather differently in the United States and Israel.[2] Also, specific "way of life" differences between the two countries in the 1950s are manifest during this period when American Jews enjoyed postwar capitalist prosperity in the suburbs while Israeli immigrants settled in tent-town *ma'abarot* and their country's welfare state system enforced economic rationing while bracing for an expected "second round" of warfare against Arab states.[3]

Nonetheless, several dynamics rode past these objective differences and drove the Americanization of Israel. Most obviously, Israel developed as a lively democracy, and American Jews could therefore identify with the spirit and substance of the new Jewish state's political system. Arguably, political affinities between the two countries go beyond their formal apparatuses of representative democracy. As commentators such as Peter Grose and Moshe Davis have argued, the founders of America's democracy were deeply inspired by images of the ancient Hebrews and even imagined that their endeavors were dedicated to the creation of a new Israel; links between America and Israel in the second half of the twentieth century, this argument suggests, were threaded by a long history of New World fascination with the Land of Israel.[4] In the postwar 1950s, such broad cultural and political overlap between America and the new Jewish state intersected with specific concerns and motivations of American Jewry. In an era saturated with Cold War suspicion about mixed loyalty, Jews in the United States had a strong incentive to show that there was nothing un-American about their love for Israel. When images of the Jewish state appeared recognizably American, a Jew in the United States who showed his or her love for Israel was less likely to deal with innuendo about a lack of patriotism. Significantly, both Israel and the United States progressed in the 1950s as victorious democratic responses to the Nazi assault on freedom during World War II. In this respect, the Americanization of Israel expressed a shared sense of triumph in both countries.

Such a roster of congruous historical forces appears persuasive, but nothing in these abstract reasons determined a particular writer's vision, or a particular audience's response. Looking out at Israel in the 1950s, an American Jewish writer could have apprehended many dynamics that were in or out of sync with norms and developments in his or her own home culture. Then, and thereafter, American Jewish artists and audiences overlooked the topic of immigrant absorption, the prevailing social issue of Israel's first years. Although the volatile and highly engaging drama of encounters between European (Ashkenazi) and Asian/African (Sephardic, or Mizrahi) Jews in Israel's tent town ma'abarot bore resemblances to relations between uptown "German" Jews and downtown "Russian" Jews in New York City at the turn of the twentieth century,[5] American Jews showed little interest in the subject. There is nothing surprising about the observation that American Jews were selective about what they saw in the young Jewish state, but it is important to be precise about the motivational basis of such selection. Choices were made on a sprawling historical canvas of Judeo-Christian links in American culture, Cold War anxieties and calculations, and postwar triumphalism, but the specific strokes that painted the Americanization of Israel belonged to the very personal identity needs of a writer.

Thus, as with everything else about the making of *Exodus*'s narrative of Israel's founding, the key to understanding how America came into the story is to be found in the writer's biography. An important reason why he wrote so passionately about the Jewish state, and why his audience found the story so compelling, is that Uris projected his own personal problems and existential dilemmas, and their imagined solutions, into the narrative.

Exodus perpetuated a long-standing pattern. As one historian has phrased it, American Jews view Israel as a "projection of America as it ought to be."[6] In Uris's case, the projected ideal—seamless harmony between Jews and Christians—radiated out of personal need and translated persuasively for millions of Jewish and Gentile readers and filmgoers. With power and effect that far surpassed any Zionist public relations effort that preceded it, *Exodus* popularized the Jewish state story partly because Leon Uris found a way to integrate into it the prevailing cultural concern of his era, that is, Judeo-Christian union in a post-Holocaust melting pot. Our argument begins with the mini–melting pot of Leon Uris's own family drama.

During World War II, Uris served as a radio operator in the U.S. Marines Second Battalion, Sixth Division, and saw some combat action at Guadalcanal and Tarawa. One of the highlights was sending home to his father a captured Japanese flag, which was auctioned with fanfare at a Philadelphia Gimbels department store to raise money for war bonds.[7] Uris served bravely, but he never attained rank higher than private 1st class, and his active service ended with the first Pacific offenses. At Tarawa, at the end of 1943, he contracted dengue fever; swollen, feverish and asthmatic, he was sent stateside. Recuperating for several months in 1944 in an Oakland naval hospital, Uris faced medical discharge, but, a quick talker, he wrangled from the Marine brass limited duty tasks in San Francisco, and waited for the war to end. His energy partially restored, Uris wrote some scripts and was arranging sponsorship for a Marine Corps dramatic production when he fell in love with Betty Katherine Beck.

She was a Marine sergeant and a Christian of Danish extract. "She just worships me, my work and everything I do," wrote Uris in late October 1944 to his half-sister Essie.[8] Betty, a twenty-two-year-old from Waterloo, Iowa, was blonde and had a "beautiful light complexion." Uris's new girlfriend had all-American traits. Betty liked to "shop, gossip, worry about her figure, cook, have fun and diet—stuff like that," Uris explained to Essie. "I need Betty very much," Uris confessed to his half-sister, "[and] she will make me a fine wife for many, many moons."[9]

Still, there was one problem. Twenty-year-old Uris worried that his family would give him the "bum's rush" because Betty was not Jewish.

As 1944 drew to a close, Betty offered Uris companionship after his "chicken shit friends in the Marine corps" backed out of sponsoring his play. While smitten with his girl, the soon-to-be veteran worried that his parents would not approve of his melting pot marriage. "It bothers me a lot to think about," Uris revealed to Essie, writing about his parents' expected disapproval of his Danish fiancée. But if his parents wanted to object, they could make a ruckus—as long as Betty agreed, "we are going to be married," wrote Uris.[10]

As it turned out, there were problems on the other side. Betty came from a comfortable, middle-class home (her father was a successful contractor) that was jarred by the thought of her seeking a happily-ever-after ending in the postwar world with a high school drop-out who happened to be Jewish. In mid-December 1944, Uris faced the first postcombat drama of his young adult life. Betty received threatening letters from her parents, one saying that her father would never see her again if she married Uris, another threatening that her mother would travel halfway across the country to stop the wedding. "The poor girl was tortured to say the least," Uris recounted; but she stood her ground. After "two of the worst days" he had ever lived through, Uris got on the phone to Iowa and unruffled the feathers. Uris was communicative and persuasive. "Things are all right now," the relieved Marine PFC wrote to his half-sister.[11]

"It doesn't make any difference to me personally whether we are married by a rabbi or a street car conductor," Uris told Essie, looking ahead to his wedding. But it mattered to his fiancée; and so, resolved that it was prudent to be "broad-minded," Leon agreed to a chapel wedding officiated by a chaplain who had served in his unit overseas. "Betty's folks came through in wonderful style" at the California wedding, delivering a $100 check as a gift.[12]

As a newlywed, Uris settled happily in the Bay Area. For him, the view from the hilltops in San Francisco looked out to everything that had been won in the war. For years, he would judge new vistas of human liberation and opportunity in terms of the glimmering view of the San Francisco Bay he saw as a young husband—in his first novel, island paradises in the Pacific; in his second novel, the rebellious hills of Nazi-occupied Greece where democratic ideals first materialized; and in his third novel, Israel's coastal city of Haifa, the venue of key events in the Jewish state's 1948 War of Independence, are all depicted as being almost as promising as what Uris and his peers saw offered to them in the San Francisco Bay Area after World War II.

In 1945, the pot of treasure at the end of the Golden Gate Bridge was filled with simple pleasures. "We enjoy football, hockey, the theater, movies, picnics, the best restaurants and cocktail lounges," Uris exclaimed.[13] Just after his discharge from the Marines in October 1945, Uris described to his half-sister what San Francisco represented in the postwar world: "Little private booths, wine, candlelight and gypsy music and all the good food you can eat for a buck, and scenery that is the masterwork of Jehovah himself." The newlywed Marine veteran had little doubts about his share of the American dream. "It's wonderful living out here," Uris told Essie, looking out toward an all-American, postwar future.[14]

At the end of the 1940s, Leon was still struggling to publish a piece of writing,[15] but he had made a comfortable home in Marin County with Betty. Leon worked as a district manager for home deliveries of the *Call Bulletin* newspaper, while Betty worked at San Quentin prison. Newspaper delivery did not stimulate Uris, who complained that his district was the toughest on the West Coast. "I am boss, father confessor and wet nurse to 33 brats ranging [in age] from 10 to 16," he wrote to Essie.[16] Still, the job had "decent hours" and it was a "good living." His block in Marin had "millions" of redwoods and just four or five houses, all solidly middle class. He presented himself emphatically to his half-sister as the fully contented suburban husband. "Kid this is it," exclaimed Uris. "I don't know if you can picture an old slum bred alley rat like me puttering in the garden, but that's what I do. We have a big front porch where we eat dinner in the summer. Inside I have a nice roomy house with a fireplace." Uris looked forward to "grand days" ahead in the 1950s when he would be able to "pay off [Betty] the way I feel in minks, diamonds, maids and Buicks."[17]

Leon and Betty had three children—Karen, born in 1946 (as a child she contracted polio, but suffered no lasting disabilities from the disease); Mark, born in 1950; and Michael Cady, born in 1953, the year of *Battle Cry*'s publication.

Uris was an energetic and capable upward climber, but he had trouble leaving his relatives' ill feelings about his mixed marriage behind him. The marriage to Betty detached him from parts of the family, particularly his mother. Uris insisted to Essie that the problem boiled down to the fact that their mother was psychologically unhinged. "I do feel sorry for her [Uris's mother]," he wrote to Essie. "She is a pathetic person." He insisted that his heart and mind were a clear slate: "I do not regret my choice in making my break and finding a life away from that former gruel."[18]

In the summer of 1948 (when Betty's cousin, Zoe Anne Olsen, was winning a silver medal at the London Olympics), Uris struggled to conceal his frustration over the rough mix created by his mother's high-strung personality and his own intermarriage. The contrast between the tolerant learning curve traced by his Protestant in-laws and his Jewish mother's dogmatic clannishness depressed Uris. "I'll tell you a secret," he confided to Essie.[19] "Betty's father and family were quite, to put it bluntly, Jew haters before we married. . . . Once she married and when they met me they've become quite fond of me, and vice versa. We've had four wonderful years without as much as a harsh word or a serious argument." In contrast, his mother's disapproving attitude toward the course Uris's life had taken was "a black spot I wish I could erase. . . . I do love mother very much, but every time I wrote to her she came back with attacks and sob stories, [and] I just couldn't stomach it." Uris hoped that the pull of the granddaughter, Karen, might end his estrangement from his mother, but he himself wasn't going to take affirmative steps in a conciliatory direction. The last thing he wanted was to have to deal with his mother on one of her off days, "when she's liable to whine what a brutal son I am, and 'what did I do to deserve this.' . . . I won't stand for any quarrels and fights. I've had enough of them, in the Marine Corps."[20]

Instead of fighting with his mother, Uris wrote *Exodus* a decade later. Essentially, the novel imagined that were the sort of marriage he had undertaken with Betty Beck to win universal approbation, Christians would support the Jews' deepest passions, and the messianic ideal cherished by Jews throughout close to 2,000 years of exile and suffering would be redeemed by the establishment of a state in the ancient homeland. Bringing the fulfillment of God's ancient promise into the mix, *Exodus* was one massive and theatrical way to win an argument with a whining Jewish mother.

Although he was resolved not to incorporate American Jewish protagonists in his book about Israel's founding, Uris was unable to avoid a number of America-related questions. These were challenges that arose naturally in any book whose primary target audience was American readers (Jews and non-Jews). How, for instance, should this new heroic narrative of Israel relate to American Jewish life? How should the quality of American Jewish life and American Jewry's connection to the Jewish state be described?

Owing to the rough edges and ambiguities of his personal situation, as the product of a radicalized, largely unhappy home where Jewish observances were ignored, and as an intermarried suburbanite who had actively pursued the American dream in the postwar melting pot while remaining acutely aware of the prejudices stirred in it by Jewish assimilation, Uris could not furnish conclusive answers to these questions. Part of the novel's appeal derived from the creative tension surrounding them.

Exodus basically related to American Jewish topics on two levels. In some oblique barbs in the text, and more bluntly in private and public comments that accompanied the novel, Uris conducted a polemic against assimilated American Jewish culture. Wisely, he restrained this posturing, or directed it against demographically limited targets (such as American Jewish authors), else he would have alienated his most trusted audience while also damaging his credibility in view of his assimilated marriage and lifestyle.

Not always with sensitivity and subtlety, *Exodus* spoke about American Jews the way Israeli culture related to them in the 1950s, as though they were orbiting around the most significant Jewish event of two millennia without really being part of it. In the long term, articulate third- or fourth-generation American Jews would not countenance this normative, center-periphery construct of Jewish life; their rebellion against it in the 1980s and 1990s, in a period when many believed that Israel's moral and political course was perturbed, became a major factor in the unmaking of the *Exodus* narrative. That, however, was far in the future.

At the time of its publication, *Exodus* ignited an empowering chain reaction of pride and creative self-awareness among Diaspora

Jews because Uris reined in the polemic and related to broad existential questions about Jewish character on another, second, level. *Exodus*'s fundamental point is that once Jewish character is shorn of the dross of servile, imitative, or obsessively defensive habits that were inculcated by centuries of life in hostile environments, a courageous and affirmative core could produce miracles. For Jews everywhere, as well as for sympathetic, fair-minded Gentiles, this was a profoundly liberating message. For over a decade, members of these two groups had been deeply disturbed by reports of the Holocaust but had lacked a readily apprehensible storyline that would dictate constructive responses to what the Nazis had done.

To put it in the simplest possible way, *Exodus* made Jews feel strong, and in the post-Holocaust world millions of non-Jews were comfortable about that. This empowering feeling dominated readers' (and viewers') response to *Exodus* and encouraged them to overlook the narrative's polemic against American Jews as an incidental feature. The polemic was *not*, in fact, incidental, but for many years this fact was conveniently ignored.

In *Exodus*'s heyday, the combined effect of these two rather contradictory levels, the argument about Israeli moral-physical superiority and the argument about the rock solid core of Jewish character, produced the fascinating dualism of Israel's founding narrative. Thanks largely to *Exodus*'s influence, when Jews and others thought about the 1948 war, they were reflecting simultaneously in national and ethnic terms—their thoughts were about the palpable circumstances of Jewish statehood and also about the intangible pride of ethnic identity.

Leon Uris had family in Israel, and he had immersed himself deeply (albeit briefly) in its life and daily routines, so he became closer to the country than most of his American Jewish readers at the end of the 1950s. Nonetheless, the author experienced essentially the same process through which hundreds of thousands of Diaspora Jewish readers were transported by his novel. For them all, the ideal image of Israel projected by the novel was an instrumental means, a remedy for feelings of insecurity and vulnerability that had lingered after World War II. If *Exodus*'s heroic narrative encouraged adulation for Israel, it also produced feelings of empowerment that spilled well beyond the borders of the Jewish state.[21] In this way, the book's title referred to a process of mass return, not so much of Diaspora

Jews to their ancestral homeland but rather of Americanized Jews to their own sense of ethnic distinctiveness.

In *Exodus,* the character who most clearly reflected the concerns and fantasies of the book's diverse ethno-religious readerships was Kitty Fremont. Understandably enough, literary critics have suggested that Kitty's character, like her relationship with Ari Ben Canaan, is "tepid," "superfluous," and "canned."[22] Some reviewers even recommended that readers skip over her love affair with Ari, as indeed apparently happened in Russian-language underground samizdat editions of *Exodus.*[23] As will be argued, this negative critique is somewhat unfair, but it arises because Uris handled Kitty as a symbolic prototype, not as a human character.

In his early drafts of *Exodus,*[24] Uris demonstrated no concern as to what sort of person this character would be. All that needed to be said about her was that (as the notes of one draft indicated) she was an "American standard like mom's apple pie," and Uris unconcernedly used all-American names for her (Katherine White, Katherine Adams) on successive pages of the same draft. What mattered greatly to the author was to generate an intelligible discussion of how Protestant, middle America viewed Jews, and then to follow how this attitude might transform when embroiled in Israel's independence struggle. Uris equivocated about the attitudes that were to be projected by this all-American woman. He realized that the credibility of the journey his narrative proposed, straight to the eye of the storm of the Jewish state's founding, depended upon whether the attitudes his American character type represented would be recognizable and relevant to readers, Jews and non-Jews. Uris knew that much was riding upon the words he put into the mouth of Kitty Fremont. This was a key creative moment in the making of *Exodus;* and if it did not yield first-rank literature, Uris's choices nonetheless produced a significant mass-culture moment in relations between Christians and Jews.

In some early drafts, Uris toyed with the idea of neutralizing Kitty's viewpoint and presenting her from the start as an advocate of an earnest, if philosophically nonrigorous, brand of 1950s ecumenical tolerance. To do otherwise and hint about forms of anti-Semitism in America's heartland, the author feared, might alienate readers. Hence, in one early version, when she is recruited for nurse work with the detained Jewish refugees in Cyprus, Kitty disavows misgivings and declaims broad-mindedly: "I haven't been around Jewish children, but I suppose they're pretty much like any other."[25]

Elsewhere, in his early drafting of *Exodus,* Uris experimented with spoon-feeding Kitty a blunt dose of polemical attack against American Jews. Thus, in one draft, a conversation between Kitty and her hometown friend, the journalist Mark Penn (eventually called Parker), is disarmingly explicit as it casts the contrast between proto-Israeli Ari Ben Canaan and Indiana Jews as being between selfless courage and selfish cowardice. Without blanching, the characters in this early draft outfit American Jews with anti-Semitic attributes. As he derides the character of "a nose-picker named Maury," the journalist refers vaguely to the extenuating circumstances of an American Jew's "inside pain," and turbulent relations with his mother. This awkwardly apologetic passage from an early draft of *Exodus* reads:

> Kitty shook her head. "He [Ari Ben Canaan] certainly doesn't act like a Jew. You just don't think of Jewish people as being, well, particularly brave. Take those in our town. The way they were terribly to themselves, awfully show-offy."
>
> . . . [Penn speaking:] The Bradville Indiana version. Just a nose-picker named Maury. Three to give he'll grow up to hate his mother. . . . Maybe their [the Jews'] nose hurts because it's been busted so many times by a deep down inside pain. Maury hurts and he pushes himself to become a big doctor so he can look down his nose at a Gentile nurse."[26]

As this repartee continues, Uris's journalist alter ego, Mark Penn (Parker), mentions that he's promised his publisher that he will never write a book about American Jews. Kitty replies, smiling, "if you did, you'd put a dozen Jewish authors out of business."

Such draft dialogue was toned down considerably in the published *Exodus,* but Uris carried on with his polemic about American Jews in private and public writings that accompanied his smash best seller. His pet peeve was American Jewish fiction, which Uris believed to be plagued by whining neuroses and self-hatred. The patriotic author of *Battle Cry* believed that American Jews had written too critically about World War II and thereby isolated their own subculture and nurtured anti-Semitic suspicions. Uris adopted an antidefamation motive in his construction of *Exodus:* his images of strong, victorious Israelis would solidly associate American Jews with the 1950s postwar culture of winners and thereby undo the damage wrought by the "Wouk-Mailer school."

"Once upon a time a book called *Battle Cry* came out and told about an outfit of men who loved each other and believed in what they were fighting for," Uris wrote to his father, as he was putting the final touches on *Exodus*.[27] Then came the turning point with the "Mailer, Wouk, 'ain't war hell' school of writers." *Exodus*, Uris "prayed to God," would be a counterturn "in which Jewish writers stop apologizing for their Jewishness." Uris then added privately to his father some pointed words he would later recycle for all the world to see. His *Exodus* would bring an end to the "neurotic ghetto characters, the brilliant doctors and brilliant lawyers and cutthroat businessmen."[28]

As *Exodus* climbed up the best-seller charts on its first printing, Uris reworked the barbs he inserted in his private letter to his father and pasted the cagiest polemic he ever wrote on the front inside pages of the paperback version. This inside cover authorial announcement, printed under the large print banner LEON URIS SAYS, warrants comment. After two short paragraphs that unabashedly herald *Exodus* as "the story of the greatest miracle of our times," Uris floated before his mass-culture audience elliptical references to Jewish character types ("sneaky lawyer," "clever businessman," "golden riders of the psychoanalysis couch") that circulate prominently in anti-Semitic innuendo. In the course of a mere seventy words, Uris identified himself variously as an American Jewish writer, as a scriptwriter, and as a member of the American public. In this very public space, he dropped cryptic references to his own testy relationship with difficult aunts and uncles in Israel, and he wrote indecisively or ambiguously about the "sneaky" and "clever" American Jews as though they were the causes of their own problems, or as though they were victimized by other fiction writers:

> All the cliché Jewish characters who have cluttered up our American fiction—the clever businessman, the brilliant doctor, the sneaky lawyer, the sulking artist—all those good folk who spend their chapters hating themselves, the world, and all their aunts and uncles—all those steeped in self-pity—all those golden riders of the psychoanalysis couch—all these have been left where they rightfully belong, on the cutting room floor.

The balance of these words appears to identify fictionalized characters as the target of Uris's objection, but the remainder of this authorial preface refers to *Exodus*'s subjects as real-life Israelis, "fighting people" who "do not apologize either for being born Jews or the right to live in human dignity." In effect, such phrases brought to life "the clever businessman, the brilliant doctor, the sneaky lawyer, the sulking artist"—these were real-life American Jews who, unlike Israelis, *did* apologize for being born Jews.

In *Exodus,* Kitty Fremont is vested with a large degree of authorial authority, even in Book One where she articulates negative generalities about Jews to substantiate her misgivings about working with Jewish children. After her initial encounter with Ari Ben Canaan, when the "strapping, handsome" Yishuv fighter turns his head and requests Kitty's help advancing his plans for the detained Jewish orphans, the all-American girl privately details her reservations about Jews to her longtime friend Mark Parker. Uris does not give the reader any reason to blame Kitty, an experienced nurse, for blurting: "I've worked with enough Jewish doctors to know they are arrogant and aggressive people. They look down on us."

Kitty is subsequently transformed in the novel by her involvement with Israel's statehood struggle, but it is important to scrutinize the terms of this metamorphosis. In the popular mind, Kitty Fremont is often remembered as having been swept up by Ari Ben Canaan and his Israeli soldier comrades in their statehood fight, as though the American woman herself were entering the melting pot of the Jewish state. This memory bears the stamp of the *film* version of *Exodus,* which (as we shall see) ends with Kitty standing in Israeli battle dress, ready to join the armed struggle for the Jewish state. Melting pot dynamics, moral hierarchies, and terms of engagement between American Jews and Israelis, and between Americans Gentiles and Israelis, are somewhat more complicated in Uris's *Exodus.*

In the novel, Kitty never definitively sheds her Americanism. Uris's well-turned plot gains much mileage from tension and conflict caused by Kitty's intention to bring her protégé, Holocaust survivor Karen Clement Hansen, back to the United States. This back-to-America plan is repeatedly forestalled by dramatic events of Israel's independence struggle, such as the need to nurse Ari Ben Canaan after he is wounded in the daring operation to free his uncle Akiva, the leader of the right-wing Irgun (Maccabee) terror underground, and Dov Landau from the imposing Acre prison fortress. However, the novel's most diehard Israelis never substantively contest the rationale of the back-to-America plan. Figures who are engaged heart and soul with the Zionist thesis that young people such as Karen can securely fulfill themselves as Jews only in Israel accept Kitty's contradictory intention for Karen with fatalistic equanimity. After all, with Arab armies on the advance against the besieged new Jewish state in June 1948, who could truthfully challenge Kitty's insistence that wearing plaid skirts at a twelfth-grade gym social in San Francisco would be a better deal for a gifted, sociable teenager who was once on course for stardom at the Royal Ballet of Copenhagen? Neither the embattled Haganah hero, and Kitty's sometimes lover, Ari Ben Canaan, nor Dr. Lieberman, the kindly doctor at the Gan Dafna children's welfare colony (characters entrusted with the most inviolable, military and medical, roles in the *Exodus* narrative of Jewish rebirth) pull knock-down arguments out of their ammunition bags and medical kits to rebuff Kitty's plan to return to America with Karen.

By the end of the novel, Kitty has, improbably, turned into a Hebrew-speaking, pro-Zionist welfare worker whose good works are rewarded in the new Jewish state via the attribution of an admiring nom de guerre, Hayedida. This nickname, which means "the Friend," in the prestate days had been given to the real-life, Bible-reading, British military officer Orde Wingate, who trained young Yishuv fighters to seize the advantage in the fight against Arabs for control of the Holy Land. The nickname is thus an imposing token of trust won by Kitty among Israelis, yet even more awe inspiring is the approval she receives from Ari's sister Jordana Ben Canaan.

Jordana is a red-headed sabra cowgirl who whisks across the pages of *Exodus*, leading Palmach military exercises at Gan Dafna, riding bareback on horses through Arab villages in the Galilee, and hot-stepping in the *hora* at a Palmach bonfire in the Jezreel Valley, where she is united with her boyfriend, the scholarly Jerusalemite and Palmach fighter David Ben Ami. Jordana originally scoffs at the American materialist frills kept by Kitty and summons all her grass-roots endogamous wiles to foil the developing romance between her Jewish sabra brother and the foreign WASP woman, Kitty. However, during the initiation rite drama of the 1948 War of Independence, Jordana embraces Kitty and eventually works to rekindle her romance with Ari. The turning point is the demonstration of Kitty's unmitigated maternal solicitude for the Gan Dafna orphans during a grueling evacuation ordeal—in the novel, this scene, which was

based on real-life episodes at Kibbutz Manara and Ramot Naphtali,[29] symbolizes the irreversible bond that has developed between
the archetypal American woman and the new children of the Jewish state. Although the sorrowful sacrifice of Karen, Kitty's primary
reclamation project in the novel, is reported at the altar of the book's
final scene, the Ben Canaan seder gathering, Kitty will apparently
continue in her adopted role as welfare nurse-mother to the rehabili-
tated Jewish immigrants and sabras of Israel.

Via these plot turns, an American visitor who initially recoils
from "arrogant" Jews becomes emotionally attached to the Israeli
statehood struggle for survival. Uris, of course, uses Kitty manipu-
latively to illustrate that Israel's circumstances as a gutsy democracy
capable of overcoming tremendous threats and obstacles can, and
should, exercise a magnetic attraction on all Americans. Israel's spirit
of frontier independence seduces Kitty. Her evolving commitment to
the new Jewish state fulfills Ari Ben Canaan's prophecy. Early in the
novel, during the Cyprus sequence, Ari observes that "Americans
have consciences," meaning that the New World nation of immigrants who themselves escaped oppression in Europe must naturally
be drawn to the plight of Holocaust refugees who seek to leave the
European slaughterhouse behind them and find sanctuary in their
ancestral homeland.

Strongly identified as she becomes with Israel's 1948 struggle,
Kitty keeps her distance to the very end, and her American identity
never loses its status as a source of high, perhaps ultimate, authority.
Through Kitty, Uris looked down from his comfortable suburban
San Francisco home at the rugged courage of his kinsmen in Israel
the way twentieth-century Americans admired the frontier spirit of
the pioneers in the Wild West. In both instances, lacing through the
vicarious identification, there remained the feeling that the desert
rough riders were a bit too dirty behind the ears.

Jordana Ben Canaan eventually embraces Kitty as an honorary
sabra, but this does not mean that the American visitor becomes fully
converted to the rough soil communalism of the kibbutz and the Palmach. "Don't tell me what makes a woman—you don't know, you
aren't one," Kitty snaps angrily at Jordana at one stage in the novel.
"You're Tarzan's mate and you behave as though you belong in the
jungle. A brush and comb wouldn't be a bad start at fixing what's
wrong with you," announces Kitty, dangling an American dress in
front of the Zionist cowgirl as an example of what real woman wear.

Kitty's American looks and sensibilities dictate the terms of the novel's central romance, her six-hundred-page on-again/off-again entanglement with Israeli superman Ari Ben Canaan. Uris does not mince words in his analysis of what draws the virile Israeli male to Kitty. As the Christian American woman wades in for a swim in the Sea of Galilee, the all-weather sabra male notices that she has curves ("Ari inspected her frankly. . . . Her body had not the angular sturdiness of a sabra girl. She was more of the softness and roundness one would expect from an American woman"). For her part, Kitty expresses her American expectations from the sabra fighter in the familiar clichés of mass-culture soap opera.[30] She wants a man who will love her as much as he loves his work, and, in what becomes the big showstopper in *Exodus,* she wants a war hero who knows how to cry. It takes untold travail, including the horrific terror murder of Kitty's protégé Karen at the novel's conclusion, but Ari ultimately obliges this request. With sententious biblical phrasing, "Ari Ben Canaan wept," Uris announces that his ultimate Israeli hero has become a man, in sentimental American terms.

That seems like an ironic conclusion to a book whose hundreds of pages are devoted to the premise that the Jews are becoming a proudly independent people in their homeland. The whole schemata of *Exodus* "makes the validation of the Jews dependent on the approval of the Gentiles," Ruth Wisse insightfully observes in her comments on the Ari-Kitty romance.[31] If the book were written as a celebration of the independence of the Jews, why do its central Israeli archetypes from the Ben Canaan family need to be tamed and civilized by the American emissary, Kitty Fremont, before they can be loved?

The answer to that question can be found on the broad level of history and ideology. From its start in late eighteenth-century Europe, the modern emancipation of the Jew hinged conditionally on the approval of the Gentile and typically depended upon the Jew's fulfillment of an externally imposed self-improvement routine. Scholars of the nineteenth-century Jewish Emancipation movement in central Europe have identified this program to civilize the Jew as the ideology of *bildung;*[32] and the program permeated subsequent Jewish political movements, including Zionism. Its echoes can be heard in the way Uris drew the novel's central romance between Kitty and Ari. His Israeli hero who (as Uris proclaimed privately to his father) "won't take shit from anybody," spends hundreds of pages dismissing and summoning the American woman whenever and however he sees fit, but in the end wins her love only by reaching a state of abject emotional vulnerability and sorrow that accords with her romantic sensibility and agenda, not his own.

In *Exodus,* as in any historical novel, plot schemata are influenced by ideological legacies and cultural idiosyncrasies of the context it describes. Yet as Uris puzzled over new variations in majority-minority, Gentile-Jewish relations posed by the establishment of the state of Israel, he was not looking as far away as bildung programs of the Jewish Enlightenment movement, the Haskalah, in early nineteenth-century Central Europe. Undoubtedly, the author's conscious point of reference were the "two worst days" he ever lived through, during Christmas season 1944, when as a convalescing marine in the Bay Area he had to pick up the phone to Iowa and pitch his qualities to prospective parents-in-law who were mortified by the prospect of their solidly middle-American Protestant daughter marrying a restless Jewish boy from a politically radical, poor, and unstable home.

In *Exodus,* minutiae of place settings and character details are autobiographical. The pivotal War of Independence scene, the escape of children down the mountain from Gan Dafna, draws from details and emotions stirred by the Uris family evacuation in the 1956 Sinai campaign; descriptions of Tivoli Gardens in Copenhagen in passages relating Karen's survival during the Holocaust are culled from Uris's experiences in the land where his wife's family had roots; Kitty grieves a husband, Tom, who was killed in action at Guadalcanal, and a daughter, Sandra, who died shortly thereafter from polio, and this sequence resembles passages in Uris's own life, in the Marine Corps, and in a frightening episode when his own daughter Karen contracted polio; and so on. Such details, however, are not the point; the entire sweep of the novel reflects Uris's personal concerns as a simultaneously assimilated and proud Jew. The overall structure of *Exodus* as a romance of Jewish history in general, and of the developing connection between America and Israel in particular, can be seen as the author's personal testament.

In literary terms, the pairing between Kitty and Ari in *Exodus* was a superficial Harlequin romance, but critics who dismiss this relationship as tawdry and sentimental miss the point.[33] Readers of the era would not have been brought passionately into the *Exodus* world had they not been deeply intrigued by the identity politics laden within the pairing between the archetypal American heroine and the archetypal Israeli hero. An elitist judgment holding that *Exodus* had a melodramatic romance at its heart and became a best seller because the reading public at the time was superficial is incorrect.

In 1958–59, Leon Uris muscled his way onto the best-seller lists at the expense of Boris Pasternak, D. H. Lawrence, and Vladimir Nabokov. Anyone who wants to make the argument that today's readers are more sophisticated culturally than Uris's audience ought to take a look at this morning's list of best-selling fiction and then consider that the same readers who half a century ago endorsed the plausibility of the union between the prim American Protestant Kitty Fremont and the muscular Zionist Ari Ben Canaan in *Exodus* were at the same time dealing with the moral perplexities and erotic adventures of Lady Chatterley's lover and Humbert Humbert's Lolita. As it turns out, Fremont and Ben Canaan were dancing the hora around Palmach bonfires at Beit Allonim in a pre-1960s high moment in best-seller fiction. The surging popularity of figures like Nabokov and Lawrence indicates that the receptiveness of mass audiences toward probing, sometimes subversive, examination of the meaning of intimate relations reached a peak precisely at the time of *Exodus*'s publication.

The complicated interplay between identity politics and romance in the popular fiction of this period is highlighted by the comparison to Pasternak's *Doctor Zhivago*, which was for many weeks *Exodus*'s competitor for the number one spot on best-seller lists. Both revolving around dramatic historical events, the two novels were written by authors who had strong personal interests in the subject of Jewish-Christian relationships and who sometimes entertained daring notions regarding union between the two religions. In publicity tours conducted in support of *Exodus*, Uris criticized Pasternak as a moral renegade for abdicating all traces of Jewish pride.[34] Yet within the covers of the passionately Zionist *Exodus*, key characters pass their days looking for new, creative ways to relate the Old Testament to the New Testament and Judaism to Christianity. In view of her background as a young Jewish teenager who is sheltered during the Holocaust by a kindly Christian couple in Denmark, it perhaps makes sense that before her engagement with the Zionist Youth Aliyah framework, Karen Clement-Hansen puzzles over the "largest riddle of all": "If Jesus were to return to the earth she [Karen] was certain He would go to a synagogue rather than a church." But Karen is not the only *Exodus* character to consider whether new angles are to be found in the Judeo-Christian relationship. In the Pale of Settlement, in Zhitomir Russia in 1884, Simon Rabinsky, a pious traditional Jew and father of the two Ben Canaan brothers who are destined to lead diplomatic-political and underground-terror flanks of the Zionist movement, confesses that as a child he considered converting to Christianity. A surprisingly broad range of religious identity politics can be traced in *Exodus*.

The Ari-Kitty soap opera romance convinced countless readers that Jewish-Christian union was not just one aspect of victory in World War II. It was, in fact, the triumph's big story. By generating romantic magnetism between Kitty, "the proverbial girl next door . . . one of those great American traditions, like Mom's apple pie, and hot dogs," and Ari, who "comes from a breed of [Jewish] supermen . . . [whose] blood is made of little steel and ice corpuscles," Uris reinforced his American readers' belief that their country's struggles had high moral purpose and were rooted in core Judeo-Christian values of tolerance.

Devoted to the miraculous Jewish rebirth in the Land of Israel, *Exodus* is also very much about the American way of life. The novel came out of a 1950s American culture that was brilliantly described by Will Herberg in his study *Protestant, Catholic, Jew: An Essay in American Religious Sociology.*[35] As Herberg hinted throughout his 1955 volume, a belief in the basic unity of religion was increasingly identified in this period as the American way of life. It did not matter so much whether one introduced oneself as Protestant, Catholic, or Jew—the imperative was to identify with religion, for failure to do so, as Herberg explained, was "somehow not to be an American." Herberg wrote about a "triple melting pot" in which members of the three faiths married their own kind, but were wedded emotionally to the American way of life. His landmark study pointed to a postwar reality in which Jews and Christians converged progressively closer to each other while still keeping some borders and distance. In the scholarly realm, Herberg set the stage for Kitty Fremont's ambivalent yet continuing approach to Ari Ben Canaan.

Even though it was set on foreign turf, Uris's *Exodus* evoked a new melting pot mode of Americanism at a moment when ideological concern passed from the remaking of immigrants as synthesized Americans to the planting of America's cultural roots in *Judeo-Christian civilization.*

In many ways, the concept of Judeo-Christian civilization developed in the 1950s as what some scholars have called an invented tradition, an anachronism created by ambitious social circles to serve a particular ideological agenda.[36] In the 1950s, adult American Jews with backgrounds like Uris's must have cracked a wry smile whenever the phrase came up: did "Judeo-Christian civilization" really mirror the rough realities they had known on Depression-era streets in Baltimore or New York? Looked at from another angle, references to Judeo-Christian traditions immediately after World War II, when ashes were still smoldering at Auschwitz and Buchenwald, and Hitler's survivors languished in so-called Displaced Persons camps, were acutely problematic. This was a concept that needed to be refined and bordered. As the scholar Mark Silk has observed, the insertion of the term *Judeo* in postwar discussions of America's religious traditions might have assuaged consciences, in line with politically correct sentiments of the time. "After the revelations of the Nazi death camps, a phrase like 'our Christian civilization' seemed ominously exclusive," writes Silk. That is surely true, but it is also likely that through the 1950s nobody knew exactly what in the real world the rhetorically improved phrase, Judeo-Christian civilization, really entailed. In other words, in *Exodus*'s cultural milieu, Judeo-Christian harmony was not a tradition in civilization but rather an American work in progress.

For hundreds of thousands of readers, Kitty was a pathfinder. They recognized the brand of detached, social anti-Semitism that Kitty originally personifies, and they followed her journey in good faith, maintaining a strong American belief in the cleansing power of earnest experience. There was no Ari Ben Canaan in the life paths of American humanitarians like Eleanor Roosevelt, but figures like Mrs. Roosevelt set an example, having rid themselves of WASP snobbery toward Jews, and they emerged in the postwar world with strong affection for the Jewish state campaign. In this way, Kitty's identity education had apprehensible expressions in postwar American social realities.

For all its literary failings, Uris's handling of Kitty Fremont can be seen as one of *Exodus*'s genuine accomplishments. It brought many thousands of readers and film viewers into an exploration of the Judeo-Christian foundations of the era's all-important value of toleration.

Uris's novel was published when public commentators were scratching their heads in puzzlement about the ultimate endpoint of concepts of Judeo-Christian harmony—that is, intermarriage. Just a few years after *Exodus*'s publication, it became fashionable to brand explicitly Jewish-Christian intermarriage as a social trend. The Jewish social scientist Marshall Sklare published an article on "Intermarriage and the Jewish Future" in *Commentary* in 1964, the year when *Look* magazine published a cover story under the sensational title "The Vanishing American Jew."[37] A few years earlier, when Uris drafted his story, intermarriage may not have been a pronounced social trend, but it could reasonably have been identified as a precious raw material to be mined in a box-office smash, or a best seller. Celebrity intermarriage generated buzz. Arthur Miller married Marilyn Monroe in 1956. Substitute the Jewish playwright's brains with Ari's Israeli muscle, hem the sex starlet's figure and put her in a nurse's uniform, and you have the stuff Uris was developing at the heart of his tale. Paul Newman and Eva Marie Saint came out of it, in the *Exodus* film.

In his thoughtful *The Jew in American Literature,* Sol Liptzin anticipated Ruth Wisse's point about the way the Ari-Kitty interfaith romance in *Exodus* is structured as a quest for Gentile validation. Liptzin grasped that Uris's book capped a series of well-known 1950s novels by American Jewish writers in which Jewish characters seek, in some deep existential sense, the acceptance of Gentile neighbors, friends, or lovers.[38] Placing Uris taxonomically with other American Jewish writers from the era (writers whom Uris himself shunned) raises an interesting question. How exactly are we to make sense of the fact that the era's most sensational and influential exploration of melting pot dynamics written by an American Jew was set offshore, in Israel?

Answers to this question point to the function of idealized versions of Israel, to images of "America as it ought to be" in the ethnic identity of American Jews. Imagined or idealized images of Israel frequently allow American Jews, and others, to continue probing everlasting existential issues after analytic resources on native grounds in the United States appear to be exhausted. In *Exodus*, this dynamic occurred because American Jewish writers in the 1950s simply ran out of space at home for their ongoing investigations of possible permutations in Jewish-Christian relationships. Elaborating upon this point in detail would take us very far from Uris's story of Israel's independence struggle, so two brief examples, relating to American Jewish urban and suburban realities, will have to suffice.

Uris's depiction of Jewish strength on the Israeli frontier compensated for lingering feelings of urban vulnerability in America. As a depiction of a bleak New York City milieu of Jewish weakness, Bernard Malamud's *The Assistant,* published in 1957,[39] a year before Uris's epic, is a bookend to *Exodus.* The text shares the same problem of redefining Jewish-Christian relations.

The Assistant portrays the bitter last weeks in the life of a hapless Jewish grocery store owner, Morris Bober. Honest but nonenterprising, Bober reads the *Forward,* speaks broken English, grieves the loss of his son to a childhood disease, and is miserably unable to guarantee a share of the American dream for his attractive daughter Helen. He eventually loses control of his unprofitable store to a hard-luck young Italian American. This figure, named Frank Alpine, is alternately repulsed and attracted to the Jewish storeowner and his family and zooms in and out of the narrative as a saintly character (as a latter-day St. Francis of Assisi) and also as a petty thief and rapist. Malamud explores the tense ambivalence and interdependence between the Jewish grocer family and its Gentile assistant as though it is a miniature both of tough, inner-city ethnic relations and also of a larger historic nexus between Jew and Christian. As *The Assistant* constructed reality, it is difficult to imagine the Catholic Frank and Jewish Helen overcoming differences and climbing up to middle-class respectability. In Malamud's New York City frontier, the Jew seemed to have run out of space. There was no room for the fulfillment of postwar values of toleration and interfaith harmony.

Herman Wouk's *Marjorie Morningstar,* published in 1955, reflects American Jewish culture's quest for suburban order.[40] As Wouk depicts it, the journey to the suburbs of second-generation American Jews is emotionally taxing, materially rewarding, and troublingly unheroic. Set mostly in Manhattan in the mid-1930s, the story migrates, relentlessly and more or less happily, toward a conclusion in which the heroine, a would-be Broadway starlet, is securely ensconced in a postwar, 1950s Westchester County suburb with four children and a capable lawyer husband. The prose is as trim as neatly cut hedges in a suburban yard, and character psychology is similarly cropped closely by the author. Settling his heroine in the Westchester suburbs, Wouk rewards Marjorie with emotional stability and material comfort but derides her youthful dream of being a Broadway actress.

In the book's final pages, Marjorie appears gray and weary, while her white-collar husband Milton Schwartz is not entirely content in Mamaroneck because he has not delivered a virginal white wife to it (such calculations suggest that an overbearing Puritanism haunts the country clubs and fund-raisers of the suburbs). In short, Wouk's *Marjorie Morningstar* displayed fatigue with the suburbs before anyone really got to live in them.

As the 1950s drew to a close and the incredible balance sheet of Jewish losses and triumphs overseas became more apprehensible to American Jewish (and Gentile American) audiences, the rational self-interest of types like Marjorie Morgenstern might have filled the suburbs, but also provided little creative spark. Uris, who emphatically refused to let his books carry endorsements from Herman Wouk,[41] never explained at length why he found books like *Marjorie Morningstar* to be so exasperating, but, in retrospect, it does not seem difficult to grasp the roots of his consternation. As they were constructed in American Jewish writing in the 1950s, the suburbs were prosaic and tedious. They were entirely inappropriate emotional space for the examination of questions of Christian-Jewish relations in the conflicted spirit of the times, following Hitler's extermination campaign in Europe and the triumphant Allies' war effort. To understand what remained, and what was new, in Judeo-Christian civilization, Uris and his readers looked away from the supermarket moms and white-collar dads of the suburbs and toward the muscular pioneering sabras of Israel.

In *Exodus*'s melting pot dynamics, non-Jews (readers and fictional characters) are swept around by a historical romance in which muscular Jews perform heroic feats. In the far-off venue of Israel, Jews are seen in heroic roles as fighters who take their fate into their own hands and not as "sneaky lawyers and clever businessmen."

Uris was not entirely able to uphold his early plan to keep American Jews out of *Exodus,* but whenever they appeared he deliberately remained ambiguous about their relation to Israel's founding narrative. In a novel rife with creative tension about late 1950s melting pot dynamics, Uris's most revealing comments belong to a minor character, the appropriately named Bill Fry, the skipper of a ha'apalah illegal immigration ship, *The Star of David,* and the only American Jew in *Exodus* who engages in any of its numerous death-defying action sequences. "I love America. I wouldn't trade what I've got over there for fifty Palestines," the captain informs a wobbly Karen Clement Hansen as they recover in captivity after being beaten by British troops in a daring attempt to run the ship up the shore of Caesarea, a beachhead that symbolizes the convergence of British and Roman imperial opposition to Jewish national life in Eretz Israel. Through this soon-to-be-martyred American Jewish hero, Uris confesses that he never really figured out how to balance the comfortable American Jewish formula of acculturation and the blood and guts heroic sacrifices of Israeli heroes of the 1948 struggle. When pressed by Karen for an explanation as to what a self-proclaimed lover of America is doing risking his life for the illegal Aliyah Bet immigration, Bill Fry frankly replies: "I'm not smart enough to figure those things out."

In *Exodus,* Uris laid it on thick with images of tough, steely Israelis in order to show Gentile Americans that his people knew how to fight and therefore deserved respect. Throughout this eye-popping exhibition of Jewish strength, the novel never conclusively addresses the issue of whether the muscular Israelis come from the same national stock as "sneaky" and "sulking" American Jews. Sometimes grotesquely, Uris symbolized his doubts about the unity of the Jewish people by punctuating the novel with Jewish figures whose bodies and spirits are out of sync. Hence, the kindly patron of the Holocaust orphan colony Gan Dafna is a hunchback; and the romantically incompetent Ari learns how to walk in his torturously convoluted relationship with Kitty only after the elegant Christian American painfully yanks a bullet out of the wounded Israeli's leg. This fascination with deformity and surgical recomposition reflects Uris's insecure misgiving that he was "not smart enough to figure out" what sort of body of men and women was supposed to take shape in the post-Holocaust vision of Jewish-Christian interaction and of America-Israel union he projected in *Exodus.*

Not prescribing any American homegrown remedies, Uris implied that the best therapy for American Jewish "golden riders of the psychoanalysis couch" would be to identify vicariously with Ari Ben Canaan as he rescues Jews from Nazi-occupied Berlin and British DP pens in Cyprus and then fights Arab enemies up and down Israel, from the Negev to the Lebanon border.

Summing up the identity politics of *Exodus,* the brave American Jew Bill Fry offers more questions than answers. He can only say that evidence of Israeli strength adds to the respect he receives as a Jew:

Bill Fry didn't seem to be convincing himself either. He stood up. "It's hard to explain, Karen. I love America. I wouldn't trade what I've got over there for fifty Palestines."

Karen propped up an elbow. Bill began pacing the tent and groping to connect his thoughts. "We're Americans but we're a different kind of Americans. Maybe we make ourselves different . . . maybe other people make me different . . . I'm not smart enough to figure those things out. All my life I've heard I'm supposed to be a coward because I'm a Jew. Let me tell you, kid. Every time the Palmach blows up a British depot or knocks the hell out of some Arabs he's winning respect for me. He's making a liar out of everyone who tells me Jews are yellow. These guys over here are fighting my battle for respect . . . understand that?"

"I think so."

"Well, damned if I understand it."

In its dealings with Jewish identity politics of the 1950s, Uris's *Exodus* furnished means for the recovery of self-respect but left a troubling list of questions to be addressed by others during the turbulent 1960s.

In Otto Preminger's film version of *Exodus,* ambiguities in Uris's novel about melting pot politics are eradicated, and the screen becomes saturated with fascinatingly explicit images of an Americanized Israel. Very little in Leon Uris's writing is subtle, but compared to the movie's emphatic treatment of America-Israel connections his written narrative seems restrained. The film's blatant Americanization of Israel's founding is part of a larger story by which Preminger lost commitment to the distinctiveness of the story and contributed (in some ways) to the unmaking of the Jewish national narrative—this deconstruction process, and how it stemmed from the complicated story of the Preminger-Uris dispute and other circumstances of the film's production, will be analyzed in the next, final chapter, which analyzes how the *Exodus* narrative began to unravel. Here we will limit our discussion to ways in which the film translated into visual images and exaggerated Uris's Americanized conceptions of the Jewish state.

As we have already noted, Uris's and Preminger's dissimilar biographies dictated important differences in the way their works envisioned topics of Jewish history and Jewish society. Not surprisingly, however, their life stories intersected in one important respect—both Jewish men intermarried, more than once. This biographical point of tangency was responsible for the basic similarity in the way both the book and the film approached *Exodus*'s melting pot politics, even though Preminger's film accentuated some of Uris's ideas about identity.

Uris's marriage to Betty Beck caused ongoing stress, though at the time of *Exodus*'s writing the author seemed to have thought of his marriage as a story with a happy ending (he eventually divorced Betty and married two more times). The circumstances of Preminger's marriage to Hope Bryce, an Episcopalian and former model and costume designer, were lighter, almost comic. After Preminger's divorce from another Gentile, Mary Gardner, became final, he married Bryce in Haifa, during the spring 1960 filming of *Exodus*. The marriage was facilitated by Meyer Weisgal, a veteran Jewish nationalist who worked tirelessly for the Weizmann Institute from 1944 to 1977. The Preminger-Bryce interfaith wedding necessitated some clever maneuvering to bypass reservations harbored by the city's rabbinate—Haifa mayor Abba Khoushy strong-armed the rabbis, threatening to cut off funding, while Weisgal relayed creative assertions about the bride's supposed Jewish ancestry and coached Bryce to recite the Jewish names of her relatives. Such help to Preminger paid off nicely for Weisgal, whose Weizmann Institute was promised royalties from Israeli screenings of *Exodus* as well as income from world premieres.[42]

The *Exodus* movie passes from the frontiers of Bunker Hill to the Wild West. The film's opening sequence, set in Cyprus and devoted to the story of six hundred DP's dramatic departure for Haifa aboard the *Exodus,* draws from American Revolution motifs; the film's later phases, chronicling struggles at the time of the Jewish statehood declaration, play out as an Israeli cowboy replay of how the American West was won.

The first time we see Paul Newman as Ari Ben Canaan, he swims ashore to Cyprus after receiving flashlight beam signals from a Haganah man camouflaged as a local taxi driver. This is a Mediterranean version of the Paul Revere story. Later, after the ma'apilim (reduced in number to six hundred from the real-life *Exodus* figure of 4,000, apparently because packing several thousand extras onto a boat was one miracle Hollywood couldn't pull off in an on-location shoot in

1960) decide to stage their hunger strike, the camera focuses on the Holocaust survivors pitching packaged foodstuffs into the sea. For viewers who miss the parallel to the Boston Tea Party, Ari redirects his repartee with the Indiana widow, Kitty Fremont, to the story of 1776. Explaining his purposes to the American woman, Ari describes the hunger strike as "a publicity stunt, a letter to the editors of newspapers, a Help Wanted ad to the official journal of the United Nations—wanted by 600 men, women and children, a country they're dying for . . . " Incredulous, Kitty exclaims, "you can't fight the whole British army with 600 people." Ari parries with the American analogy: "How many Minute Men did you [Americans] have at Concord the day the shot was fired that was heard around the world—77."

Its eye on American audiences steeped in tales of British soldiers marching in columns as easy targets for agile colonial freedom fighters, the film emphasizes the bungling of British soldiers on Cyprus. The aim, of course, is to drive home this parallel between the 1776 and 1948 fights for national independence. The worst British bungler, Major Caldwell (played by Peter Lawford), is an anti-Semite who scoffs about how he is always able to pick out a Jew, even after he peers into Ari Ben Canaan's sky blue eyes and authorizes forged papers for the DP escape aboard the *Exodus,* not realizing that the man before him is a Jewish Haganah operative disguised as a British soldier. Reviewers of this amusing scene have commented on its illustration of one skin-deep difference between the film and the novel: Uris would never have made light of anti-Semitic buffoons in this way.[43] But the difference cuts deeper.

More than any single visual item in the film, Paul Newman's blue eyes belie everything Uris wanted to say in his book. The writer of the *Exodus* novel was inspired by a profound sense of the Jewish people's return to political history in its homeland as a once-in-a-millennium experience. Whatever they were imagined to look like, readers of *Exodus* understood its Israeli heroes to be new and different types of Jews. They are recognizably different people. Yet in the film, Hollywood cast as the new Jewish man an all-American face that could be stretched to endorse any number of vapidly homogenizing 1950s melting pot prescriptions about Israel's 1948 founding experience.

The novel contextualized Israel's statehood struggle as the latest phase in history's unique story of the Jewish people's fight against the curse of anti-Semitism. In the film, Israel's founding was sanitized and presented as the latest in a line of history's revolutions, none of which were particularly revolutionary since the warriors who won independence could always be mistaken for their antagonists. As it turns out in the film, the archetypal Israeli fighter, Ari Ben Canaan, can be taken as a proper British officer ("Captain Ari Ben Canaan. His Majesty's Jewish Brigade Paratroop Division. North Africa, Lebanon, Syria and Palestine. The decorations are real," declares Ari, a British World War II veteran, to Kitty, to explain his get-up in the Cyprus caper).

Ari's Hollywood face repeatedly strays from Uris's model of a distinctively new Israeli sabra type and drifts toward assimilation in the melting pot of nations theory espoused by Kitty throughout the film. In one of the movie's better-known scenes, Kitty and Ari exit their car on a drive to his family's moshav, Yad El. As they peer at a stunning view of the Jezreel Valley, Ari reminds his Presbyterian guest about the locale's 3,200-year history as the site of scenes in the Book of Judges. Suddenly, the discussion decontextualizes, and the biblical setting becomes a mere backdrop to a lively debate about contrasting contemporary theories of the melting pot and cultural autonomy.

"All these differences between people in the world are made up," Kitty declaims. Drumming on melting pot themes of tolerance familiar in American, and American Jewish, 1950s culture, she continues: "People are the same no matter what they're called." Ari disagrees. Rubbing against the grain of 1950s conformism, he offers a stirring anticipation of what would come to be called the multiculturalism

Perched above the breathtaking, biblical settling of the Jezreel Valley, Ari Ben Canaan (Paul Newman) and Kitty Fremont (Eva Marie Saint) debate about melting pot and multicultural diversity. (*Exodus* film)

position: "Don't ever believe it. People are different. They have a right to be different. It's no good pretending differences don't exist. They do. They have to be recognized and respected."

This convention-defying conversation captures much in the spirit of the film *Exodus*. Preminger had little patience for 1950s-era demands about political loyalty and identify conformism, and (as will be noted) he incurred the wrath of American Legionnaires by crediting a blacklisted writer. Yet, as exemplified by his own Haifa marriage to an Episcopalian, Preminger was personally ambivalent about the moral and practical reach of claims about Jewish particularity. Not surprisingly, Kitty and Ari spend the film flip-flopping about the social integration versus cultural autonomy positions voiced in the Jezreel Valley scene. "People *are* different," Kitty subsequently moans, after being unnerved by the way Jewish family quarrels dominate the dining-room table at Barak Ben Canaan's moshav. "I guess I'd feel the same way on an Indiana farm," Ari tepidly responds. Positioned later in the film, early in the Gan Dafna sequences, this mutual understanding of cultural difference is so unconvincing to both heroes that their moratorium on kissing lasts just a few scenes.

Who, in the film, really is Ari Ben Canaan? His smart, white-collar wardrobe throughout the film is a grotesque protrusion in a production that went to impressive lengths to project local authenticity. The $3.5 million United Artists budget provided Preminger the means he needed to get the details right. On site in Israel, the director did an astonishing job, narrowing his script's reality gaps, lavishing the picture with striking panoramas of the Jezreel Valley, and inserting a wealth of street markings and local color (in this regard Preminger's biographer remarks aptly that the country of Israel stands out as the real "star" of the *Exodus* film[44]). Half a century later, such scene details stand up to the most scrupulous possible, pause and rewind tests that can be operated on a DVD player. In a film distinguished visually by its local realism, Paul Newman becomes the ugly duckling because of his Hollywood good looks. *Exodus* is a film production in which somebody took the trouble to dig up a 1947 street map of Haifa to hang up on the wall of one of Akiva Ben Canaan's Irgun lairs, but nobody on the set had the gumption to tell the notoriously dictatorial director Otto Preminger that a Palmach man would never have struck such a preppy look on a road trip back home to a northern moshav (later, Newman's wife Joanne Woodward, who accompanied her husband to Israel, suggested that he was too traumatized by Preminger's heavy-handed directing to even mention the *Exodus* film in public[45]). Even though the Palmach ethos held bourgeois accoutrements in contempt, the film's Ari never takes off his culturally challenged shirt after he paddles ashore in Cyprus.

In actual fact, Yigal Allon, the Palmach hero of 1948 to whose mold Uris, arguably, whittled most closely when he created Ari Ben Canaan, might have viewed Preminger's depiction of Ari in 1960 with tacit admiration.[46] After his stirring experiences in the 1948 war, when his command stints, such as the northern Yiftah operation, included events roughly similar to *Exodus* dramas such as the Gan Dafna siege, Allon tried to add some polish to his roughly hewn Israeli character via, among other things, academic study in England. Allon grew up in grinding poverty in the Kfar Tabor (Mescha) village, and his psychological motivations after Israeli statehood seem comprehensible. Tellingly, however, nobody in Israel could take seriously the post-1948 efforts of this consummate Palmach veteran to append civilized English refinement to his résumé. The accomplished biographer, Anita Shapira, devotes just a small fraction of a first-rate study of Allon to his life after the 1948 war, and she barely conceals her endorsement of the judgment of Allon's Palmach peers, such as Yitzhak Rabin, who viewed Allon's social ambitions and solicitude for considerations of international diplomacy to be pathetic.

Palmach men came from Hebrew-fixated Zionist homes and were tongue-tied in contacts with Mandatory officials, and their cultural bearing was parochial. Before the 1948 war, Nahalal-bred Moshe Dayan, who married into the Yishuv's highest, most cosmopolitan, Jewish society, traveled with his young wife to England, but quit his studies there after just a few months out of sheer disinterest.[47] The Palmach fighters were drawn to Socialist representations of Western civilization as hypocritical colonial oppression. As World War II drew to a close, they chafed at the bit, waiting for the Yishuv's political elite, led by Ben-Gurion, to allow them to attack British targets and thereby promote the campaign for Jewish statehood (in this respect, the *Exodus* film correctly identifies latent Irgun tendencies within characters like Ari Ben Canaan). When they went overseas on various emissary missions connected to the Aliyah Bet illegal immigration of Jewish DPs, Allon and Palmach fellows found it difficult to connect emotionally and work closely with the survivors—Zionist education had inculcated in them too deeply the idea that the objects of Hitler's hatred were the victims of their own *galut* self-

Uris on a visit to Kibbutz Ginosar, speaking with 1948 Palmach hero (and subsequent Israeli politician) Yigal Allon. *Exodus* hero Ari Ben Canaan drew from several sources; Allon was one prototype. (Harry Ransom Humanities Research Center, the University of Texas at Austin)

centeredness and materialist comfort in their European "exile." No less significant than anything else, the Palmach men from Yishuv kibbutzim were very poor. At key intervals in their lives they found that their objective poverty threatened the emotional empowerment they found in Zionist pioneering ideology. A poignant example is provided by Allon's family life just months before he adopted command positions in the 1948 war. A warm-spirited man and loving father, Allon had an autistic daughter, and he spent several desperate hours trying to figure out how he might pawn off the Spartan furnishings of his kibbutz dwelling to fund a visit to recommended neurologists in Europe or North America.

For these reasons, and many others, Yigal Allon and other real-life Palmach fighters bore little resemblance to the film's protagonist Ari Ben Canaan. They lacked the facility and the will to converse in perfect English with British army officers, order martinis at the King David, or even relate to Holocaust victims without self-consciousness, in terms of unfettered Jewish solidarity.

Ari's suave exterior so egregiously distorts that of his ostensible historical models that the film cannot coherently display its hero's self-identification. "Tell me about yourself," Kitty affectionately asks her new lover at one stage in the film. "Where are you from?" Ari's response is absolutely priceless: "I don't come from anywhere. I'm a sabra, a native-born Palestinian."

The literal meaning of this response is that the hero did not immigrate to Mandatory Palestine, but the figurative slip of the tongue is far more germane to Ari's situation. In the film, Ari Ben Canaan comes from no real spot on the globe. He is a figment of Hollywood mythology, a magical attempt to draw mass audiences close to the new state of Israel without ever really going there. He is the new man of Zionist ideology refashioned in mass-culture terms audiences of American Jews and American Christians could understand. He is "from" some imagined ethno-nationalist interstice where postwar American Jewish ethnicity converged with the new Israeli national character. Ari fused dominant traits of American Jewish culture to characteristics of Israel's fighting halutz pioneer culture in ways that are so overtly contradictory that they remain unnoticed or undiscussed in the film. He plays impeccable white-collar gentleman to Kitty in ways that obviously belie the socialist, Labor Zionist ethos of prestate Israel. Yet when viewed from the American standpoint, Ari lacks the paramount postwar emblem that even the ascetic kibbutz pioneers allowed themselves: a home.

Where does Ari Ben Canaan *live*? When he takes Kitty on a trip to his family moshav homestead at Yad El, he pointedly refers to the journey as a visit. This is not his home. Ari cannot be a settled figure because he is comprised of component parts drawn from two significantly different Jewish subcultures. As he fights for the birth of the Jewish state, his present is homeless; and his past, his pioneering childhood at Yad El, is a story too rough to be told. Karen underscores this point grotesquely when she tells an obviously appalled Kitty Fremont about the horrific fate of Ari's seventeen-year-old teenage sweetheart, for whom Gan Dafna is named. As (according to the script directions) a "concealed light sends a soft glow" over the statue of Ari's first lover, Karen recalls, speaking in a "voice that has grown reverent and enthusiastic": "She was a Palmach, and the Arabs caught her and they—they tortured her to find out things from her. And she wouldn't tell. So they sent her back to Moshav Yad El in a—in a sack, tied to the back of a mule. They—they cut her hands and feet off and gouged out her eyes."[48]

In the *Exodus* novel, Uris drew upon real-life legends, most notably that of Sarah Aaronsohn, a young woman from the "Nili" pro-British spy ring during World War I who endured torturous interrogation and then killed herself to avoid divulging secrets to the Turks, and reworked them to vivify what he considered to be Muslim barbarism. In the film, passing references to Muslim terror have a somewhat different purpose—functionally, they convey the filmmaker's explanation of why he cannot look too closely at where his heroes have come from. Their homes are not understandable. The graphic grotesqueness of the quotation cited above ought not to obscure Karen's suggestive comment about Dafna, "she wouldn't tell." Even under much happier circumstances, what would characters like Dafna and Ari and Jordana have to say to outside audiences about their childhood homes? Simply put, there is nothing to "tell" about the home life of *Exodus*'s heroes since the two Jewish subcultures engaged by the story had very different conceptions of home, one in America, the other in Israel.

Preminger set out to accomplish the cagey feat of producing the definitive account of the end of the Jewish Exodus and of the creation of the Jewish state without allowing his Jewish hero to go home. Ari Ben Canaan, the most heroic Jewish character ever presented to a postwar mass audience, simultaneously became the ultimate antihero for his era. Here was a baby-boomer icon without a nest. Here was a Jew who kept wandering even as he led his people home.

Belonging to a realm of invented ethnicity, an imaginary realm where the post-Holocaust world's two most powerful Jewish subcultures converged, the dashing, mercurial, Jewish hero, Ari Ben Canaan, was a walking contradiction. He was the anticolonial guerrilla who was disarmingly comfortable when he wore the empire's dress and spoke with its accents; and, of course, he was the quintessential Jewish nationalist who happened to be entangled romantically with the all-American girl. In light of these synthetically united contradictions, the film's descriptions of Ari's character could only be camp.

Why, for instance, would the febrile partisan Akiva Ben Canaan dedicate his final breaths to political taxonomic classification of his nephew ("With your fatal optimism you are Haganah; in methodology you are Irgun; and in your heart, you are Israel," the dying Jewish terrorist utters as a benediction to his nephew) rather than excoriation of the British and affirmation of the holy Jewish national cause?

The evasiveness about Ari's character was shrewdly politic. In the two Jewish subcultures, 1950s experiences were too thought-provokingly different for comment. When *Exodus* hit the movie screen, Jews in both places had for almost a generation lived in the aftermath of epochal victory, World War II in the American case, the 1948 War of Independence in Israel's. However, those victories were construed in very different ways. American Jewish life in the 1950s was postwar confidence. Israeli life in the 1950s was postwar fear of a "second round" of conflict with the Arab states (which, of course, occurred during the 1956 Sinai campaign). Second- and third-generation American Jews were settling in the suburbs and enjoying comfortable circumstances lauded by commentators as the end of ideology or as the mass-consumerist peak of the modernization process.[49] In Israel, in contrast, Jewish life buzzed with quasi-messianic state-building ideology in the Ben-Gurion Mapai Party era; new immigrants, Holocaust survivors and Jews from Arabic-speaking countries, huddled in tents in ma'abarot transit camps; and, while scarcity rationing (*tzena*) policies remained in effect, communalist traditions of the kibbutz and halutz pioneering were being readapted in the social welfare economy of the young state. To say that American Jews and Israeli Jews lived under different circumstances in the 1950s is glib understatement.

From the American Jewish standpoint, a visual exploration of the cultural and political specifics of Zionism's successful campaign to create the Jewish state might have generated the feeling that Israel was a foreign land, pretty much like any other one. But as had been the case with the novel, *Exodus* was produced for movie theaters to achieve exactly the opposite effect of Americanizing Israel.

Ari's hybrid character contributed much to that effect, but an equally obvious technique utilized as part of the movie's agenda of Americanizing Israel was its reliance on cowboy images and motifs. Although Uris's résumé included authorship of the script for *Gunfight at the O.K. Corral,* he could not have played the cowboy card more adroitly than Otto Preminger's handling of the Jezreel Valley as a frontier of biblically inspired, American western true grit. The *Exodus* film's transformation as a western should be summarized briefly.

The film's final Gan Dafna action sequences especially rely on transposed cowboy motifs. Gravely wounded during the Acre jail-break, Ari needs to be smuggled from Gan Dafna to the nearby Arab village, Abu Yesha, in order to escape a posse of British soldiers. British authorities uncover a cache of Haganah weapons just as Kitty Fremont drives off with the unconscious Ari strapped precariously to a mattress atop her car. With Ari lying rough saddle as though atop a horse, his beautiful sidekick Kitty earns her spurs and lives up to the reputation of her name (Uris, it will be recalled, slyly named *Exodus*'s heroine after Fremont Street, the scene of action in the O.K. Corral gunfight). This cowboy imagery is temporarily suspended by one of the film's other standard features, the association of Jewish partisanship and health restoration. In the film, Kitty brings Ari back to life by pumping a long needle full of adrenaline into the Israeli hero's heart.

The life-saving serum is brought by Taha, the young Arab mukhtar of Abu Yesha, who promptly takes up the role of the friendly, allied Indian. Ari's resurrection occurs in Taha's home; and though the American Protestant woman nurses Ari back to health, the dramatic energy centers on the blood brother relationship between the Haganah man and the enlightened mukhtar.

The Taha-Ari friendship has a frontier quality of emergency patronage and rustic indebtedness. Taha swears that he owes everything to the Ben Canaans. "When the Syrian Arabs murdered my father in his own mosque, Ari's father saved my life and my heritage," exclaims Taha. "Ari and I used to live together in Yad El. We shared the same room. Now to think that my house could become his tomb." Taha might owe his "heritage" to the Zionist Ben Canaans, but owing to the wild logic of the frontier he is also forced to lodge the Jews' most vile nemesis. An old Nazi is in Taha's house plotting the deployment of his own "personally trained" eighty Arab storm troopers and three hundred newly recruited Abu Yesha villagers in a ruthless attack on the Jewish children's village Gan Dafna. Not willfully duplicitous, Taha appears as an honorable but weak Indian chief who is unable to keep both the good guys and the bad guys off his lands. Taha pleads, earnestly but ineffectually, with the Nazi. "I am the mukhtar of Abu Yesha, and I will not attack Gan Dafna," he implores. When he points out that there are 650,000 Jews in Palestine, his ghoulish Nazi guest replies "temporarily."

Few of the details in this sequence make sense when removed from the binary oppositions and emotional expectations of a cowboy movie. There is no historical validity to the gruesome account provided by Taha's Nazi guest regarding his meddling. "The Grand Mufti was our guest in Berlin during the war. Since we are now his guests, we have placed our experience in handling Jews entirely at his disposal," the Nazi guest states. He explains that the strategic plan for the attack on Gan Dafna is to clear out the Jezreel Valley to guarantee passage for Haj Amin on his way to Safad, which will serve as the mufti's "provisional capital until every last Jew in Palestine is exterminated." Handicapped by outrageous errors of geography and fact, this Nazi speech does more on its own to delegitimize the Palestinian side of the 1948 struggle than anything Uris ever attempted. As we will see, in his novel Uris pointed to real-life connections between the mufti and Nazism, and he also indulged scathingly prejudicial descriptions of the Jews' Arab antagonists in the 1948 war. However, Uris never manipulated historically invalid devices to portray the fight as an updated and Palestine-transplanted chapter of the Nazi plot to exterminate the Jews.

The late sequence in Taha's home is juxtaposed against jubilant scenes from central Israel, where a city crowd throngs on a summery night supposedly in late December 1947 to hear Barak Ben Canaan announce the UN vote in favor of the partition of Palestine and the establishment of a free Jewish state. Barak's oratory implicitly recognizes Palestinian sensitivities and grievances as being at the heart of the brewing dispute: "We implore you," the veteran Zionist diplomat addresses Palestine's Arabs, "remain in your homes and shops, and we shall work together as equals in the free state of Israel." The oration is a central plot event in the film narrative (lavishing incredible energy in its filming, Preminger strained relations with his cast[50]). As Taha, Kitty, and Ari listen to a radio broadcast of the elder Ben Canaan's peroration, the mukhtar candidly spells out Palestinian objections to the land's newly approved dispensation. "You have won your freedom, and I have lost mine," Taha laments. Ari attempts to correct his friend: "We've never had freedom. All our lives we've been under British rule. Now we will be equal citizens in the free state of Israel." Taha's rejoinder conceptualizes the impending war as a fight for political power. If, as Ari insists, it makes no difference whether a group is a majority or a minority in a free democracy, why have the Zionists fought so hard to create a Jewish state, asks Taha.

That is a good question, and it can be addressed cogently by an examination of the twists and turns of Jewish history. But the climactic sequence of the *Exodus* film engages neither a serious investigation of history nor a serious political discussion of the causes of the 1948 war. Neither the nomenclature, the dates, or much else is accurate; the scene offers absurdly divergent explanations of the Palestinian cause in 1948 as either a Nazi plot or as a nationalist campaign for political power. The scene, in short, is not history in cinema, but cinema transmogrifying history as a western showdown.

At the end of his blood-curdling interview with the Nazi, Taha dutifully pays obeisance to Middle East hosting rituals by promising his hateful guest dinner. Taha then rushes to Ari's room to warn him to get the Jewish children out of the Gan Dafna village by midnight the following day, the showdown hour designated for the attack by the Nazi-trained Arab storm troopers. Wrapped in traditional white headdress, Taha comes on as a film cliché when he conveys this vital intelligence to Ari—the good native of the cowboy western genre, he personifies a conflict between the demands of blood-brother friendship with a white man and tribal honor. Warned, Kitty and Ari quickly spring into action at Gan Dafna. Subsequent dialogue establishes that, owing to British confiscation, the children's village is badly underarmed, as must be the case in any siege on the good guys hamlet in a movie western. Kitty and Ari tape shut the children's mouths and tranquilize Gan Dafna's 150 youngest residents for the daring escape, a nighttime trek down Mount Tabor, supposedly alongside a dangerous border.

Just before they trudge into the dark wilderness, Kitty and Ari share a High Noon showdown moment in their on-again/off-again American-Israeli romance. Kitty explains that she is not needed as a caretaker at Gan Dafna because the 150 older children left behind at the village can all work as nurses; so either you let me join the rescue, or this is it between us, declares Kitty. With these tough cowgirl cadences, the American Presbyterian clinches her initiation in the Israeli statehood fight.

Final images in the movie's last action scene forcibly integrate this cowboy western genre into the Israel-Palestinian 1948 narrative. Preminger might not have deliberately planted all the symbols, but decades later it is impossible to overlook how the American West conquers the Jewish Exodus in the film's last reels. By the end, with the protagonists of Israel's founding immersed in the most familiar 1950s American cinematic mode of heroism, *Exodus* is drenched with the new Israel-America synthesis.

After successfully evacuating Gan Dafna's small children, Ari leads a united Haganah-Irgun attack on Abu Yesha (he has no compunction leading the charge on the home village of his blood brother, because the mufti's men are understood to have gained control of Abu Yesha). After winding through the alleys of the deserted village with his small force, Ari stops to behold what has happened to his lifetime friend, Taha. The camera follows his gaze down a straight alley; a swastika is smeared on a side wall to herald the handiwork of the Nazi agent. Looking straight ahead, Ari spots Taha, hanging dead from a noose with a blood red Star of David branded onto his chest. The form of execution, a hangman's noose, has relatively little meaning in the terrorized landscape of the modern Middle East. But its resonance as a token of justice, or lack thereof, in the epic frontier of the western knows no bounds.

In these final minutes of the film, other cowboy symbols of condemned victims of the 1948 violence, and of their mourners, refer to the new American-Israel synthesis. After an impulsive tryst with Dov Landau at her fiancé's nighttime guard post on the Gan Dafna perimeter, Karen is abducted and murdered by Arab marauders. The following day her abused body is discovered tossed alongside a prickly

Exodus used cowboy images to Americanize elements of Israel's founding story. Here, Kitty's young protégé, Karen Clement-Hansen (Jill Haworth), is seen lying dead next to wild cacti as the victim of a western-style ambush. The cacti appear also as sabras, the prickly pears (hard on the outside, soft on the inside) that became a symbol of Israeli character. (*Exodus* film)

sabra, the symbol of a native-born Israeli who is tough on the outside and sweet on the inside. The symbol, part American Western cactus, part Israeli national symbol, comments poignantly on human sacrifice on the new Jewish frontier, and the troubled search for a new home undertaken by a serenely disposed Holocaust refugee. Karen is the protégé of Kitty Fremont, who glides in and out of the *Exodus* novel and film with plans to adopt the lovely teenager and bring her to America.

We last glimpse Kitty in the film standing grimly at the joint burial of Karen and Taha. In the film, she travels a hard full circle. A year before the plot's opening sequence, her husband Tom, a war correspondent, dies while covering a bridge demolition operation perpetrated by one of the Jewish undergrounds. Returning to Palestine as a widow aboard the *Exodus* ship, she becomes entangled in missions carried out by the same sort of partisans whose zealotry proved fatal to her husband; and so, throughout the film, she has her reasons to be wary of her protégé's engagement with the Irgun terrorist, Dov Landau. Stiff and sad as Karen is buried, Kitty stands wearing a droopy Israeli army cap. She is prepared to join the Israeli teenage boys and girls in the next battle of the War of Independence.

Nothing in the film more forcefully represents the cult of Israeli-American convergence. Ideally, the last thing a director would want to do with Eva Marie Saint is put a hat on her resplendent blonde hair. For decades after 1948, this army hat, known as a *kova tembel* (literally, dunce cap), symbolized Israeli character. In Israeli culture through the 1980s (at least), it obliquely evoked halutz pioneering and Palmach informal camaraderie, and probably also the fussy anxieties of Ashkenazi immigrant parents who worried about the exposure of their sabra children to the blazing Mediterranean sun. Israelis proudly donned the kova tembel as a token of the humorous, human side that persisted despite the daunting military demands and daily hardships of life in the Jewish state. With the funeral mourners about to disperse for the next battle in the 1948 war, Preminger put the cap atop Kitty's head the way the director in a western would have a ranch girl plop on a cowboy hat before going out to fight Indians with the boys. Preminger tips his cap and bows out of *Exodus* with this impossible Cult of Synthesis image of an American-Israeli-Cowgirl-Sabra.

More cowboy-Americanization of the Israeli War of Independence narrative. Kitty Fremont in battle dress, as though she is wearing a cowboy hat for a western showdown. The hat is a *kova tembel*, renowned as a definitive symbol of Israeli culture. (Exodus film)

With the perspective of time, what has been said about *Exodus*'s Americanization of Israel, and what remains to be said? Did it really make a difference that, building on Uris's agenda, Otto Preminger encouraged audiences to think about the Jewish state's founding by using American terms of reference? If so, can that difference be identified?

Stephen Whitfield, Brandeis University professor of American studies, exaggerates when he cites a dialogue of Jewish self-estrangement between Walter Lippmann and Felix Frankfurter (Lippmann: "What is a Jew, anyway"; Frankfurter: "a person whom non-Jews regard as a Jew") and claims that it characterizes the "general level of ideological sophistication when the manuscript of a lengthy novel by a Marine veteran named Leon Uris arrived in the office of [agent] Ingo Preminger."[51] Whitfield's point, however, is well taken. Culturally speaking, American Jews and Israelis in the 1950s were distant relatives. *Exodus* responded creatively to this culture gap, even if it did little to effectively narrow it. The film brought American Jews closer to their own Jewish identities by simultaneously cultivating an admiring, vicarious identification with Israelis. Since specifics could be distracting, and since the medium of film trades in images and can gloss details, the movie version of *Exodus* could promote its ethnic agenda in ways that eluded the printed product written by the ambitious, talented Leon Uris.

By remaining vague about what was "really" Israeli in Ari Ben Canaan's character, the film found a way to enable American Jews to dress up themselves as the 1948 war hero and to discover heretofore-unknown components of their Jewish identities. *Exodus* projected them well out of their secure but dull suburban enclaves onto a heroic frontier of post-Holocaust Jewish action and redemption. Associating the Zionist process of resettlement with physical courage and uplifting idealism and sprinkling a dash of cocktail sophistication at the terrace restaurant of the King David Hotel, *Exodus* paved an exciting imaginative path to the Jewish past and present rooted in the Holy Land.

The effects of these vicarious journeys in the mysterious realm of human identity cannot be measured with any degree of precision. Whitfield is probably right when he speculates that by "enhancing ethnic pride" among American Jews, the film version of *Exodus* "helped to undermine Theodor Herzl's premise that the *Galut* was fated to disappear."[52] Deborah Dash Moore is probably on track when she argues that *Exodus* played a crucial role in preparing American Jews for mobilization for future Israeli crises. After a lively discussion of *Exodus*'s effects on postwar Jewish communities in Miami and Los Angeles, Moore opines that "so many American Jews responded so quickly to the crisis of May–June 1967 . . . because Israel had become such an integral part of their self-consciousness."[53] The Israeli maverick journalist Uri Avineri worried sententiously and needlessly in his groundbreaking *Ha-'Olam Ha-zeh* magazine about how the "revolting kitsch" of *Exodus* would poison the minds of Israeli youth; but he was probably right when he observed that "for many millions" around the globe, the screening of *Exodus* would provide "first-time exposure to the state of Israel and its builders, and this first impression will stick in their minds."[54] However, in the end, whether a trip to the cinema to see *Exodus* provided merely a passing pat on the ethnic ego of an American Jewish viewer, or possibly spurred more sustained forms of general Jewish identification, or specific support for Israel, depended on innumerable intangibles of personal upbringing and social circumstances.

The surest thing that can be said about the effect of the *Exodus* film is that accelerating the influence of Uris's novel, it promoted a sea change in the orientation of American Jewish culture, transforming the terms of its "Cult of Synthesis." Whereas American Jewish publicists, thinkers, and artists had for decades striven to prove that there were authentic bonds between Jewish tradition and American democracy, the highly influential *Exodus* film projected to mass audiences the concept of an organic link between American democracy and the new Jewish state. Even as particular arguments and images of the *Exodus* narrative have (as our concluding chapter argues) been deconstructed in past decades, this conception of a natural link between the two democracies retains a strong, revitalizing, power.

4) After *Exodus*

History has no precise measurements for evaluating the impact of a widely read political novel. Well-known assessments have intuitive appeal to those familiar with the relevant historical context, as exemplified by President Abraham Lincoln's reported exclamation to the author of *Uncle Tom's Cabin,* Harriet Beecher Stowe: "So you are the little woman who wrote the book that started this great war!" Specific responses (astronomical sales figures, effusive reader testimonials) to the publication of a historical novel can be adequately quantified or recorded, but nothing in them can prove a causal relation between a book and the emergence of cultural attitudes or particular activities. Just as we intuitively grasp that a well-argued and widely read book can have significant historical impact, we understand intuitively that no book will cause readers to believe or act in some new way in the absence of other cultural and educational influences that encourage the same new belief or attitude.

One major reason why *Exodus*'s impact is hard to assess derives from a fundamental difficulty of classification. As suggested by the first chapter of this study, Uris's book is not easy to place in any particular category, be it political novel, historical novel, or Jewish historical fiction. That is, we cannot readily ascribe it to a taxonomic group whose members typically exert a defined sort of influence. Rachel Weissbrod has called *Exodus* a Zionist "melodrama," and some of the traits she attributes to this category (hyperbolic black-and-white characterization, division of the world between good and evil) clearly apply to Uris's work. However, other qualities that her article associates with melodrama (e.g., "no pretense at realism") are overstated criticisms of a book whose contents mix exaggerated dramatization with evocative representations of a pioneering culture that hundreds of thousands of readers continue to regard as realism.[1] No less importantly, dismissive categorizations such as "melodrama" ignore important functions in the *Exodus* narrative, particularly its educative task as a prolonged Jewish history lesson and its semiconscious aim to Americanize Israel's founding story, which this book has analyzed.

If *Exodus* is not simply a melodrama, then what is it? In this chapter we will briefly note ways in which Uris's narrative can, and cannot, be grouped with 1948 narratives written by Israelis and Palestinians—such discussion will show that the taxonomic listing of *Exodus* as a 1948 narrative is interesting, but problematic. Leon Uris emerged as a popular American writer. His own creative heroes were writers like John Steinbeck,[2] and his work before and after *Exodus* was by no means devoted exclusively to Jewish topics. Can he therefore be readily grouped alongside American writers whose novels combined fictional narrative with "real" history?

The answer to this question is uncertain. Important discussions of American historical fiction emphasize a kind of authorial self-consciousness about the border between historical fact and creative fiction that is lacking in Uris's writing. In *Exodus* the authorial voice seems deeply and passionately immersed in a sea of credulity about the history of the period under discussion, whereas writers of American historical fiction often seem tormented by the thought that the invented world of their fictional narrative could be more real than the putative facts of historical eras. The "burden of historical responsibility under the pressure of skepticism," writes Emily Miller Budick, is "the distinguishing feature of American historical romance."[3] Other critics have suggested that twentieth-century American prose is steeped so deeply in history that analytic classification about the "historical novel" or the "political novel" lacks utility. "Every novel is a historical novel," writes one critic. "During the last one hundred years, we have had many American novels that tell us as much about the history as about the society of their times, knowing of course that the two are inseparable."[4] Since *Exodus* cannot be easily grouped with any particular genre of writing about Israel, or within American culture, its historical status can be hard to measure.

Aware of such reservations, we have argued that Leon Uris's *Exodus* must be considered a groundbreaking, even revolutionary, book in post-Holocaust Jewish history. The book's pro-Zionist arguments were not original; nor was Uris's heavy-handed handling of character and plot innovative, from a literary standpoint. *Exodus,* however, virtually created its own genre. Presenting an imposing amount of history in a best-seller format, the novel was uniquely informative and argumentative. It reshuffled stereotypes with such dazzling dexterity that many thousands of readers never noticed they were being drawn to superhuman heroic types that could never exist in the real world, and also that, on some levels, the book berated their own lives as (in the words of the LEON URIS SAYS preface) "brilliant doctors" and "clever businessmen." As we have seen, one compelling indication of the book's unparalleled status is the real difficulty of contextualizing it. Desperate to win worldwide recognition for the Jewish state program, the Zionists attempted for decades, in vain, to pull off a public-relations coup of *Exodus* proportions; then, after Israel's establishment in 1948, Jews of the world maintained a preternatural silence about the Jewish state, as though they had nothing to say about an event for which they had waited in messianic expectation for almost 2,000 years. Whatever the merits of its contents, the sheer popularity of Leon Uris's book (and its subsequent film version) and its explicit treatment of Israel's founding following this decade of peculiar reticence warrants its ranking as a major event in the culture of Jewish revival after the Holocaust.

Exodus empowered Jews throughout the Diaspora to assert their ethnic pride. In some Diaspora contexts (as we will note in this book's final words) this assertion expressed itself in bold action, as though Jews were reenacting images of heroism they found in Uris's book. In broad cultural terms, the *Exodus* narrative yielded an impressive result. In an ethnic revival, countless Jews felt newly comfortable in their own skin. Partly this was because they were conscious that Gentile readers of the same book were admiring them.

Half a century after *Exodus*'s publication, we live in an age when the deconstruction of *Exodus,* of Israel's heroic founding narrative, is taken for granted, as though the discrediting and demise of Uris's story is more of an existential certainty than its original ethnic effects. Thus, in a 2005 *New York Times* report about the efforts of Israel studies academics at some universities to mollify increasingly militant pro-Palestinian voices, Samuel Freedman eulogized Uris's work as being entirely irrelevant in a twenty-first-century climate of multicultural expectation of balance between national narratives.

Lauding the effort of one professor, Ronald Zweig, to play fair with all sides of the 1948 story, Freedman noted that the Israel studies professor "lectured without sentimentality about the illegal immigration of Holocaust survivors to British-ruled Palestine. . . . This was not the romantic epic of *Exodus*."[5] The absence of any expectation of heroism in Israel's founding story spells the unmaking of Uris's *Exodus*.

Following the waning influence of any cultural item is a cumbersome task. In the broadest sense, people simply "move on" after being deeply engaged with an engrossing novel or film. With *Exodus*, so many controversial and complicated events involving Israel have transpired in the past half-century that this process of moving on has unfolded in a morass of emotion, expectation, belief, and interpretation so thick as to render impossible an attempt to isolate the lingering impact of any particular cultural influence. Nonetheless, since *Exodus*'s popularity was so unprecedented and massive, an effort to discuss intelligibly what has happened since its publication is warranted. This "After *Exodus*" chapter measures the unmaking of Uris's narrative not as a function of any deliberate political or cultural plan to deconstruct his heroic perception of Israel's founding but rather in terms of how far we have, in fact, moved on in our thinking about Israel since Leon Uris produced his influential book. Since there is no hope of analyzing, comprehensively, reasons why many people stopped perceiving Ari Ben Canaan as a literal depiction of a new sort of heroic Jew, and as a representative Israeli, this measurement of *Exodus*'s unmaking is necessarily selective and descriptive. Nonetheless, the results of this measurement—which show, simultaneously, how far-flung and long-lived Uris's influence was in some contexts, and how emphatically the influence has been erased in other contexts—are extraordinarily impressive and warrant reflection.

The measurement's first step involves being as specific as possible about what was lost. Only by meeting some of Uris's readers can we assess the impact of the ethnic revival generated by his book.

Many people read *Exodus*. The book entered the *New York Times* fiction best-seller list at thirteenth place on October 12, 1958, a week when Nabokov's *Lolita* topped the charts. Something of a slow starter as a best seller, Uris's novel clawed up to sixth place on December 2; Pasternak's *Doctor Zhivago* claimed the number one spot that week. A month and a half later, little had changed—Pasternak was still number one, and Uris clung to the fourth spot. This holding pattern continued until May 1, 1959, when the very long historical novel about Israel's founding finally made it to number one on the *New York Times* list.

From May 1959, *Exodus* topped the various best-seller lists (*New York Times, Time,* the *New York Herald Tribune*) for seventeen to nineteen weeks. When *Lady Chatterley's Lover* finally knocked *Exodus* from the top spot, the publishing world was convulsed by preparations for the sale of *Exodus*'s paperback edition. At the end of September 1959, the national press quoted excited Bantam officials as they talked about *Exodus* advance print orders of 1.5 million copies, the largest in paperback history. Bantam correctly expected massive sales of three to five million for the paperback edition of *Exodus,* whose initial cost was 75 cents.[6] Twenty years after its inception in America, paperback publishing hit its peak precisely at this interval. In 1959–60, for the first time, dollar revenue from paperbacks exceeded those of adult trade hardcover books.[7] *Exodus* was the milestone gem in the fulfillment of the paperback revolution.

Jewish readers were spellbound. Uris received letters from hundreds of American Jewish readers who thanked him for helping them reconnect with their Jewish identity and for teaching them about the moral purposes and practical accomplishments of the state of Israel.

Writing to Uris in August 1959, Lewis Glenn, a twenty-three-year-old from Morristown, New Jersey, explained: "I am a Jew, but my religious beliefs have wandered quite far from the Hebrew tradition. . . . I have come to feel somewhat ashamed of my heritage, as have many of my friends. I should like to inform you that your work has rekindled the spark in me and in many of your readers. You have forced me to have PRIDE and I am most grateful for this."[8] Another letter (August 4, 1959), from Nancy Goldberg, a sophomore at the Connecticut College for Women in New London, exemplified the exodus from the melting-pot norms of 1950s America. "You could say that we are a typical American Reformed Jewish family," the writer noted, describing her background. "When reading *Exodus* a whole new world opened up for me." Goldberg had started to ask probing questions about her own education. "Here I am taking numerous courses at College and I don't even know about my own religion." She explained that she was devoting the summer to research on the history of the Jewish people; she was making plans to work on a kibbutz or to work with children in Israel and wondered whether Uris could help with these preparations.[9] The writer replied, informing Goldberg about six-week *ulpan* intensive Hebrew courses and advising that Hadassah in New York might help place her on a Youth Aliyah children's village.[10]

American Jewish readers who were too settled in their ways to contemplate extended work-study trips to Israel attested to having undergone a deeply emotional experience with Uris's book. "I spent many hours thrilling, crying, sympathizing with the brave people of Israel," Joyce Hoffman of Brooklyn told Uris (January 14, 1959).[11] Joy Goldsmith of Burlington, Vermont succinctly described *Exodus*'s ethnic effect when she wrote to Uris (April 8, 1959): "Thank you for writing *Exodus* for making me aware of my Judaic background and once again proud to be a Jew."[12]

Other readers attested to soaring feelings of ethnic pride while hinting that Uris's handling of the Holocaust in his book about Israel's founding was critical. They found the connections Uris drew between the Jews' European tragedy and their triumph in the Middle East to be utterly convincing and wanted others to read and learn about them. "Thanks for the pleasurable hours but not for the wet hankies," wrote Harriete Giber in March 1959. She thanked Uris for "reminding me of my own identity with Israel and her fighting Jews," and added, pointedly: "I noticed on the book flap that 85,000 copies have been sold. There should have been six million."[13] *Exodus* was turning readers into advocates. For them, Uris's 1948 narrative was not a story but a testament the world needed to see.

These readers were hanging on every word of *Exodus* and almost never quarreled with Uris about major points of interpretation regarding the Arab-Israel war of 1948. During his prepublication fidgeting, Uris had worried (as he put it in a late 1957 letter to his father) that "every Jew who reads Exodus will have his own little bone to pick,"[14] and this turned out to be completely true. But such criticisms were amusing, not stringent, and they proved how readers had become completely immersed in the *Exodus* text. For instance, Inge Hirschfeld protested that the appearance in *Exodus* of November 29, 1947, the day of the decisive UN partition vote on Palestine, as a Friday instead of a Saturday was a "glaring" and "unforgivable" mistake.[15] Ralph Goldman, who signed his letter as Vice President of the American-Israel Cultural Foundation, and who was to devote a lifetime of service to the Joint Distribution Committee and many

Jewish causes, was much more diplomatic, calling Uris's attention to this "minor point" about the Friday-Saturday error while making haste to identify himself as one of hundreds of thousands of readers who were "impressed with your most dramatic presentation of the establishment of the state of Israel, and the full background you gave of its birth."[16] Uris replied: "Dear Mr. Goldman, I am a sloppy writer."[17]

From Tel Aviv, Mrs. Herzlia Levin identified herself as "an old settler" in Israel who had arrived in 1920 at the age of fifteen, and who joined the Irgun ten years later. "What was the reason for the cruel unfairness of hiding the true name of Ezel [Irgun], while you used the true names of Haganah and Palmach," she asked Uris.[18]

Inscribing Hebrew salutations on his letter, Louis Forgash, from Weirton, West Virginia, pointed out that an innocent reference to "pigs" as part of the livestock and landscape of Abu Yesha, a Muslim village, made little sense.[19]

When Dr. Nathan Izbicky from Chicago complained in March 1959 that Ze'ev Jabotinsky was not mentioned by name in *Exodus*,[20] Uris dropped his guard, for a moment. "It is said that next year the eight of nine thousand people who have questions will converge on the Coliseum in Los Angeles and re-write the book," he replied to the Chicago physician.[21]

Outside of the Jewish community, dozens of readers wrote to Uris, thanking him for exposing them to story they had known little about. Ronald Dunn's letter in January 1961 exemplifies the spirit of these responses: "I was young at the time when all this was going on, and never knew about the Jewish people till I read your book. I never realized how much people, despised by others, could fight for a country."[22]

More often than not, when Uris received letters from non-Jewish correspondents who brought up Arab claims and circumstances, the writers' viewpoints accorded with Uris's perspective about the 1948 war. Some such Uris admirers were long-standing supporters of Zionist aims and projects. For instance, soil conservationist Walter Clay Lowdermilk, whose 1944 *Palestine: Land of Promise* influentially argued that the land of Palestine was sufficiently fertile to support large-scale Jewish immigration, wrote enthusiastically to Uris in February 1959, on letterhead of the American Sponsoring Committee for the International Farmers Convention in Israel. "Your industry in getting at sources and first hand accounts makes *Exodus* a must reference book. . . . You have done a masterful job," the soil expert told Uris. Lowdermilk added a sharply dismissive line about the Palestinian side of the story of 1948: "I call the evacuation by Arabs under orders of the Arab High Committee a military maneuver that failed, and such it was."[23]

In months after *Exodus*'s release, Uris claimed that he received eighty speaking requests a week. That number is hard to verify since many such requests were fielded by his agent, and several might have made their way to his Encino home via an array of intermediaries. At any event, Uris's papers amply reflect this deluge. For example, during the first six weeks of 1959, the following organizations and invitations formally invited Uris to speak: Beverly Hills Circle literary club, Temple Beth Am (Los Angeles), Temple Sinai (Philadelphia), Jewish Community Center (Chicago), *Jewish News* newspaper (Newark), West Oak Jewish Community Center (New Jersey), Fresno Hadassah Chapter, Glendon Book Fair (Los Angeles), Hillel Institute (San Jose), Scarsdale Hadassah Chapter, Great Neck United Jewish Appeal, Brooklyn United Jewish Appeal, Women's Canadian ORT, Hillel City College of New York, and Temple Sholom (Philadelphia). And in the month of July 1959, the invitations were still pouring in, coming from (among other institutions): Boston Hadassah Chapter, Montreal Hadassah, American Jewish Congress (Valley Stream), Palestine Economic Corporation, Worcester Chapter National Council of Jewish Women, Baltimore Associated Jewish Charities and Welfare Fund, Congregation Bnai Jeshurun (New York), Temple Miskan Tfillah (Boston), and Brooklyn Council of Pioneer Women.[24] Clearly, Uris was a much-sought-after speaker who had star power and who could talk about Israel as a success story in idiom Americans keenly appreciated.

By the end of 1959, Israeli officials openly described *Exodus* as a godsend for the country's tourist industry. "More tourists fly in to Tel Aviv with *Exodus* than with the Bible," declared Yohanan Beham, director of the Israel government tourist office.[25] Tourism to the country had jumped 70 percent in 1958 as a result of Israel's tenth anniversary celebrations, Beham stated. His office had expected tourism figures to decrease in 1959, but in December of that year Beham proudly cited a 20 percent rise. *Exodus* was his explanation as to why tourism momentum stayed in effect after the conclusion of the tenth anniversary celebrations.[26]

Soon enough, *Exodus* became a cleverly packaged trade name in Israeli tourism. This process hit a peak as the *Exodus* film was being prepared for screening in movie theaters. In 1960–61, El Al airlines offered a special two-week *Exodus* tour. For $1,024, El Al promised, "you will visit the cities and villages, the valleys and the mountain ranges, and the seacoast where Ari Ben Canaan and his companions struggled for a towering ideal. You will see the battlegrounds where they fought." The tour's promotional materials pitched the excursion as being "modeled directly after the novel, read by millions." Travelers received a complimentary copy of the Bantam edition of the novel as well as a picture book portraying Otto Preminger's adaptation of the story for the silver screen. The tour promised stops to Kibbutz Nahal Oz, the basis of *Exodus*'s Nahal Midbar, where Karen is killed by Arab fedayeen; Kibbutz Lohamei Hagetaot, "founded by survivors of war-time ghetto rebellions, like Dov Landau"; Kibbutz Hanita, the original of the book's Hamishmar, "founded by Ari and his love, Dafna, who was killed there"; Yemin Orde, "a children's village like Gan Dafna of the book"; the Druze village Daliyat al Karmel, "where the wounded Ari was sheltered after the Acre prison break"; the Hula valley, the region of Ari's home colony of Yad El; and the "hilltop ruins of the British fortress of Nebi Yusha, the book's Fort Esther and the scene of bitter fighting."[27]

Just as the novel's sales started to skyrocket, contemporary reviewers of *Exodus* were generally appreciative of the reasons for its success. In one especially insightful review, Dan Wakefield observed in *The Nation* (April 11, 1959) that "the novel of Israeli life Americans had been waiting for had to be written by an American." Although *Exodus*'s characters were "typecast," the novel's plot was so exciting that its figures become engaging as well, "not," this reviewer explained, "because of their individuality or depth, but because of the historic drama they are involved in." Wakefield spoke for countless other readers and hit the nail on the head when he identified the "real achievement of Exodus" as "its skillful rendering of the furiously complex history of modern Israel in a palatable, popular form that is usually faithful to the spirit of the complicated realities."[28]

Exodus did not win paeans of praise as great literature, but most critics found something very special, even monumental, in Uris's book. In a finely turned phrase, Maxwell Geismar referred to "a kind of underground power in his [Uris's] writing." More than other reviews, this response (published in the *Saturday Review* September 27, 1958) must have riveted Uris, since it described the writer's abilities and accomplishments in ways that matched the self-analysis Uris sometimes shared with his closest confidants, particularly his father. "Perhaps a more sophisticated writer than Mr. Uris might never have attempted to relate this epic tale at all, and a less talented writer could never have brought it off," Geismar opined. The "underground power" of Uris's writing compensated for its occasional lack of tone and the tendency of his characters to be "social types rather than individual portraits." Geismar's final lines spoke for tens of thousands of readers: "No other novel I have read recently has had the same capacity to refresh our memory, to inform our intelligence, and to stir the heart."[29]

Still more complimentary was the response of Harold Ribalow, a knowledgeable critic of Jewish fiction. *Exodus*, Ribalow insisted, "is the best one volume history of Israel and the Jewish people a reader can obtain at this time." Ribalow praised Uris for boldly painting on a broad canvas of fifty years of history rather than focusing on "a corner of Israeli life, on the kibbutz, or the Yemenites, or isolated battles with the Arabs," as "some Israeli novels do." He added: "I have yet to read a Hebrew novel as ambitious, as sweeping in emotion and scope, as exciting." In this review (*Pioneer Women's Journal*, January 1959), Ribalow was ahead of the critical pack when he recognized that *Exodus*'s enduring contribution to public perceptions of Israel was the way it historicized the founding and circumstances of the Jewish state.[30]

Not all reviews were positive. *Time* grumbled that "too often the author's flag-waving enthusiasm for Zionism diminishes rather than exalts the achievements of Israelis." Yet negative reviews typically revolved around recognition of *Exodus*'s extraordinary status as a cultural milestone. For instance, for all its dismissive barbs of Uris's work as "pornographic" and "genuine trash about Jews," Midge Decter's *Commentary* review (October 1961) reinforced a sense that *Exodus* was an event in the history of Jewish books. This reviewer, a future neoconservative leading light who wrote after the publication of *Mila 18* but directed the brunt of her remarks to *Exodus,* inserted an eye-popping comment: "By now it is unlikely that more than a handful of literate Americans have not either read one of his [Uris's] Jewish novels or been engaged in at least one passionate discussion about him with someone who has."[31] Despite its pejorative slant, this review's diagnosis of the source of *Exodus*'s appeal sounded uncannily close to Uris's own statements about his purposes and method. In *Exodus*, this *Commentary* review noted, "one is relieved of all the nagging, whining, doubting of most current literature, and provided instead with the refreshment of characters who think simply and act, act, act all the time."[32]

Jewish newspapers across the country lauded *Exodus*. For instance, in July 1960, the *Jewish Times* gloated about how Uris and his followers were doing something that had eluded Zionism for decades. "A highly placed Israeli personality said some time ago upon return from America that *Exodus* had done more for the popularity of the Zionist idea than 50 years of Zionist propaganda," noted this periodical, correctly.

In Christian media, responses to *Exodus* were appreciative, though some reviews found the book excessively pro-Zionist. Most critical was a review written in the *Christian Science Monitor* (December 4, 1958) by Geoffrey Godsell. While he recognized that "Uris is a skillful and lively writer," the reviewer was noticeably uncomfortable about how *Exodus*'s author "is convinced of the divine right of the Jews to Palestine."[33] The *Monitor*'s criticism of Uris's Zionist partisanship was not the Christian media standard, however. In *Christianity Today* (February 29, 1960), Marie Malmin Myer was neither distracted nor troubled by Uris's Zionist outlook. "That Uris is deeply himself involved in the story he is telling does not detract from the importance of the picture he draws," Myer wrote. She found Uris's history sections about European Jewry to be very enlightening and useful antidotes to prejudice.[34] The *Catholic Star Herald* (March 16, 1960) made the same points but in a more elegiac voice. *Exodus*, it wrote, "is worthy of epic poetry." Although the book "may be sentimentalized" and "written from a highly partisan point of view," it is nonetheless "searing in intensity and illuminating in insight."[35] In mid-June, in the *Michigan Christian Advocate*, Allan Gray attested: "I have had little understanding for the Zionist movement and not too much sympathy for Israel. After reading this book, there is almost a complete reversal of my opinions."[36]

Motivated by compelling personal experiences and worthy ideals, Uris had labored hard to create a zone for Israel and world Jewry in the postwar atmosphere of democratic triumph. He did so without obscuring the slightest trace of the gruesome setbacks Jews had suffered during World War II, and he presented a wealth of information about Israel's purposes and struggles that had been mostly unknown outside a core of committed Zionists. The world appreciated the results.

A photograph of an address, "The Faith You Have Kept," delivered by Uris at the National Conference of the United Jewish Appeal (UJA) in New York City on December 12, 1959, captures the excitement and unifying power of his accomplishment.[37] Uris stands at the podium of a large hall that is packed to the gills with charity-givers dressed for the occasion. Cynics could say that the room is filled with the mechanical blandishments of the fund-raising circuit, but just as surely the image projects a newly forthright assertiveness about American Jewry's links with the Jewish state. The large unfurled American and Israeli flags to the right and left of Uris arrest-

The Faith You Have Kept: Uris speaking at a UJA fundraiser, late 1959, in the eye of the explosion of ethnic pride ignited by his novel. (Harry Ransom Humanities Research Center, the University of Texas at Austin)

ingly reflect the capacious American patriotism and Jewish idealism he projected in his writing.

Uris, who often claimed to find little enjoyment from public speaking, maintained an engagingly candid testimonial tone at this 1959 UJA event. He confessed that in his youth, "I live[d] my life away from the Jewish community. I would run into the house in which I was raised and grab a drink of wine on the Sabbath, and run out the back door." As he grew older he heard about all the stories of how "so-called assimilated Jews have come out of nowhere to take over the leadership of their people." But he was no Moses or Herzl. What he meant to say was that "there comes that day when every Jew, no matter how far he has gone astray, must look at himself in the mirror and say, 'this is what I am, and this is what I am going to do about it.'"

No single thing caused him to write *Exodus,* Uris recalled. Over the years he felt himself drawn inexorably to the story of how "Jews for the first time in thousands of years were taking their destiny into their own hands." As a veteran of the Marine Corps, Israel was speaking in "a language that I understood too, and I said to myself, this is the kind of Jew I want to be." Uris decided, "I didn't want to spend my life apologizing for being a member of a minority which has contributed far beyond its numbers to this country's greatness." As he began a career as a writer, Uris added, "I decided I was not going to be one of those young American Jewish authors who psychoanalyze themselves in print, and berate the Jewish people. I was determined not to be a Jewish beatnik."

Uris bluntly acknowledged the continuing conflict in Israel, but at this 1959 high-point event in his own *Exodus* saga, the writer sounded optimistic. He seemed to be speaking with authority when he appealed to Jewish unity as a lasting remedy for Israel's challenges. "It is my feeling that with the peace treaty that eventually must come, our little Israel, and I say that with affection and not possession, will take a leading part in the greatest renaissance the world has ever seen," Uris proclaimed in this UJA address. "The Arabs have a parable saying that patience destroys mountains. To that, I answer, a mountain built of love is indestructible."

Just days before the start of the 1960s, nobody in Jewish America was speaking the language of ethnic revivalism with more persuasive power than Leon Uris. As the photographic image and words of this December 1959 New York event illustrate, the writer's narrative of

Israel's 1948 War of Independence had unusual power in the unification of world Jewry for a common purpose. For all that narrative's prejudicial blind spots and historical inaccuracies, its deconstruction in decades ahead would come at the Jews' peril.

The waning of *Exodus*'s influence proceeded on several parallel tracks. First, contemporary criticism brought up morally problematic or factually inaccurate aspects of the narrative. *Exodus* was an empowering, unifying book, but it related to an inherently controversial topic, and its vision could never have appealed to all of the various groups that imagined themselves as having a stakeholder interest in the 1948 story. Some Israeli partisans who fought in the War of Independence resented that their sacrifices and triumphs were popularized by what they regarded as a Hollywood outsider; some American Jewish critics objected bitterly to the values Uris's narrative attributed to Jewish rebirth after the Holocaust; and pro-Palestinian writers observed angrily that the "Other Exodus," the Arab version of 1948 events, was misrepresented in some parts of Uris's narrative and was simply ignored in other parts.

Second, Uris's prejudicial writing about Arabs could not attract new, liberal-minded generations of readers to his particular vision of Israeli power and moral rectitude. As decades passed by, *Exodus* continued to be widely read, and (presumably) many readers who did not agree with Uris's characterizations of Arabs, or even found them to be repugnant, overlooked this aspect of *Exodus* and drew inspiration instead from the novel's description of Jewish pioneering and valor. Readers have typically not known about Uris's own socialization in the World War II culture of ultimate showdowns between forces of absolute right and absolute wrong or his employment as the scriptwriter for a popular cowboy movie; but it has never been difficult for them to understand that *Exodus*'s treatment of Arabs is beholden to a venerable popular culture universe wherein one side's goodness depends on the total delegitimization of its adversary, as in the way Indians are robbed of their humanity in westerns. Such understanding, however, has a shelf life. Lines of latitude given to *Exodus*'s prejudices shortened over time. The novel's treatment of the Israeli-Arab dispute appeared increasingly dated as popular culture became, in time, a bit less locked in Manichaean simplification.

Uris's public work and writing after *Exodus* reinforced the outlooks of those readers who shared his basic skepticism regarding

Arab politics and culture, yet it did little else to renew interest in his major novel about Israel's establishment. Uris had very little to say in his later writings in tribute to the Israelis who built the Jewish state in the 1950s, 1960s, and 1970s; readers who admired (and who continue to admire) *Exodus*'s enthused appreciation for Israel's founders were left hanging by this omission. Uris never gave them reason to be interested in the next, postfounding, chapters of the Jewish statehood narrative. Instead of providing updated and perhaps more sophisticated images of heroic Israeli state-builders, he kept bashing Arabs. The attacks on Arab society and politics in Uris's 1984 *The Haj* are so vehement that many (though by no means all) readers wondered about Uris's objectivity regarding the Middle East; at least for some readers this Arab bashing damaged the credibility of all of Uris's writing about Israel and so contributed to the fading influence of his *Exodus* narrative.

Third, the *Exodus* story was (and continues to be) brought to the attention of hundreds of thousands of nonreaders by a film that lacked Uris's commitment to the distinctive features of Jewish history, including the events of Israel's founding. The *Exodus* film, of course, popularized the novel's basic storyline and cultivated strong support for Israel among viewers who would never otherwise have been exposed to Uris's narrative. However, whereas Uris treated his subject as though it had no parallel in any other nation's history, Preminger was not particularly interested in the historical background of Israel's founding and of the Israel-Arab dispute, and his morally relativistic vision looked ahead to future eras when news watchers, filmgoers, and readers expect "balance" on the assumption that there are always "two sides to the story." Like the *Exodus* novel, Preminger's film lavishly praises and celebrates the Israeli fighters who created a modern state in an ancient land; unlike the novel, the film seemed far from certain that those fighters were unlike other partisans who brandish guns and make sacrifices. The film's final image of two 1948 war heroes, a Jew and an Arab, being buried alongside each other can be seen as an uplifting tribute to ideals of peaceful coexistence; it also strikingly repeals Uris's conceptualization of 1948 as a story of Jewish triumph and previews an era when 1948 is thought of not as the recovery of an ancient people after genocidal horror but rather as a competition between two morally equivalent national narratives.

Fourth, and finally, as Israel's political circumstances became
ever-more complicated and controversial following the conquest of
densely populated Palestinian territories in the 1967 Six Days' War,
the frightening setback in the early part of the 1973 Yom Kippur War,
the first Lebanon War, and then the first intifada uprising, groups of
scholars, activists, and others began to ask new, challenging questions about the circumstances of Israel's founding. Whereas Uris and
his readers conceptualized the 1948 story as heroic redemption of the
crimes committed against Jews in modern times, these groups critically combed Israel's founding narrative for evidence of tendencies
and dilemmas that (they argued) left the Jewish state incapable of resolving future disputes. The sociological backgrounds, motivations,
and claims of these American Jewish and Israeli groups are diverse,
but it suffices to describe their deconstruction of Israel's founding
narrative in broad terms: whereas Uris and his readers viewed Israeli
statehood as the solution to all the woes Jews had endured before
1948, the post-Zionists and other critical groups focus on heretofore
ignored problems of the 1948 experience and view them as precur-
sors of Israel's subsequent controversy and suffering.

These critics have bones to pick other than *Exodus*. Nonetheless, all forms of criticism of Israel that evolved in the past quarter
century are responsive to heroic images of the Jewish state's founding, which Uris popularized; various indirect or direct links between
disillusioned American Jewish commentators and *Exodus* can be
traced. This leaves little doubt about the context of *Exodus*'s waning
influence. We will conclude this section with some comments about
Exodus's relation to revisionist rethinking about the circumstances
and meaning of Israel's founding—these comments are not intended
to be analytically comprehensive and instead aim to mark how great
a distance has been traversed in half a century of discussion about the
meaning of the founding of the Jewish state.

Liberal American Jews, partisan Israeli veterans of the 1948 War of
Independence, and pro-Palestinian writers spearheaded criticism of
Exodus. They aired their views two or three years after the novel's
publication, around the time of the film's screening.

Speaking in 1961 at a Loyola University symposium on "Needs
and Images of Man" sponsored by the Anti-Defamation League, the
young American Jewish writer Philip Roth upbraided Uris's statements in favor of refashioning the Jew in cultural products as fight-

ers rather than golden riders of the psychoanalytic couch, as being "bald, stupid and uninformed."[38] Roth excoriated Uris as a commercial writer who falsified Israel's 1948 history for profit. He brought up a *Time* report that cited *Exodus* ship captain Ike Aranowicz's objection that the heroic types described in Uris's novel never existed in Israel. Uris's glib reported reply to this accusation about historical misrepresentation—"just look at my sales figures"—infuriated Roth, who could not accept that a book's popularity was a measure of its veracity or quality. *Exodus,* Roth declaimed, "is neither history nor literature."

Exodus's offshore investigation and melodramatic vindication of 1950s melting pot values infuriated Roth. He implied that Kitty's original state of mind about the Jews was entirely natural, whereas everything else that happens in the book as she becomes bonded to Ari and the Jewish state was mischievous alchemy. "Why shouldn't the Gentiles have suspicions," wondered Roth. "The fact is that, if one is committed to being a Jew, then he believes that on the most serious questions pertaining to man's survival that he is right and the Christians are wrong." Roth perceived *Exodus* as the sappy endpoint of 1950s processes of contrived collaboration between natural antagonists and of relentless exercises in middle-class cooptation. "They are presently holding beatnik parties in the suburbs," remarked Roth, "which does not convince me that all men are brothers." Nor was he persuaded of that principle when Israeli Ari wept and hugged Christian Kitty.

Uris's images of superhuman Israeli heroes redressing history's horrors mortified Roth. Interestingly, he suggested that a key factor in *Exodus*'s success was the way it let Christians off the hook for the Holocaust by telling them "you don't have to worry about Jewish vulnerability and victimization after all, the Jews can take care of themselves." With *Exodus*'s transformation as a popular motion picture, a few quick-fix images of tough Dov Landau (played by actor Sal Mineo) avenging crimes against the Jews allayed uneasy consciences and supplanted authentic forms of ongoing reflection about the "raw, senseless, fiendish horror" of the murder of six million Jews. Just as he resented *Exodus*'s position on Jewish-Christian communion as cheap sentimentalism, Roth rejected as cheap expiation *Exodus*'s handling of the Holocaust: "One week *Life* magazine presents on its cover a picture of Adolf Eichmann; weeks later a picture of Sal Mineo as a Jewish freedom fighter," Roth scoffed. "A crime to which there is no adequate human response, no grief, no compassion, no vengeance that is sufficient seems, in part then, to have been avenged."

Roth sensed that the apotheosis of military might, coupled with a religiously infused sense of Eretz Israel as a Jewish country, could possibly produce a new, bitterly violent phase in the Arab-Jewish conflict, a stage in which avengers of the "other," Palestinian, exodus might fight for restitution on the basis of their own interpretation of God-given birthright. It seemed, in fact, that Roth was looking ahead warily to Israeli circumstances after the 1967 Six Days' War. Uris's *Exodus,* Roth feared, was precariously leading Jews away from the moral high ground: "Fine then. Welcome aboard. A man with a gun and a hand grenade, a man who kills for his God-given rights . . . cannot sit so easily in judgment of another man when he kills for what God has given *him,* according to his accounting and inventory." Iconoclastically critical of *Exodus* at the time of its release, Roth's philippic previewed the attitude of a later generation of American Jewish liberals. A few decades later, when growing numbers of critical American Jewish commentators came to see military power in Israel as causing as many problems as it solved, their thoughts echoed Roth's dissent from *Exodus.*

In Israel, one fly-in-the-ointment philippic against *Exodus* was penned by Uri Avneri, who in future years would lobby tirelessly for peaceful accommodation with Palestinians from the far left fringe of Israeli politics, but who in spring 1960 worked as the editor of a highly influential magazine, *Ha-'Olam Ha-zeh* (the Hebrew name, meaning "This World," has an appropriately secular ring).[39] As Rachel Weissbrod has pointed out, several Israeli writers and critics attacked *Exodus,*[40] but Avneri's review stands out as a colorful diatribe against the Americanization of Israel.

Throughout the 1950s, this antiestablishment but widely popular journal was a weekly exercise in ambivalence about the United States and the West. Avneri stamped on the magazine's cover glossy photos of American actresses and models and relished publishing letters of irate readers who regarded these well-dressed starlets as pornographic harlots. Periodically, *Ha-'Olam Ha-zeh* would publish manifestos forswearing the West and proclaiming the country's national identity as Middle Eastern—the Canaanite movement, which sought to minimize Diaspora and Jewish religious influences and to reconstruct Israeli identity exclusively on historical and contemporary

Middle East foundations, echoed strongly in these proclamations.[41] This anti-West ideology motivated Avneri to publish in 1953 a remarkable series championing the rights of the country's Eastern (Sephardic) population, immigrants from Asian and African countries who languished in transit tent camps and low-income towns. Even as it hammered away at the prejudices and elitism of Western (Ashkenazi) Jews in this series, the magazine used American idiom and analogies to document the discrimination faced by Sephardic Jews in ma'abarot tent towns. Israel's under-class Eastern population, *Ha-'Olam Ha-zeh* wrote, were "Israel's blacks."[42] *Exodus* tapped deeply into this magazine's Americanized dependence on anti-Americanism. In Avneri's critique of *Exodus*, the engineer of Americanized media in Israel inveighed against the Americanization of its founding myths.

In his not-subtly titled "Don't Let the State of Israel Certify the Perpetuation of Literary Abomination" (*Ha-'Olam Ha-zeh* March 9, 1960), Avneri passionately called for the state of Israel to ban the screening of the *Exodus* film in Israel (his request went unheeded, of course[43]). He complained that the novel *Exodus* turned Israelis into "ridiculous Cowboys." The life-and-death struggles of three generations of Israelis were vulgarized as "revolting kitsch" in Uris's narrative, which is so trashy that it could only have been written by "an electronic, robot brain, not a human mind." *Exodus* packed within its covers "all the clichés, cheap superlatives and hyped-up descriptions parroted by tourist guides or fund raisers at Zionist *schnorer* events," Avneri complained. Uris "didn't miss a single cliché."

The source of *Exodus*'s appeal, claimed Avneri, was the neurotic psychology of *galut* Jews. The novel's brawny imagery and cowboy action scenes offered psychic release to these emotionally stunted Diaspora Jews: "They've put into this book all the secret longings of the conflicted *galut* Jew from the American ghetto, all the inferiority complexes of a man who deals all his life with contempt—and whose sacred dream is that one day he [the ghetto Jew] will be similar to his tormentors."

Avneri believed that *Exodus*'s characterization of the new Israeli man, Ari Ben Canaan, was pathetic and demented. Uris's Ari, Avneri decried, is seen as a "higher mortal who grows up with a whip in his hand, as a kind of Jewish SS figure who lacks a soul." Ari is the kind of prototype that "could only arise in the heart of a *galut* Jew . . . someone who has a pathological fascination with power."

Why was Diaspora Jewry's fantasy about muscular Israelis harmful? Avneri acknowledged that many Israelis evinced a practical appreciation of the novel's effects, even though they discounted its veracity. Avneri quoted an Israeli army officer, "the type of person Uris worships as a God," who admitted that "an Israeli who reads *Exodus* will crack up laughing by the 30th page, if he gets that far. But [asked the IDF officer] if a Jew in Brooklyn . . . is enthusiastic about all of this, and then gives money to the UJA, well what's wrong with that?"

Avneri, who as a ten-year-old in 1933 immigrated to Israel from Germany, and who fought in 1948 and authored a combat journal (*B'Sdot Pleshet*) about the war, grounded his response to this question in the realm of national honor. Israelis who milked Jewish and non-Jewish tourists by selling them tall tales about the country's founding were like white conquerors of lands who sold natives glass beads—"a country which gives its endorsement to *Exodus* sells itself, its heart and soul."

Avneri spoke for Israelis who sought to control the story of their own state's founding. He wrote for countrymen who were disturbed by the exodus of the experience that defined their national identity from youth-movement campfires, school classrooms in ma'abarot tent towns, and other carefully structured Israeli rituals and settings to the commercial, homogenous realm of mass culture. For all his chest-thumping about *what* was said in *Exodus,* Avneri's real concern seemed to be *who* had the right to talk about 1948. Israel's story was for Israelis, not an American Jew, to tell. "It took infinite *chutzpah,*" he announced, for Uris "to position himself as the one and only historian, the ultimate arbiter and sole interpreter of a period he knows nothing about, and of events in which he played no part."

The American Jewish critic Philip Roth charged that Uris's apotheosis of Jewish power offered specious formulas for Jewish-Christian relations after the Holocaust, and the Israeli critic Uri Avneri objected that *Exodus* Americanized his country and injured its honor. These were blistering, intelligent reviews, but they lacked the one single phrase that captured the gist of all serious future criticism of *Exodus.* In contemporary criticism of Uris's novel, this slogan was coined by a pro-Palestinian writer.

The phrase "Other Exodus" circulated in an influential article published by Erskine B. Childers in the London weekly *The Spectator* on May 12, 1961, less than three years after the publication of

Uris's novel.[44] Childers hailed from a family of prominent Irish patriots (his grandfather, Robert Erskine Childers, was executed during the Irish Civil War, and his father, Erskine Hamilton Childers, was president of Ireland), and later in the 1960s he began a distinguished, twenty-two-year career as a UN civil servant. Childers had devoted time and thought to the Palestinian situation. In 1960 he published a volume, *Common Sense about the Arab World*, that tried empirically to rebut various claims about the Palestinian refugees.[45]

In his 1961 article,[46] Childers charged that Israel's founding had mercilessly spawned thirteen years of inhuman neglect of Palestinian refugees, whose number had swollen to 1,145,000. He recalled his own dealings with the exiled. He ended his piece with a ringing indictment: "It is shaming beyond all brief descriptions to move among these million people, as a Westerner."

Childers openly disputed Uris's interpretation of the refugee situation in *Exodus*. Denying the contention of one of Uris's spokesmen that the Palestinian refugees were "kept caged like animals in suffering as a deliberate political weapon," he insisted that these 1948 victims lived in camps outside Israel's borders on their own volition. The Jewish narrative's explanations of how and why the Palestinian refugees ended up where they were, Childers charged, were "demonstrably and totally hollow." Examining sources such as BBC records of Middle East radio broadcasts in 1948, he could find "no primary evidence" to corroborate Israeli suggestions that Palestinian villagers and townspeople had received evacuation orders from their own leaders.

Rebutting explanations of the mass refugee departure offered in the 1950s by prominent Israeli officials such as Abba Eban, Childers suggested that upholders of the Jewish narrative were propagating a huge human rights cover-up. Referring to *Exodus*, he bemoaned how a political myth, "reproduced around the world," has been "soothing our highly pragmatic Western conscience." The time had come to tell the other side of the story. "It is clear beyond all doubt that official Zionist forces were responsible for expulsion of thousands upon thousands of Arabs," concluded Childers. A radically different way of looking at what had happened in 1948, this new narrative of the Other Exodus was beginning to take shape.

Uris, demonstrably, never saw this other narrative. The blind spot in the making of *Exodus* can be seen vividly today in one incident that occurred during Uris's preparatory research trip to Israel on May 1, 1956.

That day, Uris attended a funeral held at Kibbutz Nahal Oz in a scorched desert area in Israel's south, close to the Gaza Strip border. The funeral was for a nineteen-year-old Nahal Corps soldier, Roe Rutenberg, whose mutilated body had been tossed back to the Negev kibbutz by fedayeen guerillas who a day earlier had snatched the IDF man and taken him across the border. Uris's response to the funeral is extremely revealing.

It touched him to the core. At the time, he wrote movingly to his father: "Here on a sun-baked mound overlooking Gaza 1000 people gathered. There was not one tear, not one word of revenge against the poor, ignorant Arab." Uris added that mourning kibbutz members, mostly young people in their early twenties, told him that such tragedies only strengthen them.[47] Moved, the author took photos of

Uris's own photograph of a rifle salute at the funeral of slain kibbutz pioneer and IDF soldier Roe Rutenberg. In *Exodus*, Uris pictured Rutenberg's murder as a symbol of Zionist martyrdom; ironically, in Israeli culture, the same funeral became famous due to IDF chief of staff Moshe Dayan's unconventional references to Arab grievances. (Harry Ransom Humanities Research Center, the University of Texas at Austin)

the stark landscape and of the rifle salute at the funeral. In fact, if any single event on the 1956 research trips fashioned Uris's admiring respect for native-born Israeli sabras—admiration that constituted the dramatic core of *Exodus*—it was this Nahal Oz funeral.

The kibbutz members' calm bravery never left his memory. Nahal Oz appeared to him as a kibbutz colony planted on scorched dead earth at the end of nowhere (in *Exodus*, the American Kitty Fremont's scathingly dismissive descriptions of the landscape around "Nahal Midbar," the fictionalized Nahal Oz, reflects Uris's own view of the terrain); for the author, the kibbutz members' determination to carry on under hellish circumstances of desert deprivation and Arab terror symbolized the sabras' capability to overcome everything. For years, whenever he spoke publicly about his own journey in the writing of *Exodus*, Uris brought up the Nahal Oz funeral.

The glimpse of sabra endurance at this kibbutz determined the final plot twist in *Exodus*, in which young Karen, the Holocaust survivor and handpicked favorite of the novel's American heroine, Kitty, is murdered by terrorists at Nahal Midbar. Uris received tear-stained letters from readers who were upset by this conclusion. "The purpose of this letter is to protest the senseless killing of Karen," two high school seniors wrote to Uris in July 1959, about a year after the novel's publication.[48] Uris, who was not at liberty to respond to hundreds of readers' letters, replied to this heart-felt complaint. A few years before, he responded, "I stood on a sun-baked hill" facing the Gaza Strip and "watched a young person about Karen's age lowered to the ground, after being mutilated by Arab gangs." At Nahal Oz, Uris explained, "I asked myself exactly the same question: why the senseless killing. And *Exodus* is my protest to the killing of children like Karen."[49]

But that is not all that could be said of the Nahal Oz funeral. Everything that went into the making of *Exodus* played out on one conceptual field. From start to finish, the whole story was about Jews overcoming tragedy to build a life of their own. Uris had compelling personal and ethical reasons not to look beyond the horizons of this particular field. Nonetheless, there were always other conceptual zones at play in Israel's story, and it is intriguing to observe them entirely passing by Uris's field of vision during his *Exodus* research in 1956. Indeed, what became known as the Other Exodus of Palestinian dispersal and suffering was always an unseen part of Leon Uris's story. In his fiction and in his correspondence and public addresses,

Uris devoted many words to the Nahal Oz funeral, and there is not a trace of recognition in any of them that the same event became remembered in Israeli culture in ways that differed qualitatively from the tone and substance of the *Exodus* narrative.

In his remarkable eulogy for the slain Roe Rutenberg at Nahal Oz, IDF chief of staff Moshe Dayan spoke out of a tragic, compassionate understanding of the Israeli-Palestinian conflict as a contest between two morally legitimate sets of claims. His words caught notice. They sounded confessional and very far removed from the prevailing mid-1950s conception in Israel, which held that Arabs everywhere were preparing for a second-round attempt to annihilate the Jewish state. "Let us not cast blame on Roe's murderers," stated Dayan. Who could wonder about their burning hatred for us, he asked. "For eight years they have been sitting in refugee camps in Gaza, witnessing with their own eyes how we have transformed the lands and the villages, where they and their fathers dwelt, into our own hearth and home." Claims of morality converged enigmatically with security interests in Dayan's words as he urged Israelis to consider the Arab point of view. "Let us not be deterred from seeing the loathing that is inflaming and filling the lives of hundreds of thousands of Arabs who live around us. Let us not avert our eyes lest our arms weaken."[50]

To many Israelis, Dayan's Nahal Oz eulogy seemed to point ahead to a future era of mutual political recognition between two peoples. Whether or not it was Dayan's intention to anticipate a two-state solution in this famous 1956 funeral oration, he spoke eloquently about the need to understand the Palestinians' side of the story. But that was not something the American Jewish writer Leon Uris had come to Israel to do.

In Uris's research, the 1948 war was fought entirely on the conceptual field of Jewish redemption and righteousness. He fully accepted conventional 1950s Israeli explanations of the reason for the mass departure of hundreds of thousands of Palestinians—Uris found no reason to probe the empirical basis or to look beyond these political-military explanations.

This blind spot also appears in Uris's notes on Operation Dani and the IDF capture of Lydda (Lod) and Ramle on June 11–12. This event, destined to provoke considerable scholarly and political discussion about whether the Haganah participated proactively in the expulsive transfer of Palestinians,[51] was perceived by Uris entirely through the prism of Israeli heroism as an exemplification of new-found forms of Jewish courage. Without naming Moshe Dayan as the architect and main agent of a new, daytime rapid-raid strategy, Uris cited in his notes the well-known, daring Palmach blitz right through the heart of Lydda: "the column, headed by a captured Legion armored car with a two pounder gun nicknamed the Terrible Tiger . . . speedily drove through the city, shooting everything in sight." Palestinian departure after the fighting in Lydda and Ramle appears in Uris's notes as an inconsequential outcome ("the Legion attackers were routed, and many of the inhabitants left with them"). Whether or not he heard or knew anything about Haganah involvement in the arrangement of the Arab exodus from the two towns, Uris did not consider it to be a noteworthy or important possibility.

Where occurrences of Arab flight were on a scale that could not be ignored, Uris absorbed and rehearsed mainstream Israeli accounts of what happened. This is particularly true in his analysis of events in Israel's largest northern city, Haifa. The main strategy underlying Uris's Haifa explanation was to blame Palestinian hardship upon the mufti of Jerusalem, Haj Amin al-Husseini. Since the mufti had spent months during World War II in Berlin as a pro-Hitler propagandist, the defeat of his Palestinian followers in 1948 was associated generally in Uris's mind with a grand Manichaean narrative about a contest between forces of ultimate good and ultimate evil. On that narrative, it was nonsensical to worry about hardships endured by losers.

Uris believed partisan accounts about Haifa relayed to him by former Haganah commanders and Israeli spokesmen because he was not positioned emotionally to process ambiguous circumstances in the 1948 war and complex and confusing dilemmas faced by Jewish soldiers. As far as he saw it, the Haganah, along with civilian Yishuv/Israeli leaderships that managed the results of its battles, could only have done the right thing. This viewpoint produced an entirely partisan account of what happened in Haifa, a battle summary that reflected in miniature *Exodus*'s outlook of the 1948 war as a whole: "The Arabs capitulated and agreed to stay in the town [Haifa] under Jewish terms of surrender, but the Mufti phoned from Beirut and demanded evacuation, and the Arabs with British aid left by boat to Acre. Jewish leaders went from house to house persuading the Arabs to stay, but only 5000 decided to live under Jewish rule."[52] During his visit to Israel in 1956, and over the next year when he resettled in

California and worked on drafts of *Exodus,* Uris occasionally fielded questions about the 1948 war. Whenever he spoke publicly about Israel's independence war, Uris was anything but apologetic. As far as he was concerned, the right side won a very tough war, and whoever wanted to quibble about costs of that victory simply did not understand what the Jewish cause was about. In moral terms, Israel's military victory translated as the creation of a new sabra identity utterly devoid of the shtetl Jew's self-defeating obsessions about other peoples' problems. For Uris, the very meaning of exodus was entirely singular—there could not be any other, Palestinian, exodus. In Israel, Jews had finally resolved to look after their own problems. To worry anybody else's exodus was to impose defeatism upon a miraculous triumph for which Jews had yearned throughout 2,000 miserable years.

In late November 1957, two weeks before he finished the composition of *Exodus,* Uris delivered a lecture in Beverly Hills, and a woman in the audience urged the author not to write that "the Jews drove the Arabs from Israel." This prompted an outburst from Uris. Such shtetl finesse was a blueprint for self-destruction. Nothing would make him apologetic about a war the Jews had won after centuries of powerlessness. He later recalled his outburst: "The Jews not only drove them [Arabs] out, but also knocked down their villages so they wouldn't return. It is nothing to be ashamed of. The Arabs meant to throw them into the sea and it is time the Jews stop apologizing for the refugee problem. The Arabs brought it upon themselves."[53]

In the *Exodus* novel, Uris's polemical attack against Arab politics latched largely upon Haj Amin al-Husseini, the mufti of Jerusalem.[54] "The leader of the dreaded El Husseinis was the most vile, underhanded schemer in a part of the world known for vile, underhanded schemers," wrote Uris, summing up *Exodus*'s interpretation of leadership and politics on the other side of the 1948 conflict. Since the mufti is so central to the politics of *Exodus,* a few schematic points about how Haj Amin was perceived in the "real world," by Zionist leaderships in the 1920s and 1930s are warranted.

During the Mandatory period, the mufti was loathed as a terrorist by Yishuv Zionists. Yet, rather like the on-again/off-again attitudes toward Yasser Arafat evinced by their Israeli political descendants generations later, the Ben-Gurion leadership of the prestate Yishuv lacked the luxury of remaining rigidly doctrinaire toward a figure it reasonably and rightly regarded as an enemy. Toward the mid-1930s, Ben-Gurion searched for ways to open dialogue with the mufti and his associates. Not necessarily assuming that the Palestinian leadership was evil incarnate, the Zionist leader reasoned that the Yishuv and his Labor Zionist movement were sufficiently empowered to see whether a practical deal could be brokered with Palestinian antagonists on land, immigration, and sovereignty issues.[55] In Mandatory times (as in later periods) the most damning and accurate objections the Israeli collective could raise against the Palestinian leadership is that it resorted to terror to promote its political agenda, and that it refused to commit to a two-state partition formula that entailed recognition of the Jewish state's right to exist. These are very serious complaints, but they are not tantamount to proposing that the Jewish state's founding was opposed by Arab forces of absolute evil.

Exodus explains that Haj Amin seized his position as mufti in order to control funds for retention of holy sites in Jerusalem, a city whose holiness follows only Mecca and Medina in Muslim tradition. Besides the opportunity to line his pockets with donations and fees, Haj Amin grabbed the post as custodian of the Old City holy sites because he knew that the "Palestinian fellaheen were ninety-nine percent illiterate," and so "the only means of mass communication was the pulpit."

In a breathtakingly manipulative two-page synopsis of the politics of the Arab-Jewish dispute in Mandatory Palestine in the 1920s, Uris compresses realities to extenuate Jewish involvement and to blame the mufti and the British for events they could not possibly have caused. On his telling, the conniving Haj Amin murders rivals and grabs the mufti post and then whips "up a mob of fellaheen with hatred of the Jews" so that they terrorize defenseless, pious Jewish communities on a Moslem holy day celebrating the birth of Moses. That is an interesting sequence, since the Nebi Mousa riots of April 1920 occurred a year before Haj Amin became the mufti.[56]

More seriously, the effect of *Exodus*'s inaccuracies is to impute diabolical design to all the confused and inchoate religious, economic, and nationalist raw materials of the Israeli-Arab dispute. Arguably, as in Arafat's case, at key junctures of his career Haj Amin al-Husseini duplicitously told Western power brokers whatever he thought they wanted to hear; but he was not necessarily far from the truth when he described chaotic and violent events in the 1920s as spontaneous Palestinian actions. In contrast, on Uris's account, Palestinian rejection of well-known Zionist arguments about mutual benefits to be reaped by modern, scientific Jewish settlement in Eretz Israel has no explanation, apart from the mufti's psychotic hatred. Uris writes: "The early friendships, the fact that the Jews had raised the standard of living of the entire Arab community, and the fact that Palestine had lain neglected and unwanted for a thousand years in fruitless despair until the Jews rebuilt it was all forgotten in the face of the Mufti's tirades." However irrational it might seem when measured by standards outside of the realm of nationalist experience, the refusal of one national movement to accept economic benefits that come attached with the strings of a second national movement's political agenda, is not obstinate apoplexy. Such refusal is the logic of nationalism itself.

Uris's narrative had no room for a Palestinian voice that objected to Zionist arguments about increased standards of living as neocolonist noblesse oblige. Nor, as Jeremy Salt pointed out in an important 1985 article, was there place in Uris's story for numerous nineteenth-century travel reports attesting to rural continuity and charm in Palestine and other Ottoman areas.[57] With the partial exception of the picturesque hilltop Druze village where Ari Ben Canaan recuperates after the daring Acre prison break, nothing in *Exodus* is ever seen outside Jewish Palestine, the Yishuv, other than dirty Arabs. The narrative has no other way to portray Arabs.

On a hike up Mount Tabor, Ari Ben Canaan and Kitty Fremont are forced to accept Bedouin hospitality at a small encampment. Encountering "the dregs of humanity," the Israeli and the American, themselves paragons of courage and self-sacrifice, spend the scene holding their noses. Kitty recoils from Bedouin women who are "encased in black robes, and layers of dirt. She was not able to smell the goats but she was able to smell the women." The American-Israeli couple sit down to partake in Bedouin cuisine that features a "greasy lamb leg," "unwashed fruit," and "thick, sickeningly sweet coffee in cups so filthy they were crusted." The Israeli then coaches the American how to deal with the culture of the Middle East: "Be a good girl and eat whatever he [the Bedouin host] offers you. You can throw it up later."

In *Exodus,* the dirty backwardness of the Middle East is not the by-product of one religious faith. Christian Arabs and Muslim Arabs are in the filth together. When Kitty and Ari visit the boyhood home of Jesus Christ, the narrative reports: "Nazareth stank. The streets were littered with dung and blind beggars made wretched noises and barefoot, ragged filthy children were underfoot. Flies were everywhere." In Nazareth, Ari, the Jewish Israeli, offers an exception to the rule of Arab political recalcitrance. "At least the Arabs are friendly," he says. "They are Christians." Kitty, the Christian American, is not convinced. "They are Christians who need a bath," she retorts.

This is, in short, rigidly zoned historical fiction that has no real estate for pilgrims, missionaries, and explorers who did not talk about dirty Arab villages when they described Holy Land landscapes.

The moral failure in Uris's narrative was its narrowly self-serving explication of Palestinian loss. To this day, Palestinians charge that the Western countries ought to have taken responsibility for the settlement and rehabilitation of the remnants of the "Jewish Question," since that "question" was posed exclusively in Christian Europe. Why should we be the "victims of the victims," wonder the Palestinians. The question has logic, even if it tends to resonate among those who are disposed to Arab claims in the controversy about Israel for deeply rooted reasons that do not depend upon interpretations of historical sequences.

For millions in the West, Uris's narrative preempted the Palestinians' question. In *Exodus,* Palestinians are not victims of victims. If they are seen as victims at all, it is as victims of their own leadership and of their own politics. Dealt a choice between Zionist-stimulated economic progress or Nazi ideology, the Palestinians selected the latter. For the Palestinians, Uris suggests, rejection of the opportunities afforded by Zionist settlement was not a nationalist necessity but rather the legacy of Nazi malice and irrationality. By far the prevailing victim image in *Exodus* is not of Palestinians but of Jews victimized by a Nazi-Arab axis of evil. Their worst enemy's junior partner is the Jews' antagonist in the 1948 war.

The *Exodus* film, it will be recalled, falsified history by describing Nazis as on-site conductors of Palestinian fighting during the 1948 conflict. Uris never doctored the historical record in this fashion; instead, he discredited Haj Amin by blurring moral distinctions between Hitler and the Palestinian leader. During the World War II era, Uris wrote, "Haj Amin went to Germany where Adolf Hitler greeted him personally as a brother. The two madmen could work through each other for mutual personal profit." In Uris's storyline,

Haj Amin's Nazi-like fanaticism is morally to blame for everything that goes wrong in Arab-Jewish relations. Thus, during the 1936–39 Palestinian uprising, "Husseini's henchmen" slit the throat of Kammal, the mukhtar of the fictional Abu Yesha village in the Upper Galilee and the one Palestinian notable in the novel who accepts the argument about the health, education, and welfare benefits to be accrued by collaboration with the Zionists. Kammal is the conciliatory Arab who cedes land for the creation of the Gan Dafna asylum for the *Exodus* ship's refugees, near Abu Yesha. His murder by the mufti's terrorists symbolizes the end of hopes for beneficial Palestinian development alongside, or within, the Jewish state. Kammal's weaker-willed son Taha, who grows up as a kind of Semitic blood brother to Ari Ben Canaan, is unable to resist the vortex of tribal hatred in the 1948 war and eventually allows his village to be used as a base for blood-curdling attacks on the ultimate victims, the Holocaust orphans of Gan Dafna. The *Exodus* orphans are thus besieged in the novel by its demonic axis of the Nazis, the British, and the Palestinian mufti.

With the Palestinian leader delegitimized as a Nazi agent and the embodiment of ultimate evil, Uris's descriptions of Israel's enemies in the 1948 War of Independence flowed mechanically. There is never any doubt about the moral balance of forces. From the prestate period onward, the Jewish armed force, the Haganah, did not face antagonists who represented conflicting positions on issues of land, immigration, and political sovereignty. Instead, they faced antagonists who represented everything that is wrong in the world. That perception is exemplified by *Exodus*'s description of the mufti's military wing in the late 1930s Palestinian uprising:

> From outside of Palestine came an answer to the Mufti's appeal. An Iraqi officer named Kawukji saw the Palestine "revolt" as his long awaited chance to seize power and make a fortune as the Mufti's military arm. Kawukji was obsessed with himself; his egomania knew no bounds . . . With money extorted from the Palestinian Arabs by the Mufti, Kawukji went about recruiting his army outside the country. He got together a band of thieves, dope runners, white slavers, and the like with the lure of the many Jewish women they could rape and the "Hebrew gold" they could loot. They were as

vicious, degenerate and brutal a gang as had ever been assembled. Under Generalissimo Kawukji they poured in from Lebanon to save the great Islam martyr, Haj Amin el Husseini.

Exodus contextualized the unimaginable Jewish tragedy of Europe and the Jewish-Arab conflict within lingering, World War II–era genres of Allies against the Axis, good guys versus bad guys. These extremely polarized images of ultimate Jewish good against ultimate Nazi-Arab evil suited the way mass culture processed (and continues to process) extremely complicated political disputes. It is easy to upbraid Uris for writing without an anthropological sense that Arab resistance to Zionist rhetoric about raised standards of living stemmed from a desire to preserve a way of life. But had he written in such a vein, *Exodus* would never have become a mass-culture commodity; so, in effect, such criticism is pointless. An unquestioned sense of Western superiority was the mass-culture story standard. Red-faced savages in cowboy films were not exactly understood to be whooping and tomahawking in the name of the preservation of a way of life.

It is, however, misleading to view *Exodus*'s prejudicial treatment of Arab politics entirely within the context of mass-culture Manichaean simplification. With respect to Arab images, we cannot readily generalize about the *Exodus* narrative—Otto Preminger's film, which also catered to the sensibilities of a mass audience, distorted the history of the Arab-Jewish dispute in ways Uris never attempted, yet it also presented utopian visions of future Arab-Jewish alliance the novel dismisses as delusional. The extremism of Uris's novel is thus not necessarily a function of commercialized, mass-culture dynamics. Instead, somewhat disturbingly, it is characteristic of the ultranationalist zealotry inherent within many *literary* narratives of Israel's founding. To illustrate this point, we will observe presently that Palestinian narratives of the 1948 Naqba catastrophe, the "other Exodus" of 700,000 Palestinian villagers and townspeople, are not particularly liberal minded in their descriptions of Zionist and Israeli realities. The purpose of this brief comparison is not to offer an apology for *Exodus*'s failings under the pathetic rationale that "two wrongs make a right." Our argument is that literary narratives have not, to this day, promoted cross-national and cross-religious dialogue in the embittering Jewish-Arab dispute.

Although written by a Lebanon-based author, Elias Khoury, *Gate of the Sun*[58] in many ways warrants description as the Palestinian *Exodus*. As in the case of Uris's product, Khoury's novel, originally published in Beirut in 1998 under the Arabic title *Bab al-Shams*, has been adapted as a film; screened in makeshift settings among Palestinians in Israel's Galilee, the movie attained cult status.

Gate of the Sun is narrated by a Palestinian fighter named Khalil Ayyoub, who was born a few years after the Palestinians' 1948 Naqba catastrophe, and who has never set foot in Israel, apart from a few border encroachments on violent fedayeen attacks.

Khalil has few memories of his father who was shot down at his home doorstep by unknown assailants in Lebanese factional fighting of the late 1950s; the mother, whose grief was compounded by the death of a child not long after her husband's murder, abandoned the young Khalil and is reported to have reinvented herself as a nurse in the West Bank city of Ramallah.

As a young adolescent, with virtually no formal schooling, Khalil joins up with fedayeen movements and takes part in nondescribed assaults on Israeli targets. He fights with Palestinians in the September 1970 debacle in Jordan and then in the horrific Lebanon civil war. Wounded in action, he is sent to China for more military training but ends up being reclassified as a medic; instead of evacuating to Tunisia with other Palestinian fighters, he stays on hand in Lebanon after Israel's ill-fated 1982 war and witnesses the mayhem of the Sabra and Shatila massacre. Khalil remains apart from processes that lead Palestinian compatriots—soldiers and politicians—to the Gaza Strip and West Bank by the mid-1990s.

This is not a placid curriculum vitae. In the book's more introspective second half, Khalil describes himself as a kind of Übermensch Palestinian soldier who is impervious to everyday moral constraints: "I really can't say there had been no crimes. We, too, killed and destroyed, but at that moment I sensed the banality of evil. Evil has no meaning, and we were just its tools. We're nothing. We make war and kill and die, and we're nothing—just fuel for a huge machine whose name is War." Khalil speaks for a generation of Palestinian militants who were born in the immediate aftermath of the Naqba and whose moral compass has no coordinate other than a burning hatred of Israel.

Khalil's first, fleeting glance at the Jewish state occurs in 1969. Based in Kafar Shouba, in Southern Lebanon, as a teenage political commissar for the fedayeen he sees the country when Israeli planes attack and the sky lights up with flares. Conversely, Khalil's mentor and surrogate father, Yunes al-Asadi, retains his humanity in his secret meetings with his wife in the darkness of the Bab al-Shams cave, located on the slopes of the Dir al-Assad village in the Western Galilee. The meaning of this sequence of symbols is clear: No natural light can be found in the Jewish state, and the Palestinian struggle for survival and rebirth within it ensues in the primal darkness. In direct contrast to the decades-long use of light as an image of moral enlightenment by Zionist writers and their predecessors in the Jewish Enlightenment (*haskalah*) movement, Israeli light projects onto the Palestinian narrative as a symbol of primitive violence. In this narrative, the state of Israel that arose from the Naqba must necessarily be an unnatural entity; since its genesis in 1948 was a primal mistake, any light that comes from Israel portends injustice, violence, and death.

The point is illustrated by Khalil's account of the Sabra and Shatila massacre, which is misleadingly said to have been "carried out by Israelis and Phalangists in '82." Various accounts of the slaughter of hundreds of Palestinians in the Beirut refugee camps by Christian Phalangists note that the killing spree was facilitated by flares fired from a nearby IDF compound.[59] Khoury's characters indeed regard the IDF's flares as the prime mover of the Sabra and Shatila tragedy. The following confession of one Phalangist thug is revealing because it shows how conceptualizations of victimization and oppression rotate oppositely on Muslim-Christian-Jewish axes of meaning in these 1948 narratives. The Phalangist murderer is confessing to an atrocity identical in detail to a horror attributed to a Nazi in Uris's Jewish epic of 1948, *Exodus*. In the Jewish narrative, the recollection of horror serves as an unassailable justification for the rekindling of the Light of Israel in the ancestral homeland. In the Palestinian narrative, the Light of Israel leads the Nations of the Galilee to wanton cruelty and violence. Meanings and symbols of *Exodus* are completely reversed in this Naqba narrative:

> I took out my revolver. I wanted to find out how far a shot from a Magnum could go. One of the children slipped off onto the floor. The light was burning our eyes, and I asked my comrade to turn his face away. . . . I went up to them [two Palestinian children in the refugee camp]. I wanted to

tie them up and then move back from them but I couldn't
find a rope, so I jammed them together, put the muzzle of
the revolver close to the head of the first one, and fired. My
bullet went right through both heads, so they died right off.
I didn't see the blood, I couldn't see it, in that strange Israeli
light.[60]

In *Gate of the Sun*'s thickly textured narrative of recollections, not
every tale encourages Palestinians to dream of some far-off day of
total solutions and messianic salvation. In the end, however, uncompromising nationalist agendas muscle away all loose ends, nuances,
and indefinite recollections. "What small minds the Jews have!"
Khoury's hero, Yunes, exclaims at one stage. His point is that Israel's and the West's antiterror operations are futile. Jews have small
minds because they do not understand that Arabs have time and are
working in stages to overturn the Naqba. Through Yunes, the Palestinian narrative mocks Zionist ideology. Whenever Jews talk about
their attachment to the land, they are saying the opposite and unwittingly expressing their fundamental insecurity. This provocative line
of thought suggests that the Jewish need to reassert and popularize long-standing claims to the Holy Land, via narratives such as
Exodus, is ultimately a sign of weakness and insecurity: "What is
this silly slogan of theirs—'Jerusalem, Eternal Capital of the Jewish
State'! Anyone who talks of eternity exits history, for eternity is history's opposite; something that's eternal doesn't exist. . . . And now
they come and tell us that Jerusalem is an eternal capital? What kind
of shit is that? It's foolish—which means they are becoming like us,
defeatable."

As a pro-Palestinian counterpart to Uris's novel, Khoury's *Gate of
the Sun* suggests that narratives of the 1948 experience typically lean
out from the ledge and view the bitter fighting and the exchange of
refugee populations from extreme angles. The delegitimization of the
other side's story can be endemic in writing about Israel's founding.
Khoury's hero mocks as "foolish shit" Jewish passion for Jerusalem
as the moral center of an inspiring story of return, analogously to
Uris's narrative diatribe against Arab fighters.

Such observations about well-known stories of Israeli statehood
reinforce a growing corpus of research studies and educational initiatives that tend to conceptualize "narratives" as a veritable autono-

mous force in the national lives of Palestinians and Israelis, as though the way members of both groups have been telling stories has caused violence between them, or as though modifications of existing storylines will make the violence go away.[61] Stories, however, do not fire guns. People do. A narrative is a tool in the hands of a creative author, not the other way around; and so, as we have emphasized in this book, the most reasonable way to analyze why a narrative operates in a certain fashion is to examine the life experiences and expectations that bring an author to tell his or her version of the story. A narrative may be presented as a national biography, but it can have no life independent of the specific biography of the individual who produces it.

Dramatic as Israel's founding circumstances were, there is absolutely no evidence to suggest that these events were so complex and potent that they had to "carry away" any writer who attempted to formulate them in a story. The heart and mind of a creative writer—and not the mesmerizing logic of nationalism and narratives—dictated the way the 1948 story would be told. Thus, in order to justify the biographical emphases of this study, it does not suffice to cite a Palestinian novel that substitutes anti-Israeli images for the anti-Arab images of *Exodus*. It is important to find examples of writing that challenge conventional nationalist formulas and that illustrate how authors could produce influential texts while avoiding the trap of delegitimizing the "other" side of the 1948 conflict. Such examples remind us that Leon Uris made creative choices when he depicted Arabs as the evil other, and that these choices need to be assessed in light of the interaction between Uris's own life circumstances and motivations and the identity assumptions of his audience. An example of one Israeli short story, written very close to the events of the War of Independence, a decade before the publication of Uris's novel, sheds light on the pro and con extremism of Uris's characterizations of Israeli and Arab antagonists.

S. Yizhar, an author from a distinguished literary family who was elected to serve in the first six Knesset (Israeli parliament) sessions, published his story "Hirbet Hizah" in 1949.[62] The tale depicts a stage of the War of Independence in which the military facts of Israel's victory are understood by combatants, but the moral implications of the conquest of Arab villages have yet to be fully absorbed by the young Jewish soldiers. Yizhar is deliberately vague about the story's setting; his intention is to raise general questions about the essence of the new Jewish state's founding experience and about the nature of war. What makes his tale "Hirbet Hizah" so intriguing and unsettling is that it is entirely devoid of the salient questions of Jewish politics that had percolated in Hebrew and other Jewish writing for generations since the late nineteenth century.[63] In "Hirbet," nobody is really asking "what should we do," or "where should we do it?" Yizhar's story does not compel an astonished reader to ask "could Jews," or "must Jews," do what they are seen doing—forcibly expelling a defenseless community from an Arab village. The narrator of the story asks these questions in a markedly aimless way. The point is that there really are no questions. The plain, demoralizing fact is that Jews are now going to have to live with what it takes to create a state.

From its opening lines, the story projects itself into the Israeli moral future. Although Yizhar fictionalizes incidents that occurred just months or weeks before he drafted "Hirbet Hizah," his narrator begins the tale in a Conrad-like vein of moral contrition, as though he is confessing to wrongs of the 1948 war years after the establishment of Jewish statehood. Yizhar's dramatic opening also ignores the developing Israeli idea that the new state only uses force in self-defense, upholding the principle of "purity of arms." Yizhar presents the army command as an amoral bureaucracy that grinds out expulsion orders in obtuse euphemisms. The narrator's unit receives field orders that refer hysterically to the danger of "infiltrators," "gangs," and "terrorists sent on hostile missions"; the order for the expulsion of the Arab villagers is formulated as a phantasmagorical mandate to "burn, explode, ban, pack up and send away." No evidence of actual village hostility emerges in the narrative. Although the unit commander, Moishe, refers loosely to reports of locals who "aid and abet the enemy," the villagers encountered by the Jewish soldiers turn out to be cowering, terrified old men and young mothers.

The soldiers exchange hateful, colonialist remarks about how the Arab villagers "are not people," and cowardly abandon hundreds of acres of cultivatable, desirable land. They muse about how their own Jewish grandfathers would have died for any miniscule portion of the land that is now being frantically abandoned by craven Arabs. "They're just like animals," contemptuously snarls one of the Jewish soldiers as Palestinians board trucks for expulsion. Other soldiers mercilessly complain that the large number of lame, blind, and elderly villagers makes it harder for them to execute their orders to "burn, explode, ban, pack up and send away." From a nearby hilltop, they fire shots to scatter the villagers; even the narrator, who is the most morally hesitant Jewish figure in the tale, admits that he and all the others enjoy taking potshots at frantic Arab notables and watching them drop to the ground after they appear to be hit.

In an insightful and informative essay about the reception of Yizhar's story,[64] and also about a well-done 1978 television film version of *Hirbet,* the historian Anita Shapira notes that Yizhar's story sold an impressive 4,354 copies in the first eighteen months of its distribution and was adopted on the high school syllabus for national matriculation exams before the Six Days' War. After reviewing extensive discussion of *Hirbet* in Israeli literary and political organs of the day, Shapira concludes that "in the early 1950s intellectuals and critics apparently did not hesitate to openly address the expulsion issue." The basic message in this line of analysis about *Hirbet* recalls Uri Avneri's scalding condemnation of *Exodus:* there was never in Israel unanimity of opinion in favor of an *Exodus*-type narrative of independence war heroism.

For Yizhar's readers, the supreme irony of victory in the 1948 War of Independence was that the fulfillment of the Zionist platform of Jewish statehood resulted in statelessness for the land's expulsed Palestinian population. Achieving deliverance from the curse of powerlessness, the new Israelis passed along the harshest excrescence of Jewish history to Palestinian losers of the war. The climax of "Hirbet Hizah" occurs when the narrator grasps hold of this overwhelming irony and conceptualizes this transference not merely in physical terms as the transformation of Palestinian villagers as refugees and the appropriation of their homes to serve as dwellings for Jewish refugees from the Holocaust and from Arab persecution outside of Eretz Israel. At this ruined Arab village, the experience of exile is being transferred on an existential level, as a curse of historical experience. The pity and irony of this transference transcends the real estate rivalry on the ground, in which kibbutz cowsheds vie against Palestinian olive groves.

Yizhar's narrator relates to the politics of state consolidation with scornful sarcasm. The last sentence of the passage cited below stands *Exodus* on its head. Whereas Uris persuaded millions of readers that Israel's founding should be viewed as the victorious *culmination* of a long, often terrifying, historical process, some Israeli heroes of the 1948 War of Independence left the battlefields with the most basic question of all on their minds. As they posed this question—"What the hell are we doing in this place!?"—Jewish politics entered a new, post-1948 phase. Whether Jewish intellectuals really wanted it to be there or not, the unmaking of the heroic perception of Israel's founding was on the agenda of this politics:

> Yes, alas, of course—that was it! Why hadn't I thought of it from the start? Hirbet Hizah was ours. There were the questions of housing and immigrant absorption! Hurray for housing and absorption, in spades: We'll open a canteen, set up a school, and maybe a synagogue. Political parties will come here, and argue about all sorts of things. They'll seed and cultivate the fields, and grow crops. The Hebrew Hirbet Hizah! And who will remember that there was once here that other Hirbet Hizah, from which we evicted and inherited? We came, we shot, we burned, we blew up, we repulsed and shoved off, and we drove into exile.
>
> What the hell are we doing in this place!?

THIS DECONSTRUCTION PROCESS passed Leon Uris by. The author never deviated from his understanding that *Exodus* relayed the essential truths about 1948. Decades went by and confusing Middle East realities and popular perceptions of them whirled about him. Uris stood his ground, never changing his basic outlook. In this vortex, what seemed like a forward-looking appreciation of democratic triumph in 1958 appeared within a few decades as a right-wing, neoconservative viewpoint that would be assailed by many. Nothing Uris wrote about the Middle East after 1958 approached the impact of *Exodus*, but his situation in this later period deserves brief comment to close the biographical circle in this analysis of the waning influence of his life's major work and to identify his later situation as a symbol of a half-century of upheaval in the politics of the Arab-Israeli dispute. In 1958, Uris wrote for a consensus of enlightened Western opinion in *Exodus;* upholding similar viewpoints about the dispute a few decades later, he came across as a highly partisan (and rather illiberal) writer.

In 1981, Uris went on the stump for the United Jewish Appeal.[65] His comments on the Middle East were explicitly responsive to the upcoming twenty-fifth anniversary of *Exodus*'s publication and to the Islamic revolution in Iran and the 444-day ordeal of the kidnapping of U.S. diplomatic personnel in the Teheran embassy. Not mincing words, Uris told audiences that Israel "is trapped in the vortex of a cyclone." Claiming that his scathing remarks about realities outside of Israel's borders applied to "90% of the Arab world," Uris elaborated upon the "bizarre behavior" of Islamic societies. Even in settings pocketed by multi-million-dollar mansions of the oil rich, "[Arab] streets are unpaved and neighborhoods are unkempt because there is a near total absence of communal responsibility." The vast majority, 85 percent, of Arab women is illiterate, Uris claimed, and he referred to hundreds of ritual blood murders of Arab women each year. Child mortality in the Arab world is high, and diseases like cholera are rampant, "because there is little connection in their [Arab] minds that lack of hygiene is a cause of disease." In Arab lands, work is "not considered an ethic but a curse." The Arab world, claimed Uris, "holds no laughter." The Arabs are a people "whose religion has told them that life itself on this earth has no value." As Uris saw it, Arab societies were plagued by paranoia and produced a "mutated human condition."

During the 1948 War of Independence, Uris told Jewish audiences in 1981, Israel harbored "no policy to stampede the Arabs out of Palestine." The Arabs fled because of infighting in their clans, because "their top echelons were in self-disarray," and "because their leadership deserted them." He added: "In the beginning, the Israeli leadership made a sincere attempt to allow a great portion of the refugees to return." Delivering precisely the same message he had pounded home in *Exodus* and its accompanying publicity a quarter century earlier, Uris declared that Jews had absolutely no cause to feel guilty about Palestinian hardship after 1948: "No Jew has to apologize for the creation of the refugee problem which the Arabs brought on themselves."

By the end of 1981, before Israel's ill-fated Lebanon War, Uris started work on a novel about the Middle East, originally titled *Beirut*. An early draft described realities outside of Israel's borders; Uris decided (in his words) that his original plan for the novel "sucked," and decided to refocus its plot on familiar territory, Israel.[66]

Although he changed locales, Uris's key creative choice in what became his 1984 novel, *The Haj*,[67] was wrong from the start. Instead of *defending* the essential image of *Exodus*—that of a new, strong, and independent sort of Jew—by rounding off two-dimensional aspects of Ari Ben Canaan's character, Uris went on the offensive and launched an intemperate attack on Arab individuals and societies.

He found it impossible to add touches of realism to the *Exodus* New Jew positive stereotype. This creative impasse was symptomatic of aspects of Uris's own Jewish identity and of circumstances that led to the composition of *Exodus* a quarter century earlier. As will be recalled, Uris's original creative impulse was not to write a realistic account of the new types of Jews who were emerging in Israel, but rather to find inspiring symbols of Jewish empowerment. Because such symbols seemed unconvincing when they were planted in the Pacific as U.S. Marines, Uris turned to the more credible setting of the Jewish state—that is, in psychological and creative senses, the Ari Ben Canaan figure was an instrumental means to express a vision of Jewish strength. As *The Haj* showed a quarter century later, Uris lacked interest in the prosaic, everyday realities of Jewish character in Israel.

The most important Jewish figure in *The Haj* (the novel's Ari Ben Canaan counterpart) is a veteran of the old Jewish guard (Hashomer) groups from the days of the early, pioneering *halutz* colonies, Gideon Asch. Uris's depiction of Asch is outlandish. The Jewish soldier secretly has sex with lonely Arab women in caves, shares secrets with village mukhtars over glasses of whiskey, runs Jewish spy rings in Iraq, and appears to have no home life of his own on the Shemesh kibbutz of the Ayalon Valley. Uris dispenses with Asch's personal biography in a page and a half and then uses this fictional Jewish hero's courage and wisdom as a mechanical standard against which the novel's hero, Haj Ibrahim, the mukhtar of Tabah in the Ayalon Valley, is measured.

The Haj has very little to do with the Jews. Instead, it is an extended polemic against Islamic Arab society. Bereft of any real positive content, Uris's writing about Israel's 1948 experience ended on an apocalyptic note. When he turned to the Middle East a quarter century after *Exodus,* Uris could not resurrect the liberating sense of empowerment, return, and redemption he expressed in his landmark novel. Instead, in *The Haj,* Uris took his bow as the most internationally renowned writer of Israel's founding by saying that the Jewish return has triggered the Armageddon of Arab terror. The following passage, appearing in the final pages of *The Haj* and uttered by one of the novel's few positive Arab characters (a noble-spirited and peace-oriented archaeologist), bridges between different eras. In the *Exodus* era, Uris's perspective appealed to liberal-minded people who conceptualized Israel as part of a post–World War II story of triumph. Decades later, Uris's negative messages in *The Haj* appeal today primarily to a pessimistic, neocon mentality that has redirected its interest from Israel's founding narrative to a timeline that runs between Iran's Islamic revolution and the September 11, 2001, attacks:

> The return of the Jews has unleashed that hatred, exploding wildly, aimlessly, into a massive force of self-destruction. In ten, twenty, thirty years the world of Islam will begin to consume itself in madness. We [Muslims] cannot live with ourselves; we never have. We are incapable of change. The devil who makes us crazy is now devouring us. We cannot stop ourselves. And if we are not stopped we will march, with the rest of the world, to the Day of the Burning. What we are now witnessing, Ishmael, now, is the beginning of Armageddon.

In *The Haj*, Uris identifies sexual frustration as the prime determinant of Muslim rage.[68] The family drama at the center of the novel focuses on generational tensions between a son, Ishmael, who occasionally narrates the story, and his father, Tabah's mukhtar, Ibrahim (of course, the names of father and son leave little doubt about Uris's ambition to write about generational issues on an epic scale). The father enjoys privileges as his village's leader, including the luxury of multiple wives and concubines, so he is not a sexually deprived character. Nor is he politically obtuse; in fact, at climactic moments in the story, Ibrahim takes great personal risk as he preaches accommodation with the Jews as an apostle of Palestinian moderation. Nonetheless, his doing and undoing in the story revolves around his sexual immaturity and patriarchal obstinacy.

Ibrahim's family collapses because of his high-handed chauvinism toward an attractive, precocious daughter, Nada. The father shaves her head, protects her modesty, and tries to stage Nada's betrothal, as tradition dictates. After the daughter rebels in devil-may-care acts of personal liberation in Damascus, Ibrahim butchers her in the street. The son Ishmael, the educated offspring who comes of age by ingeniously devising methods to keep the family together after its exodus from Tabah and thereby becomes his father's favorite, is maddened by this blood murder. Ishmael, who grew up in an incestuously charged climate, angrily reveals dark secrets of rape and

travail endured by the women in the family. Ibrahim's heart stops
dead. Ishmael, the would-be symbol of a new generation of capable, thoughtful Palestinians, ends up strapped up in bed as a lunatic,
mumbling incoherently about Armageddon. "I am so very tired,"
blabbers Uris's lunatic young Arab hero at the end of the novel, and
his words surely speak as well for many readers' feeling about Uris's
hundreds of pages of diatribe about Arab society and politics.[69]

The Haj is a part of our story of the making and unmaking of
Exodus because Uris's inability to negotiate a distinction between legitimate critical analysis of a subject and sheer delegitimization of the
topic is not primarily a *moral* failure. Uris was not insensitive about
the specific facts of Palestinian suffering, but he remained trapped
by a storyline that conceptualized Zionist righteousness as an all-or-
nothing commodity.

The writer of *The Haj* is not sadistically entertained by the Palestinian hardship he portrays. The reader gains a limited but genuine sense of the ordeal experienced by thousands of villagers—the
passing physical hardship of lack of food and shelter, the more prolonged bewilderment caused by the collapse of traditional lines of
village authority, and the everlasting agony inculcated by the loss of
home—are all portrayed in some detail by Uris. However prejudicial
in effect, Uris's sporadic use of a Palestinian narrator, Ishmael, is an
interesting creative attempt; much as outraged pro-Palestinian commentators point to factual inaccuracies in Uris's depictions of Middle
East landscape and society,[70] he undeniably learned *something* about
Palestinian suffering caused by the Naqba.

Fascinatingly, *The Haj* shares imagery and reference points with
Naqba books written by Arab authors whose antithetical agenda is
to undermine characteristic Israeli claims and perceptions about the
1948 experience. For instance, as with Khoury's *Gate of the Sun*, Uris
uses cave imagery to depict the pathos of Palestinian homelessness.
Also, as in pro-Palestinian Naqba novels, Christian icons flit about
The Haj, as though to express Palestinians' hopes that their own
martyrdom would realign sympathies in power balances between the
world's three monotheistic faiths (at one point, Ishmael sees Jesus
in a dream; through various plot twists, the vision ends up bringing
his family out of the caves in Qumran and back to human society).
None of these devices, however, would do much to insulate *The Haj*
from virulent attacks lodged by persons sympathetic to Palestinian

claims about 1948 (in the last years of his life, Uris admitted that *The Haj* incited a storm of criticism among groups of readers, though he insisted defiantly that his portrayal of Arab society was accurate—he even claimed that "our [U.S.] military and State Department people read *The Haj* as a text book before going to service in that part of the world [the Middle East][71]). But these observations suggest that the source of *The Haj*'s ineffectuality is not moral viciousness. Uris had some real grasp of Palestinian suffering, and concerns raised by his book about patriarchy and ignorance in Arab societies circulate commonly in liberal Western media and other public discourses.

In *The Haj*, Uris wrote that Palestinian departure from towns and villages was coerced by the false promises and threats of Arab religious, political, and military leaders. Setting a negative example, the panic, self-interest, and cowardice of elite Arab families also figured decisively in the mass departure. Patterns of solidarity and hospitality utterly vanished during the Palestinian scattering; eschewing norms of mutual aid, absentee landlords, warlords, and leaders from communities on the outskirts of the military conflict cruelly preyed on the acute vulnerabilities of Palestinian refugees. Jewish communal settlements that neighbored Arab towns and villages were brought reluctantly into the conflict; they offered support and sanctuary to Arab neighbors who sought it. Israeli war policy (e.g., Plan D, which, interestingly, is cited by name in *The Haj*) was devised with the defensive intent of protecting every Jewish community in Eretz Israel. When the fighting ended, Israel's leadership was prepared to support the return of 100,000 Palestinian refugees, as a start. Arab regimes surrounding the new Jewish state used the Palestinian situation as a ploy to further their own interests—not Palestinian restitution, but control in Jerusalem and over the West Bank interested Jordan's King Abdullah, and similar points could be made about the policies and intents of Egyptians and other Arab states. After the war ended, Palestinians fostered blind hatred of Jews in schools, mosques, and homes; fedayeen terror against Israel resulted from religious fanaticism cultivated by the Muslim Brotherhood and other radical groups and also from the cynical expediency of corrupt Arab regimes. Similarly, the refugee crisis was symptomatic of the lack of solidarity and the cold-blooded expediency of politics in the Arab world. Used to score propaganda points against the Jewish state, stranded in the squalid misery of refugee camps around the Middle East, capable

Palestinian operatives in the 1950s proved unable to rebuild their lives. They languished in a dream world of judgment day vengeance conjured by Gamal Abdel Nasser and others.

This, in a nutshell, is the politics of *The Haj*. None of these claims would be fully corroborated by subsequent scholarly research conducted by New Historians such as Benny Morris. In many instances—such as Uris's conceptualization of Plan D as a purely defensive measure, or his various hints about semisecret expressions of Israeli magnanimousness on the refugee issue (e.g., the 100,000 offer)—political claims embedded in the plot of *The Haj* would soon be conclusively refuted by scholarly research.[72]

However, as a work of fiction, it is misleading to judge the politics of *The Haj* solely in terms of the content of its specific claims. More significant is the novel's utterly uncompromising Zionist advocacy spirit. Uris's perspective is that *nothing* the Palestinians say about their 1948 misfortune could possibly be true because their cultural world is depraved.

By the time Uris got around to writing *The Haj*, the Palestinian story was known to millions around the world. It was narrated voluminously at the United Nations and championed widely in the third world and in left-liberal circles. To pretend that it had no viable content was to isolate oneself within an old story and ignore all sorts of friction and background noise in real-world arenas.

Inadvertently, Uris contributed to the unmaking of his own *Exodus* narrative. By defensively issuing denials or jaundiced characterizations of central claims in the Other Exodus narrative, he demonstrated the vulnerability of his own story of Israel's founding and perhaps damaged its credibility. Fair-minded readers in the mid-1980s, or after, might plausibly wonder whether a writer who couldn't face basic facts about Palestinian nationalism was totally forthright to begin with about the accomplishments of Jewish nationalism in 1948.

It is, however, misleading to argue that the unmaking of Leon Uris's *Exodus* was "caused" in part by his own prejudices. Although the narrative's simplification and distortion of Palestinian issues offended later generations of readers, its Manichaean presentation of ultimate good versus ultimate bad was also (and, for many readers, remains) a key technique underlying its popularity. In light of the simplistic way mass culture constructed cowboy and Indian type narratives, it is less problematic for a historian to identify *Exodus*'s polarity of heroic Israeli Jews versus evil Arab antagonists as a contributing factor toward *Exodus*'s popularity than it is to pinpoint the text's Arab bashing as a causal factor in its waning influence. Nonetheless, it is impossible to ignore *Exodus*'s prejudices and to wonder about ways in which they might have deflected later readers away from the pro-Zionist messages Uris wanted to inculcate.

A similar point should be made about the *Exodus* film. It would be much too paradoxical to suggest that the movie version contributed directly to the waning influence of Uris's story. This excellent movie disseminated Uris's images of heroic Jews to many thousands of viewers who would not otherwise have been exposed to the *Exodus* story; so in this incontrovertible, basic sense the film contributed to the story's success. As noted by a recent biographer of the film's director, Otto Preminger, the *Exodus* movie is "imbued with Zionist fervor," and "expresses the commitment of a Jewish director to a Jewish homeland."[73] Like the novel, the *Exodus* film provided a powerful antidote to lingering, post-Holocaust feelings of Jewish weakness and vulnerability. However, in terms we are exploring in this chapter, Preminger's film version came "after *Exodus*" (the novel), and it contained elements that drove contemporary viewers, or later generations of viewers, toward conceptualizations of Israel's founding that are rather unlike Leon Uris's interpretations. In sum, a film that glorified Ari Ben Canaan, Dov Landau, and other Israeli fighters cannot exactly be identified as a cause in the deconstruction of *Exodus;* but it is nonetheless part of an "after *Exodus*" process in which millions of people around the world have come to see things in Israel's 1948 founding that Leon Uris never imagined.

The power and the problems of the *Exodus* film are concisely conveyed by one of its most arresting sequences. It occurs two hours into the long movie, immediately after Ari and Kitty bring the young teenage survivor, Karen Hansen Clement, to her devastating reunion with her father, the renowned former university professor who survived the Holocaust only in nominal, physical terms. The father sits in a silent vacuous stupor throughout the meeting with his angelic, expressive daughter Karen. The scene takes place in a Jerusalem asylum that is suggestively decorated with various emblems of German Jewish modern psychoanalysis and religious Christian iconography.

Ari and Kitty shoulder the saddened Karen as she leaves the institution, no longer able to deny the total ruin wrought by the Holocaust to her family and European past.

Suddenly, the camera tracks straight along the side of the Jerusalem stone building and focuses directly on the King David Hotel in the not-so-distant background, where white smoke billows into the clouds after an Irgun-sponsored terror attack. In a split second, virtually all of the narrative's concerns stitch together in a camera shot of the immediate aftermath of a terror strike. Preminger could not have plotted all of the image's ingenious components, nor could he have fully anticipated how posterity would relate to his intelligently orchestrated extenuation of violent Jewish redress. The picture's meanings converge in a matrix that transcends authorial intent, and thereby reinforces an essential fact of Israel's 1948 founding experience: partly because the 1948 events are continually compared to episodes and processes that unfolded in subsequent decades, the Israel independence war story's possibilities and circumstances exceed the control and comprehension of any single author or film director.

In this film version, the King David Hotel attack is masterminded by Ari Ben Canaan's mercilessly partisan uncle, Irgun leader Akiva Ben Canaan, and is carried out by the teenage Holocaust survivor Dov Landau (played with terrific theatric gusto by Sal Mineo). Dov, the viewer knows, was raped by Nazis and compelled to work as a *sonderkommando* at Auschwitz, blowing holes into the ground and burying Jewish remains. The film provides wide latitude to Dov's unquenchable thirst for revenge.

Now, just after she has witnessed irrefutable proof of the Nazi decimation of her father, Karen stands on the staircase of the asylum and observes the results of Dov's biggest dynamite job. We see the smoke wafting over the ruined south wing of the King David Hotel through her eyes, and also through those of Kitty's and Ari's (whose relationship is in some ways an adult version of the Dov-Karen teenage pairing). As the audience peers directly at the YMCA tower and the shattered King David Hotel behind it, our view is bordered by black railing on the right side and the building's Jerusalem stone on the left. The view has the feel of railroad tracks, and shadows in the middle of the track are aligned, accidentally, as a crucifix. The building's multilingual sign on the left describes its function as a mental health institution and implicitly raises the issue of how lines of sanity have reconfigured after the Holocaust.

The King David Hotel explosion. The complex image conveys an argument about the use of terror as historic restitution; its shadows, signs, and stark lines deliberately or unwittingly evoke associations of mental health, railway transport to concentration camps, and the cross. (*Exodus* film)

Much of the dialogue in the movie pivots around moral issues raised by the use of violence by Jews in their struggle to create a state, but the images in this one shot compress the *Exodus* film's point of view more provocatively than its garrulous script. Irgun terror is seen mostly as a natural sequence in which the human need for redress propels the Jews toward a state of their own in their ancestral homeland. The smoke bellowing over the King David Hotel is horrific (we later learn that ninety-one charred, dead British bodies are cleaned away after this attack), but it represents the Jews' progression from passive victims to active fighters for their own liberation.

To deal with viewers who might fail to grasp the point about how the King David Hotel attack symbolized a turnabout in Jewish fortunes, Preminger cuts, right after the hotel explosion scene, to an image of its perpetrator, Dov Landau, crawling up out of a sewer grid to reconnoiter with his Irgun cohorts. The orphan who survived the Holocaust by cleaning up the remains of murdered kinsmen from gutters has now gone underground to fight savagely for Jewish freedom.

The film rearranges 1948 war chronology to enhance the rationale of the King David attack. In real life, the attack occurred in late July 1946, almost a year and a half before the passage of the UN partition resolution, and significantly complicated the Yishuv's status in international diplomatic spheres. In contrast, in the film's truncated chronology the attack comes on the eve of the British pullout from Palestine and is thus perceptible as a spur to that longed-for event. As happens in other key moments in the film, Preminger uses symbols after the King David bombing to exonerate Jewish zeal and to evoke a sense of Christian forgiveness for acts of post-Holocaust Jewish violence. In this case, Dov shakes off British security men by weaving in and out of Jerusalem's Ethiopian Church and hiding behind Christian relics and clergy processions.

Hard as it tries to make peace with Jewish terror, the *Exodus* film cannot find a knockdown image that would once and for all allay anxieties about Jews tossing sticks of dynamite around Jerusalem, Acre, and the Hula Valley. In fact, the film manages simultaneously to exonerate Jewish terrorism and to display neurosis about it. As soon as the King David Hotel bomb goes off and the characters on the asylum's ledge grasp what has happened, Karen collapses in a nervous attack and is carried off by the ever-gallant Ari Ben Canaan. In the film *Exodus,* this teenage Holocaust survivor bravely endures a hunger strike aboard the embargoed ship in Cyprus, does not bat an eye at a frightening guard post at her besieged Jezreel Valley children's village, and endures other traumas; but, even at a safe distance from the scene of the attack, she crumbles as a reflex to the King David Hotel explosion.

Karen's collapse after the King David bombing reveals something about the creative explosion that ripped apart the planned collaboration between Otto Preminger and Leon Uris. In his novel, Uris understood the Jewish heroes of 1948 as living extensions of historical processes; because he attributed centuries of experience and yearning to those processes, his characters behaved as courageous automatons, without a shred of qualification or doubt. Much less interested in Jewish history, Preminger did not believe that screen images of unadulterated Jewish heroism would be believable. Such reverse stereotypes of supermen Jews, Preminger must have reasoned, would have been psychologically unnerving to viewers who entered the cinema with rather different images in mind.

In the film, completely unlike the novel, something about the remaking of Jewish character after the Holocaust always seems traumatic. In the movie, wherever there are acts of outright Jewish partisanship, doctors are to be found scrambling about. For instance, aboard the ship in Cyprus, a kindly German Jewish doctor persuades Ari to exempt children from the hunger strike on health grounds (nothing of the sort happens in the novel, of course); or, as the Jewish orphans rehabilitate at their village Gan Dafna, located in the

Jezreel Valley in the film, another doctor cheerily replaces Ari's sister, Jordana, and takes some young women Palmach trainees through weapons-handling drills. The same holds true in this arresting depiction of the King David Hotel bombing. As soon as Karen swoons, uniformed nurses come running out to the balcony. In Uris's novel, Ari Ben Canaan and his steely colleagues never display emotional misgiving; in contrast, on Preminger's screen, medical or psychological care is continually provided to the teenage Holocaust orphans who are trying to refashion themselves as militant Israelis by carrying out intimidating terror acts of merciless retribution. At least subconsciously, the film associates the Jewish statehood struggle with psychological disorder—no such association is possible in Uris's universe.

By its adroit use of religious, political, and historical symbols, the film's King David Hotel image grants a form of immunity to Holocaust survivors and implies that survivors of genocidal measures have the right to transgress moral limits in their own struggle for national survival. Preminger, however, was unwilling to extrapolate from this premise and conceptualize Israel's founding and the 1948 war as a morally exceptional historic experience.

Fundamental differences in Uris's and Preminger's approaches to the subject of Jewish statehood exploded in the rancorous story of how the movie rights for *Exodus* were acquired and how its film script was written. What really happened between the writer and the filmmaker has long been clouded in mystery. Uris never told his side of the story, but he dropped dark hints about nefarious behavior on Preminger's part. In a very late, 2002, interview, the still-incensed writer explained that he had to keep mum about the movie since he had a "fifty-year reputation to consider." However, he could not resist adding that the handling of the *Exodus* movie rights "was a monstrous experience. Otto was a terrorist—he's Arafat, a Nazi, Saddam Hussein—who never knew the difference between lying and not lying."[74] Since they are connected to the way the film departed from the novel's substantive content, heretofore unknown details of their acrimonious dispute should be summarized here quickly.

Uris originally contracted simultaneously with Random House and MGM to produce an Israel book and movie script.[75] The contracts were signed on January 25, 1956; Uris's product was tentatively called "The Big Dream," and he was represented in the contract negotiations by Ingo Preminger. The film deal guaranteed Uris staged payments of $25,000, somewhat more than half of what he was promised for the novel. MGM was to receive a screenplay between 110 and 160 pages in length. Through United Artists (Carlyle-Alpina), Otto Preminger obtained rights to Uris's screenplay from MGM (Loew's Incorporated) on July 2, 1958, in a deal that sweetened Uris's share by guaranteeing him $40,000. Uris's arrangement as *Exodus* screenwriter with United Artists was short-lived and was terminated formally by mutual consent on November 13, 1958; Uris was relieved of all writing obligations but received the $40,000, along with a small share of the net profits of the *Exodus* film.

This buy-out was a source of excruciating ill-feeling in Uris's life; he was a proven scriptwriter before the novel *Exodus* was released, and he lost control of the film version of a story in which he had invested untold emotion and years of effort and that succeeded beyond anyone's wildest expectations as a novel. Financially, the film was no windfall for Uris. Over the years, Uris's earnings mounted impressively from his writing career. From a net worth of $122,000 in 1959, Uris's financials in the mid-1980s attest to a net worth over $5 million. Profits from the film *Exodus,* which grossed over $20 million by the end of the 1980s, were a very small part of this financial success—by 1988, Uris had received less than $200,000 from the film.[76] This shrunken share of the *Exodus* film profits embittered Uris. In the 2002 excoriation, Uris declaimed: "I got a royal fucking from the Preminger brothers, who were a couple of Viennese thieves."[77]

Before this alleged shakedown in the mid-1950s, Uris happily presented himself as a novelist who also liked to write for Hollywood. Riding on the crest of *Battle Cry*'s success in this period, Uris released press statements in this period describing himself as "a rare two headed monster from outer space, a living author who actually likes Hollywood."[78] Just weeks after the novel *Exodus* was released, United Artists' publicity agent Mort Nathanson issued upbeat statements about the upcoming film, which was to be a collaborative effort between the well-known director-producer Otto Preminger and scriptwriter-author Leon Uris. Just days before United Artists terminated its connection with Uris, the studio was still issuing glossy photos of Preminger and Uris standing side by side, reviewing a script purportedly written by the latter. The caption announced "The Script Looks Good."[79]

Preminger never really believed that to be true. Over the years, the film director issued anti-Uris put-down explanations to explain why the novelist was muscled away from scriptwriting work on *Exodus*. These are largely self-serving and unreliable accounts, but the novelist nonetheless does not seem to have been on the top of his game when he sat down with Preminger in autumn 1958 to hammer out a script. Uris never got past early drafts of the opening Cyprus scenes of the film, but the documents that remain from this unhappy episode in his life are enough to show that he was overreaching, setting-up psychological dynamics that would have been impossible to develop on screen, while also proposing some truly hokey images.[80]

In Uris's proposed screenplay,[81] Kitty and Ari's early meetings feature red-hot banter. Unlike the novel, where Kitty first appears as a detached widow with a vague distrust of Jews, Uris pictured the screen version of Kitty as a member of a United Nations Commission of Inquiry. At one point, to prove that he is not dogmatically anti-British, Ari drops his shirt to reveal shrapnel scars dating from his fighting with the British army during World War II. Unimpressed, Kitty growls "I know all about you Jews," and threatens to turn Ari in to British authorities on Cyprus. Later, Kitty tenders her resignation from the UN commission due to its refusal to support Jewish claims. Also in this never-used draft script, Ari runs about, occasionally espousing bitterly anti-British positions (which Preminger understandably feared would alienate audiences), crying out at one point: "Give me tanks, machine guns to drive them away! The British are just another in a long line of Pharaohs who have been pushing us around for 2,000 years." While leading the three hundred Holocaust orphans aboard trucks, during the escape from the DP camps to the ha'apalah ship, Ari is apprised by a Haganah comrade that "these kids have been taken on too many truck rides; they can smell panic." Ben Canaan proposes a musical balm: "What's the name of that thing the Americans sang, something about a Scotsman's farm." Ridiculously, Uris then pictured the *Exodus* children belting out "And on this farm he had a pig," and the other verses of "Old MacDonald Had a Farm," while riding to the harbor in Cyprus.

Preminger canned the script and booted Uris off the ranch after a few weeks. Speaking frankly, his wife, Hope Bryce, recalled that "whatever he [Uris] wrote was unusable, totally bad."[82] In his 1977 memoir, the filmmaker Preminger explained: "I began to work on the script with Leon Uris. We labored though almost a third of it, but it was hopeless. Uris is a good storyteller, but he cannot write a screenplay."[83]

That last judgment was not accurate. When Preminger purchased film rights to *Exodus,* Uris came as a package deal. The filmmaker's brother Ingo, along with literary agent Malcolm Stuart, represented Uris jointly as a proven author and a proven scriptwriter; Otto Preminger knew he was being offered a package and worked aggressively to acquire it. As Otto told the story, in fall 1958, he saw his brother lugging around a cardboard box with a manuscript inside it; Ingo let him read the *Exodus* text but warned Otto that he could not have the story because it belonged to MGM. Otto, on his own telling, stayed up through the night and couldn't put the book down. "I was terribly excited by it—it had everything, the first full account of the founding of Israel, action adventure, suspense," he subsequently told the press. In a legendary maneuver, Preminger stormed his way into MGM's offices, where he persuaded its president, Joseph Vogel, to sell rights to the film version of *Exodus* for not a penny more than the $75,000 the studio had invested in the project. "It is a great book, but if you make it the Arab countries will close all MGM theaters and ban all MGM films," Preminger reported telling Vogel. "You can't afford an Arab boycott, but I can. Since I am an independent producer, they can't hurt me too much."[84]

Preminger's story has loose ends, though it is basically true. The story's most credible detail is its suggestion that the politics of *Exodus* stirred anxieties in Hollywood, where executives worried that Uris's forthright, impassioned Zionist perspective could jeopardize the mass appeal of his dramatic story. In the end, Preminger bowdlerized *Exodus*'s Jewish messages by universalizing key images in the film; the movie's taming of *Exodus*'s militant Zionism is so evident that it puts to rest questions about why Preminger and Uris found it difficult to work together for any length of time. The two men had different ways of seeing the world and the Jews' place in it.

Politics, not screenwriting talent issues, whisked the script of the *Exodus* film away from Uris's typewriter. Preminger acknowledged this fact in a Canadian Broadcasting Corporation (CBC) interview given in February 1961. These 1961 words about political differences have credibility because they are contemporary, whereas the filmmaker's damning words about Uris's lack of skills as a screenplay writer were conveyed in a memoir published in 1977, after years of bitter, public recrimination between the *Exodus* novelist and the

Exodus filmmaker. Preminger told CBC:

> You see, I would be willing to defend my film of *Exodus*
> against some really big enemies of Israel, like Nasser. I would
> be willing to sit down with him, and let him tell me why he
> felt this picture was unfair. Because I knew it isn't. But the
> book by Uris has a pox against all the enemies of the Jews
> in it, and that is difficult to defend. This is part of my whole
> outlook of the world: I am basically an optimist. I don't be-
> lieve that there are any real villains. If somebody is a villain,
> I try to find out why. I don't necessarily excuse him, but I try
> to understand why.[85]

Uris corroborated that politics was the crux of the dispute about
the *Exodus* script. "Otto wanted to soften my treatment of the British and Arab characters, an approach I could not condone or toler-
ate," the novelist recalled toward the end of his life.[86]

After booting Uris off the project, Preminger promptly chose Dalton Trumbo, a left-wing writer who at the time was blacklisted as one
of the Hollywood Ten, to bang out a script. Later, Trumbo's name
appeared on the film credits in bold defiance of Cold War blacklist
conventions (in fact, around the United States some patriotic groups
protested screenings of the film). As a human liberation story, *Exodus*
provided leverage as Preminger and Trumbo scored a point against
Hollywood vestiges of 1950s Cold War witch-hunting hysteria; but
this anecdote about Trumbo also points to the distance between the
new scriptwriter's own political horizons and interests and the story
of Israel's founding. Trumbo's biographer touts the new scriptwriter
as a pragmatist who removed biblical baggage from *Exodus,* "refusing to go back to Old Testament times, and follow the Jews through
the centuries of the Diaspora and the horror of the Holocaust."[87]
Neither Trumbo nor Preminger shared Uris's historical sensibility;
they abandoned the novel's insistent presentation of Israeli character
action as a consequence of long historical processes.

Preminger wanted a scriptwriter who worked fast. Working together, he and Trumbo pounded out the film script in forty days.[88]
In sharp contrast to Uris, who memorably logged thousands of miles
of on-site observation in Israel before writing *Exodus,* Preminger's
new, hired-gun scriptwriter had never set eyes on the country, and
it showed. The finished script contained several odd set descriptions

and stage directions that reflected the screenwriter's imaginary pil-
grimage to a land he had never seen. For instance, setting up the stage
for the Acre jail break (a lavishly produced scene in the *Exodus* film),
the script strangely pictured the historic Crusader coastal port city
as though it were located in the Sahara: "Bearers, camel-drivers and
others are gathered around campfires which dot the place, or feeding
their animals, or sleeping. On all three sides of the area may be seen,
in night silhouette, and in startling paradox to what might be a desert
wilderness, the buildings of Acre which ring the place about, and, if
possible, the minaret of the Mosque of El Jazzar."[89] Preminger won
backing for his film project from Arthur Krim of United Artists. Krim
had strong pro-Israel inclinations.[90] He met his wife, Mathilda, an
alluring figure of speculation among historians interested in developing connections between Israel and the United States under the Lyn-
don Johnson administration,[91] when she was a research scientist at
the Weizmann Institute. Brought up in Europe by a Catholic mother
and Protestant father, Mathilda converted to Judaism and settled in
Israel, largely due to the influence of her first husband, an Irgun partisan; and so aspects of his wife's own biography must have reminded
Arthur Krim of dynamics in the lives of *Exodus* heroes Kitty Fremont
and Karen Clement Hansen and enhanced his attraction to the film
project. Krim agreed to back a $3.5 million budget for Preminger's
Exodus.

Otto Preminger's highly anticipated film version of *Exodus*
(1960), a lavish, two-hundred-minute production, became a block-
buster. Advanced ticket sales for *Exodus* of $1.6 million set a record,
and screening revenue quickly surpassed the film's $3.5 million pro-
duction cost.

In some ways, the fault line running between the *Exodus* film and
novel attests to Preminger's creative sophistication, in contrast to the
fire and darkness Manichaeism of Uris's writing. Preminger had a
realistic and sympathetic understanding of the complexities of human character, and he revised the *Exodus* text to eliminate one-sided
caricatures of figures in the 1948 drama, such as the novel's condem-
natory portrayal of various British officials. The talented filmmaker
used an arsenal of devices, including comedy, to round off some of
the book's harshest elements.

Yet the film's fundamental flaw is that it is always looking for
ways, no matter how awkward, to transport the Exodus story's car-
dinal themes and contrasts (terror versus diplomacy in a national

struggle; retribution versus forgiveness) out of their specific, dramatic context, the lead-up to the 1948 war. In Preminger's film, the story of Israel's founding is often depicted generically as a modern Jewish version of perennial debates between political idealism and Machiavellian politics of ends justify the means. This tendency is illustrated by one episode where Ari finds his way to his uncle's hideout in a second-floor apartment perched close to the Golden Dome in Jerusalem's Old City and proposes a united Irgun-Haganah alliance for the purpose of fighting the impending war against the Arabs. Ostensibly accepted by his uncle, the union proposal incites a rollicking discussion of tactics and ideals in the Jewish revolutionary struggle. Ari says his Palmach-Haganah orientation has created a civilian infrastructure for the Jewish state and has provided crucial diplomatic leverage for the Zionists; meantime, his fugitive uncle tinkers with the samovar and tosses around soggy teabag adages about where democratic freedom comes from. "Population is the most valid argument we have to bring to the United Nations for our freedom," announces Ari. "I don't know of one nation now or in the past that was not born in violence—terror, violence and death are the midwives which bring free nations into this world," replies uncle Akiva.

In the novel, Uris concocted imagination-popping fables to frame this modern Jewish political debate about high ideals and violent expediency. In Uris's story, the two Ben Canaan brothers respond with impassioned retribution and unbelievable acts of physical exertion to family tragedy in late nineteenth-century Pale of Settlement pogroms. Uris piled on historical facts out of a reasonable belief that the extreme circumstances and particular formulations of Jewish politics on the eve of the 1948 war were determined by a very complicated and unusual historical experience. To understand what an Irgun partisan meant when he derided a Haganah fighter as a naive rhetorician, and to reach educated judgments about Irgun terror strikes, you have to pay attention to the history, Uris believed.

In the film version, Preminger tossed no more than passing glances at where the contrasting ideologies of the Ben Canaan brothers had come from. In a speech welcoming *Exodus* ship youngsters to Gan Dafna, Barak drops one fleeting reference to how he and his brother Akiva walked from Russia to the Jezreel Valley forty-seven years before. The Holocaust orphans are too gainfully employed in Zionist rehabilitation to pay attention to any such explication of the historic background of a dispute that is about to engulf them. Theirs is a veritable workshop of halutz Zionist pioneering industry and culture, with hammers banging in a carpentry workshop, pointed sticks hoisted in Palmach training, and sleeves of blue proletarian garb rolled up so that string instruments can be played in the village's youth orchestra. The script directions describe a regime of Zionist reconstruction at Gan Dafna, which leaves no time for thought about what all the children are rehabilitating *from:*

> A nursery school room for toddlers; and, outside the building, children mowing the lawns, working on shrubbery; small children engaged in the serious business of tending a small garden plot; a farm truck, manned by youths, loaded with freshly harvested calisthenics, under the tutelage of one of the teenage villagers. Beyond this last group we see in background a squadron of teenagers going through military maneuvers under the command of Jordana [Ari's sister].[92]

In fact, nobody in the film *Exodus* has any time to investigate how the Jewish past bequeathed the bewildering intensity of the agreements and disagreements between the brothers Ben Canaan and their allies. It ruins Kitty Fremont's supper at the Ben Canaan moshav when Barak bangs with his fist and bans anyone from mentioning the name of his ostracized brother Akiva, and viewers of the film must have a hard time blaming her. Can politics without regard for the past ever seem like anything more than bad manners?

Preminger seems to have conceded the point in retrospect. In his memoir, he hinted that plastering Jewish political dilemmas of 1948 on the silver screen was a thankless task. His method of showing both sides of the story in the Jewish debate, without any substantive layering of historical antecedents and context, pleased nobody. Preminger recalled that Labor Zionist (Mapai party) stalwarts of the time, ideological descendants of the fictional Barak Ben Canaan such as Ben-Gurion, Golda Meir, and Moshe Dayan, complained to him that *Exodus* furnished too much credit to right-wing partisans of the Irgun for Israel's victory in 1948. Standing his ground, Preminger dipped into the well of Akiva Ben Canaan rhetoric in his response to these Mapai leading lights: "I said politely that I didn't think Israel would have emerged as a nation without the terrorists," the filmmaker rejoined. "I don't like violence but that unfortunately is the truth. The British would never have given in without the high pressure from the radical element."⁹³ Later, however, it turned out that this equal time-for-Akiva perspective was not sufficiently militant for Israel's right wing. Akiva's most renowned real-life counterpart, Menachem Begin, lunched with Preminger during the filming and complained that the film did not give enough credit to the Irgun. By trying to play fair with two Israeli versions of the Jewish statehood narrative, the film pleased neither side.

The *Exodus* film projected images of a political and cultural exodus from the Jewish narrative of 1948. Many such images were unwitting; all were politically ineffectual. Preminger did not mean to advocate provocatively a Palestinian counternarrative to the Israeli story; instead, he toned down Uris's anti-Arab bashing due to the same even-spirited, moderate impulse that drove him to qualify Uris's anti-British bashing. Then, or now, Palestinians would derive little solace out of the few moments of equal time Preminger gave to their side of the story. Justifiably, from their standpoint, they would view the film as several insufferably long hours of pro-Israel propaganda. Still, there is a qualitative difference between Uris's story and *Exodus*'s film version, and the difference ultimately derives from the storytellers' orientations toward Jewish history.

Uris found cause to put a lot of it in his text. Preminger saw fit, as his scriptwriter's camp put it, to "refuse to go back to Old Testament times and follow the Jews through the centuries of the Diaspora and the horror of the Holocaust." Uris was overwhelmed by the power and the pity of the Jewish past; his analysis of the lessons of that past was rational, but his study and his pronunciation of its results were galvanized by a quasi-religious sense of devotion and appreciation. Whatever one says about the literary quality of *Exodus*, Uris's creative process and its result retains the quality of personal testament: the author was bearing witness to something he deeply believed to be special.

In many ways, the movie's production is more shrewdly balanced than Uris's text, and Preminger and United Artists lavished energy, funds, and creative ego in the project. In the end, however, this *Exodus* was not testament, but a film. Relativism is just around the corner of every moshav, hotel, and fortress in the movie. Key exchanges of dialogue in the film point to some other Exodus. Every image can be seen in another way.

"One can argue the justice of Arab claims on Palestine just as one can argue the justice of Jewish claims." This statement does not be-

long to a university professor in charge of an introductory course on
Middle East politics but rather to the film's patriarchal Jewish militant, Akiva Ben Canaan. The pronouncement comes in the middle
of another hopelessly entangled, tea-sipping apologetic for Jewish
terror. Akiva's speech to his nephew is chock-full of self-contradic-
tory propositions. He derides the concept of justice as a meaningless
"abstraction," and in the next breath complains bitterly about past
injustices suffered by the Jews.

We do not expect Kantian philosophical rigor from our film heroes
and antiheroes, but it is nonetheless disarming to watch the *Exodus*
film's most hardened, zealous Jewish fighter acknowledge the moral
equivalence of Palestinian claims to the disputed land. Very much
unlike the historical personalities, such as Menachem Begin, upon
whom they are based, none of these movie *Exodus* heroes, not even
Akiva Ben Canaan, wholly and consistently believes in the singularity of his people's experiences and efforts. The film is interested not in
their distinctive circumstances but rather in the dramatic effects (not
to mention box-office repercussions) of those circumstances.

In this way, the film initiated a process of mass-media demeaning
of the Eretz Israel epic. All of the details that are missing in a contemporary CNN news report about a bus bombing or an IDF mission—
among other things, that the heroes or victims of the incident in question are immigrants, or descendants of immigrants, who underwent
a profound identity transformation during their Aliyah journey to
Israel, and in some objective measure typically had cause to regard
that migration as an Exodus escape from anti-Semitism—are missing
in the film. The same objectionable mechanics of facile comparisons
and dangerous parallels inculcated by equal time standards in today's
mass media coverage of Israelis and Palestinians permeate the *Exodus* movie's images. Nothing in the film story is invested with a quality of timelessness; since "one can argue the justice of Arab claims . . .
just as one can argue the justice of Jewish claims," is there anything
that protects and secures the film's images of Jewish heroism? Nothing in the Jewish narrative is anchored in a claim of moral particularity, so what is to stop viewers in subsequent eras from superimposing
upon those heroic images latter-day feelings about right and wrong,
power and powerlessness, freedom fighting and terrorism?

It is therefore a safe bet to assume that fifty years later, when
viewers observe *Exodus*'s aforementioned riveting image of smoke
rising above the demolished King David Hotel, their thoughts turn

invariably to the Twin Towers, and the story of September 11, 2001. When pressed, many, if not most, such viewers might hazard the thought that what the Irgun did to the King David is "just like" what Al Qaeda did to the World Trade Center. Such statements reflect the collapse of the moral certitude, of the reasoned belief in unique historical process, that electrified Uris's novel. They bear witness to an era captivated by moral relativism and by the mass replication of core religious values. They speak to a time when Our Exodus is "just like" Your Exodus, except that the names, religions, and addresses of the refugees have changed.

At the end of the film, Taha, the Arab mukhtar who fell short of his dream of friendly coexistence between his village and the Ben Canaan moshav, is buried alongside Karen, the Holocaust orphan whose murder cuts short her personal fulfillment of the quasi-messianic Zionist agenda of the Ingathering of the Exiles. "We have no kadi to pray over Taha's soul, and we have no rabbi to pray for Karen," mourns Ari Ben Canaan. "I swear on the bodies of these two people that the day will come when Arab and Jew will share a peaceful life, in this land they have always shared in death."

Articulated falteringly by an actor who was angry with his director, these are nonetheless gripping, inspiring words.[94] But they preview a new era, one in which a story about Jewish revival and restoration after the European genocide is not what the year 1948 prompts people to think about. Fascinated instead by the continuing inability of two great religious civilizations, Judaism and Islam, to find common ground in the Holy Land, they search for two sides of the story of the 1948 war. Hence, buried in the ground at the end of the film version of *Exodus* lies Uris's, and the Zionists', hope for cultural control of the story of the state the Jews established. Buried in the ground, but not lost, is the movie's two-story conceptualization of Israel's founding in 1948. Thrust into the real world of prolonged dispute and terror would come the era of two narratives, a time when all that remained of Leon Uris's heroic attempt to tell a story the whole world would understand and accept is the Jews' own privatized view of history, Our Exodus.

The conventional, pro-Israel conception of the 1948 War of Independence was challenged by a complicated sequence of events and ideological revisions that ensued in past decades, particularly after the 1967 Six Days' War triumph. Jewish and non-Jewish writers,

thinkers, and activists responded to an array of controversial or troubling developments—these included the rise of religious Zionism and
disputes about the Jewish settlement movement on the West Bank
and the Gaza Strip, the end of Labor Zionist hegemony in Israeli
politics and culture ushered in by Menachem Begin's victory in the
1977 elections, two embittering Lebanon wars, and two Palestinian
"intifada" uprisings in the post-1967 territories. It would be a stretch
to say that Uris's *Exodus* was uppermost on the minds of American
Jewish, Israeli Jewish, or non-Jewish commentators as they pondered
the implications of Jewish statehood in response to such events.

In the case of Israeli creative rethinking of the 1948 founding
story, the most that can be said is that Uris's symbols have sometimes been unwittingly reversed. One example of this unintentional,
but nonetheless striking, deconstruction of *Exodus* in Israeli literature can be found in Meir Shalev's brilliant debut novel about the
legacy of Israel's pioneering tradition and founding, *Blue Mountain*
(the novel was originally published under the Hebrew title *A Russian
Novel* in 1988).[95] Drawing from American frontier, Paul Bunyan,
traditions of pioneering tall tales, *Exodus* features one particularly
improbable pictorial representation of the modern return of the Jews
to their homeland: the Rabinsky (later Ben Canaan) brothers' walk
from the Pale of Settlement through Georgia and the Caucasus to
Ottoman Palestine. In Shalev's *Blue Mountain,* such a foot trek never
happens, but this outlandish idea of an exodus hike from European
anti-Semitism to the Promised Land is imprinted indelibly and ironically in the folk memory of a pioneering moshav in the Jezreel Valley.

In Shalev's novel, for decades, the commune's high-spirited, irrev-
erent, and strong-willed founders tell the story of Shifris, a member
of their Zionist circle in the Old World, who refused to board the
train at Makarov for the start of the journey to Ottoman Palestine.
"Comrades! To the Land of Israel we should go on foot, like pilgrims!" reportedly announced Shifris. *Blue Mountain*'s narrator, a
burly thirty-eight-year-old bachelor named Baruch Shenhar, relates
that he grew up in the belief that Shifris is "still trudging along on his
way, the last pioneer to arrive." For years, Baruch grills his grandfather, a revered Second Aliyah pioneer, about Shifris and the "borders
he had crossed clandestinely, the rivers he had forded." Late in the
novel, a pile of documents transferred to the village's crazed local
historian is said to include a letter-in-transit from the long wandering
Shifris, but its authenticity is disputed. "That's enough about Shi-

fris," Baruch's grandfather eventually announces. "He really did say he would walk," Mirkin (the grandfather) recalls. "But after a few days he must have run out of steam. Or something else happened to him on the way—maybe he got sick or hurt himself. . . . There's more than one thing can nail a man down to a place."

The legend of wandering Shifris is one of many comic tokens in *Blue Mountain* that beguile the village sons and feed an obsessive need to dispute, authenticate, reenact, or destroy the heroic legends of their parents' transition from the enslavement of Old World anti-Semitism to the rebirth of Jewish national life in the pioneering Jezreel Valley. Shalev's wrestling with Israel's founding story features elements of amused irony, magical enchantment, and outright bitterness that are nowhere to be found in Uris's militantly pro-Israel novel; and it is very doubtful that he contrived his story of the mythical Shifris as a conscious rebuttal to *Exodus*'s superhuman symbol of the Rabinsky brothers' trek.

While unwitting, the contrast is striking. In the late 1950s, an impassioned American Jewish writer presented a foot journey from the Pale of Settlement to Eretz Israel as a serious symbol of the end of Jewish galut wandering and of the pioneering start of the Jewish statehood campaign. Three decades later, a gifted Israeli novelist stood the same symbol on its head to cast doubt on whether the pioneering circumstances of the Jewish state's founding retain relevance, or even seem real, in aging Israel.

Exodus never really was in the educational repertoire of Israelis who grew up following the Six Days' War (a fact that would have relieved critics such as Uri Avneri), and so the novel's unmaking cannot reasonably be located in the context of Israeli rethinking about the meaning of 1948 and the founding of the Jewish state, even though the tumultuous "post-Zionist" debates toward the end of the twentieth century tackled issues such as the causes of the mass Palestinian departure that are relevant to Uris's book. As this study has argued, *Exodus* was, first and foremost, a novel about Israel's founding written by an American Jew in response to the identity needs of American Jews. Much to the chagrin of critics like Philip Roth, *Exodus* very much was part of the Jewish educational repertoire of American Jewish writers and thinkers who came of age as the events and disputes broached above (the 1973 Yom Kippur War, debates about the post-1967 territories, etc.) unfolded.

Partly because there is no authoritative historical account of the evolution of American Jewish liberal-left thinking about Israel in the postwar period,[96] comments about conscious or unconscious motivations in the unmaking of Israel's founding narrative in American Jewish thinking and debates must remain speculative. Existing accounts of liberal-left American Jewish criticism of Israel, such as Michael Staub's excellent discussion of Breira, an organization that emerged after the Yom Kippur war with a vocal commitment to the "land for peace" formula of resolving the Israeli-Arab dispute, stress gaps between American Jewish dissenters and the American Jewish organizational "establishment."[97] On Staub's analysis, what irked Breira activists was that American Jewish organizations were allegedly stifling debate about Israel's war and peace options.[98] However, it also seems plausible to propose that as debates ensued in the 1970s and 1980s about Israeli settlements on the West Bank and the Gaza Strip or about the first Lebanon War, American Jewish leftists were troubled by the gap between inspirational, *Exodus*-type images of Israel's heroic founding, upon which they had been reared, and continuing reports of a different sort of militarily aggressive, religiously zealous, or politically uncompromising Israel in their contemporary reality.

As suggested by Steven Rosenthal, the author of a study about burgeoning tensions between American Jews and Israel in the eras of the first Lebanon War and the first intifada, American Jews who came of age in the 1960s and 1970s conducted a "love affair" with Israel, and this romance was significantly nourished by *Exodus*.[99] Those American Jews who subsequently voiced criticism of Israel, starting with organizations like Breira, behaved like disenchanted lovers; as this romance waned, disaffected American Jews were wondering about how their youthful infatuation had been sparked by the novel and film *Exodus,* among other factors.

American Jews who were raised in comfortable, suburban settings of the 1950s did not share identity insecurities that troubled Uris's Depression-era generation. Adult Jews who read *Exodus* in months and years after its publication found comfort and strength in Uris's systematic reversal of images of Jewish vulnerability and weakness; younger American Jews who read the novel, or who saw the film, in the 1960s, were inspired by images of Israeli heroism (symbols that were simultaneously vindicated by Israel's impressive triumph in the Six Days' War), but they subsequently had time or reason to wonder both about whether *Exodus*'s claims about Jewish weakness in the Diaspora really corresponded to the circumstances of their suburban upbringing, and whether *Exodus*'s brave, pure fighters such as Ari Ben Canaan were really like the Israel Defense Forces soldiers they saw in news reports about the first Lebanon War or the first intifada.

By the end of the 1980s, liberal American Jewish critics routinely reversed the conceptual universe of *Exodus*. Their analysis, which often relied on tools of social psychology that Uris abhorred, targeted the very subject that Uris touted as the symbol of Jewish salvation after the Holocaust: Israel's army. At least in some moral sense, claimed left-wing American Jewish journalists or scholars, Israeli soldiering weakened and compromised Jewish identity. *That* was the one conclusion about modern Jewish experience Uris could never have tolerated.

Roughly thirty years after the publication of *Exodus,* liberal-left American Jews were putting Uris's formula of Jewish empowerment well behind them. In the unmaking of Uris's narrative, nowhere was greater emotional distance traveled than in this gap between the formulas of *Exodus* and the vision of liberal-left American Jews at the time of the first intifada. This point cannot be adequately substantiated here; two brief examples of this yawning gap must suffice. Our point is not that these explicit efforts to deconstruct Israel's founding narrative are representative of the way all, or most, American Jews have thought about Israel since the 1990s—in fact, they are not. However, these proto-post-Zionist attempts to erase entirely heroic conceptualizations of the establishment of the Jewish state have won a measure of acceptability, not just in small academic circles; and, in terms of responses to Israel and Zionism, they reflect the emotional journey of some American Jews, from sheer affection to publicly displayed alienation.

From its inception in 1987, writers attempted in the left-wing journal *Tikkun* to redefine and circumscribe the terms of liberal American Jewry's engagement with Israel's fundamental principles and policies. As early as the magazine's second issue, its charismatic editor Michael Lerner warned that Israel would have to change its ways in order to keep liberal American Jews behind it. In his piece on "Twenty Years on the West Bank," Lerner editorialized: "Eventually the liberal forces which have defended Israel in the U.S. will find themselves unable to justify repressive policies and unwilling to lead the fight for Israel."[100] In a subsequent article,[101] published in fall 1989 at the height of the uproar about Israel's intifada policies, Lerner clarified the reasons that (he believed) dictated a reappraisal of Israel's self-perceptions. In this revealing piece, "The Pathology of the Occupation," the *Tikkun* editor combined shrewd political commentary and forecasts with what appeared to be gimmicky psychobabble. Lerner's piece merits mention because it provides detail and color to the story of the unmaking of Israel's heroic founding narrative.

In his "Pathology of the Occupation," Lerner explained that he had some years before spent six months at Tel Aviv University researching "psychological dynamics that shape the self-perception of Israelis and Palestinians." Lerner confessed that his own understanding of Palestinian society was limited, but he proceeded nonetheless to hazard a psychological analysis of pathologies that (allegedly) crippled both peoples. Both national movements emerged from "different historical experiences," yet they shared experiences of "*real* powerlessness," and both peoples had "developed psychological frames of self-understanding that make them more powerless than the current reality requires." The two traumatized peoples behaved with self-defeating suspiciousness because they had not overcome the psychological effects of powerlessness.

What did Lerner mean when he announced that "dealing with the underlying psychological dynamics is the most effective approach to bringing peace to the Middle East"? At one point in his "Pathology of Occupation," Lerner intoned about how Israelis should contemplate holding ritual bathing *mikva* ceremonies for reserve IDF soldiers when they return to civilian life after serving in the territories. The purpose of the mikva ceremony would be to "convey symbolically the notion that current service in the Israeli army in the West Bank necessarily leads Israelis to perform acts that pollute the soul."

Influenced by 1960s-style spiritualism, Lerner's mikva recommendation can serve as a symbolic outer frame in this "After *Exodus*" discussion of the waning influence of Uris's heroic narrative.

In the *Exodus* world, traumatized Holocaust orphans must undergo psychological rehabilitation at the Gan Dafna utopia in order to be baptized anew as New Jews fit for military combat in Israel's epoch statehood struggle. In the *Tikkun* world, traumatized IDF heroes must be cleansed in the ritual waters of the mikva so that their immoral Israeli exterior can be undone and their healthy Jewish souls can be restored. *Tikkun*'s mikva recommendation entailed the unmaking of Israel's heroic narrative—the emblem of Israeli heroism, the IDF soldiers, needed to be cleansed because the use of Jewish power had become, at least in the post-1967 territories, pathological.

This embryonic post-Zionist vision radically stood upside down concepts of moral geography (pathology and cure, exile and return) that had been popularized in the *Exodus* narrative. As Lerner saw it, religious ritual joined forces with clinical psychology in the unhinging of the ailing Israeli exterior from the pure Jewish soul. This California-style neotraditionalism was diametrically opposed to the partially sublimated Soviet-style social realism of the Zionist movement, the unreflective faith in social engineering that allowed Uris to churn out new Jewish identity models like Ari Ben Canaan.

Michael Lerner predicated his interesting reflections about paradoxes of "surplus powerlessness" upon a brief period of several months' research at Tel Aviv University. That sounded superficial, but the *Tikkun* outlook in this intifada period of the unmaking of Israel's heroic narrative found footing in impressive scholarly research.

David Biale's *Power and Powerlessness in Jewish History,* published in 1986,[102] was a book-length, well-researched attempt to deconstruct the Zionist conceptual framework popularized by Uris in *Exodus.*

Biale's thesis was that Jews had neither been as powerful in their homeland in antiquity nor as powerless in the dispersion after the destruction of the Second Temple as the Zionist narrative contended. Biale argued strongly against this simplistic dichotomy between power in the Eretz Israel home and powerlessness in Diaspora exile. "The key to the Jews' remarkable survival never lay in either one of these polarities, neither of which exists in pure form in the real world,"[103] he contended. This scholar's use of historical examples to substantiate a compellingly provocative hypothesis could be contested by a discussion of the empirical evidence regarding each case; but it is more important for our purposes to observe that folded tightly within this scholarly text was a moral polemic entreating the deconstruction of Israel's founding Zionist narrative.

Contending that the conventional *Exodus* dichotomy between Exilic powerlessness and Return empowerment had produced abnormal circumstances in Israel, Biale anticipated the moralistic campaign that later appeared both on the pages of *Tikkun* and in the polemics of post-Zionism, a term that appears to have made its intellectual debut in his book.[104] The line of analysis in Biale's book identified an ironically poignant problem: formed to solve the so-called Jewish question of Europe, the Zionist narrative was, allegedly, producing new forms of pathology in intifada-era Israel.

Biale, who opened his book with critical allusions to the misuse of Jewish power in Israel's recent Lebanon War, denied that the Zionist narrative had empowered Jews in qualitatively new ways. At places in his book, he belittled Israel's democratic system by derogating it to status inferior to that of medieval Jewish communities in Europe. "Without a constitution, the state of Israel lacks the coherent identity that Jewish political theory provided to the medieval Jewish community, and remains torn by contradictions between differing interpretations of the meaning of Jewish sovereignty,"[105] wrote Biale. Preoccupation with the Holocaust trauma produced the misuse of excessive Israeli power, he added, in words that echoed in this period in Lerner's *Tikkun* articles. By replacing caricatures of powerless Diaspora Jews with overblown images of Israelis as military heroes, the old Zionist narrative cramped "normal" Jewish development. A nation of would-be Ari Ben Canaans, suggested Biale, could not be psychologically normal. Passages in his book suggested that retention of the old Israeli narrative was perpetuating abnormality in Jewish life. Biale, for instance, contended: "Between the Jew as a victim and the Jew as a military hero, the ideal of the Jew as a normal human being has begun to disappear. A legacy of powerlessness becomes the justification for the exercise of power."[106]

The popular image of Israel has transformed over the past half-century. Whereas its story was once about the reestablishment of the Jewish nation-state in its ancient homeland in the aftermath of a horrendous catastrophe, it is now understood as being the locus of an everlasting conflict between two peoples. To some indefinable but important extent, *Exodus* served as the foundation for the former popular conception; today's perception is represented in media, education, and other spheres by methods that frame 1948 as a tale of two stories, one of Jewish return, the other of Palestinian exile.[107]

For the time being, nothing really can be seen on the horizon beyond the two-narratives approach. That is to say, in the next few decades, the two-narratives perception will, in all likelihood, become standardized. Veteran peace activists who have devoted decades to dialogue efforts between Palestinians and Israelis predict that nothing in the foreseeable future can forestall this segmented perception of 1948 as two separate stories. Referring to this polarized view of

1948, Mordechai Bar-On, a former IDF chief education officer and a longtime observer and participant in Israeli-Palestinian rapprochement efforts, concludes soberly: "Bridging conflicting narratives of past events and the meaning of past processes in our case seems to be impossible."[108]

A glimpse at Israel's conceptual future, and a striking symbol of how far popular perception has moved in half a century, since Leon Uris's story of Jewish rebirth captivated millions of readers and film viewers, is provided by the Peace Research Institute in the Middle East (PRIME) project.

PRIME, initiated in 2002 by Professor Dan Bar-On from Ben-Gurion University's Behavioral Sciences Department and Professor Sami Adwan from Bethlehem University's Education Department, involved several Palestinian secondary school teachers (from the Gaza Strip and the West Bank) and Jewish Israeli teachers. The teachers prepared materials for three booklets that have, to date, been published under the PRIME banner.[109]

The booklets' format is more important than their content. Each booklet, written for high school students, presents the Israeli narrative on one side of the page, the Palestinian narrative on the other side, and leaves some blank lines in the middle of each page for pupils to transcribe study notes.

PRIME has a pedigree. Originally backed by the U.S. State Department under the Wye agreements and subsequently funded by the European Union, the Ford Foundation, and other backers, its two-stories methodology accords with the way concerned outsiders and even government delegates want Israel's situation to be conceptualized. This dual narratives approach has proven popular internationally—the first booklet was translated into English, Italian, French, German, Spanish, and Catalan, and made the best-seller lists in France in summer 2004.

A project like PRIME wins international support and is a cutting-edge harbinger of future methodologies, largely because people outside Israel encounter the Jewish-Arab conflict through the prism of media reports, which increasingly rely on dual narrative notions of balance. Yet, at the start of the twenty-first century, how popular is the dual narrative approach among the participants of the conflict themselves? Addressing this issue, PRIME's directors claim that the Israeli and Palestinian narratives "represent about 60 percent or 70 percent of their societies"—that is, the authors believe that a majority of Israelis would agree with the way the "Israeli narrative" is written, and the same holds true with regard to Palestinian attitudes about the Palestinian narrative. That may not be precisely true, since the Israeli narrative in PRIME tends to veer a bit left of the country's political mainstream, and the Palestinian narrative is more secular than the current, Hamas-led, Islamicized style of Palestinian politics, particularly in the Gaza Strip. These percentages, however, beg the question. The issue is not how many Israelis would concur with the way their own narrative is presented by PRIME, but rather how many Israelis and Palestinians could possibly become reconciled to the introduction of the two-narratives method in public school classrooms.

In Israel today, virtually nobody would be prepared to educate their children *mainly* via the two-narratives method, whereas a small percentage of citizens would feel that it is crucially important to expose their children to *both* the conventional (Zionist) curriculum and to the two-narratives method (as the parent of three children who have received their primary education at an innovative Jewish-Arab elementary school in the Galilee, I am familiar with these percentages; they are small). At present, a fairly significant number of Israelis (and Palestinians) might agree to incorporate two-narratives booklets like PRIME in a supervised, limited fashion as a passing *supplement* to their society's regular school curriculum. They would not feel that this supplement is crucially significant to their children's future, but they perhaps would be willing to give an experiment like PRIME a chance.

These schematic remarks relate to the origins, and limits, of a new, relativistic way of apprehending 1948 as the tale of two national narratives. At present, particularly outside of the Middle East, the liberal-minded, progressive way of looking at Israel is to break down its founding story into two parts. From the historian's standpoint, the fact that this transition has been reached after half a century is remarkable—PRIME represents an extremely different way of looking at 1948. In 1958, Leon Uris was a Stevenson Democrat who correctly expected that his book about Israel's founding would appeal to liberal-minded people as a complete package report about a triumphant struggle for human freedom. At the time, many *Exodus* readers would have been amazed by a prediction holding that within a few decades Uris's vision of Israel's founding would be derogated by well-intentioned, free-thinking people and tolerated as "just one side of the story."

The unmaking of *Exodus* was never a process that occurred at the same time, in the same way, in each Jewish-Christian context. Instead, aspects of the story Uris told have been made and unmade and remade in different places, each in their own way.

Exodus was never merely "about" Israel's early history. Nor was it about the passive relationship between a reader and a book, or between a viewer and a movie. Instead, as a potent agent of ethnonational revival in the post-Holocaust world, *Exodus* belongs to Modern Jewish History.

If it was about any single thing, *Exodus* was about Jewish pride. Uris's novel empowered readers and viewers who understood Israel's founding story as being their own. *Exodus* was an event, and not just a book or a film, because the fictional Ari Ben Canaan was never inseparably detached from the millions of Jews who became acquainted with his story. Although (and, in some ways, because) his exploits were recorded with fantastic exaggeration, Jews after the Holocaust associated with his heroism out of emotional necessity.

After Auschwitz, Ari was the Jewish Everyman. Yet in America and Israel, the two main theaters of Jewish recovery after the Holocaust, life after the 1960s and 1970s seemed too politically confused and morally turbulent for continuing identification with an image of unadulterated Jewish heroism. In contrast, in the Soviet Union, realities in the 1980s remained drawn in line with the moral structure of *Exodus* as a setting where Jewish revival could tip the balance for democracy in an ongoing fight between forces of freedom and forces of tyranny. For this reason, Ari Ben Canaan took his final bow in Modern Jewish History behind the Iron Curtain. There, a quarter century after Uris published his novel, whenever ordinary Jews reached within their hearts and minds for a vision of liberation from Soviet bondage, the *Exodus* image of Ari Ben Canaan kept popping up.

More than any other Diaspora community in the postwar world, Soviet Jews adopted and personally enacted Uris's formulas, seeking a new home in the Jewish state in their exodus from totalitarian persecution. Their journey deserves the last word in this book because it exemplifies the longevity and contextual diversity of its main premise about *Exodus*'s extraordinary status as an ethnically empowering text.

In 1985, Leonid Volvovsky was sentenced by the Gorky regional court to three years imprisonment and "corrective labor" for anti-

Soviet activity. Among other offenses, Volvovsky was penalized for disseminating Leon Uris's *Exodus* among fellow Soviet Jews. In its sentence, the Gorky court condemned Volvovsky for having had in his possession three copies of *Exodus*. "The book is Zionist in content, telling about [how] Russians drew up a program for the gradual liquidation of Jewry," ruled the court. Uris, it elaborated, wrote in *Exodus* about "the absence in the Soviet Union of a Jewish theatre, press, schools, public life, and the closing of synagogues."

When Volvovsky was sent to prison in 1985 partly for subversively disseminating *Exodus,* he had compiled an eleven-year record of Jewish activism and defiance of Soviet procedures he considered to be anti-Semitic.[110] Born in 1942, he grew up and received his education in Gorky, where he completed a graduate degree in electrical engineering. He finished his doctoral work in computer science in Moscow, where he filed for immigration to Israel in 1974. Within hours of submitting his Aliyah request to the Soviet authorities, Volvovsky lost his job at an elite research institute and spent the next decade supporting his wife and daughter by working at odd, manual-labor jobs and privately teaching mathematics and physics. In these years he was harassed and detained periodically by Soviet authorities; however exhausting and frightening, these experiences prepared Volvovsky for his 1985 arrest. In 1985, he managed to frustrate KGB interrogators by refusing to speak anything but Hebrew throughout the contorted Soviet Star Chamber process that led to his three-year Gulag term.

Both Volvovsky's parents were Jewish, but he grew up in a secular Sovietized household where Jewish observances were not upheld, and little or nothing was heard about Israel. When it came to Jewish matters, his mother, the primary parent, had nothing to say other than expressing the hope that Leonid would find a Jewish woman when the time came to get married. Under the assimilated circumstances of his upbringing, this demand seemed too Jewish for Volvovsky's enlightened taste. "The woman I marry should be a good person," Volvovsky would tell his mother. "That's the only thing that matters."

Israel's stunning victory in the 1967 Six Days' War awakened the twenty-five-year-old Volvovsky to Jewish matters, but he found it difficult to quench his surging thirst for Jewish information and activity. Reports about Israel's victory were hard to come by, and he was surrounded in his daily routines by Gentiles. One day a Jewish

friend gave him a stack of typed, onionskin papers to read—but just
for one night. Volvovsky and his Jewish wife Ludmilla kept pouring
cups of coffee as they turned page after page, entirely mesmerized.
They were reading a Russian translation of Leon Uris's *Exodus*.

"In the morning, I was a totally different person," recalls Volvovsky. "I learned that the whole world hates the Jews, but I also saw
that nothing is impossible."

Exodus ignited Volvovsky's Jewish passions, and he felt an "ob-
ligation" to circulate the book among Soviet Jews. Over the next
several years, he developed a number of Jewish interests, such as
studying Hebrew and religious texts and also taking part in Jewish
theater productions. He expressed his Jewish identity in defiance of
the repressive Soviet regime in original and courageous ways. For
one two-year period, he worked as a Jewish *shochet,* a ritual slaughterer; he was the only one of two million residents of Gorky to wear a
Jewish skullcap. Volvovsky earned a deserved reputation as a courageous, resilient Prisoner of Zion, but no single action undertaken by
himself or any of the other creative, energetic *refuseniks* in the Jewish
revival movement in the Soviet Union could ever match the impact of
Exodus.

Uris's novel, Volvovsky recalls today, "stirred a revolution"
among Soviet Jews. "It was simply amazing." Volvovsky's estimate
echoed in late 1980s Western news reports about his arrest for circulating *Exodus*. An April 26, 1987, article published in the *New York
Times,* "'*Exodus*' in Samizdat: Still Popular and Still Subversive,"
conveyed one telling evaluation. Jerry Goodman, then executive director of the National Conference on Soviet Jewry, opined that for
Soviet Jewish activists, *Exodus* was "probably more meaningful than
even the Bible." Goodman recalled: "Most of the Jewish activists in
the late 1960s and early 1970s always cited to me the importance of
the book [*Exodus*], They didn't treat it as a literary experience; it was
history, the only knowledge they had of the Jewish experience."[111]

Asked to explain why *Exodus* kindled fires of Jewish passion in
the Soviet Union, Volvovsky's assessment today echoes the positive
judgment of critics who wrote in *Exodus*'s late 1950s heyday about
the "underground power" of Uris's writing.[112] Volvovsky thinks that
the key to *Exodus*'s success in Russia was its "populism." "This
book," he explains, "showed us that the simplest, most humble person can be a hero."

In Russia, as everywhere else, *Exodus*'s main effect was ethnic empowerment rather than fulfillment of the Zionist agenda of Aliyah immigration to Russia. While *Exodus* became an integral part in the Jewish identity revival of Soviet Jews like Volvovsky who eventually settled in Israel, it is wrong (as Volvovsky himself explains) to reduce complicated personal odysseys that result in immigration to the reading of a particular book. Instead, *Exodus* was an identity stepping-stone that allowed thousands of Soviet Jews to move from Jewish self-denial to Jewish self-respect.

Volvovsky recalls that he grew up in a setting "where being Jewish was neither appealing nor accepted." Providing proof that Jews who began in abject persecution and humiliating repression could work miracles, *Exodus* inspired Volvovsky, "who had never grown up thinking that I was the sort of person who could do something heroic," to endure tremendous hardship and gain recognition in the U.S. Congress as a freedom fighter worthy of consideration as a human-rights case at the late 1985 Geneva Summit between U.S. president Ronald Reagan and Soviet premier Mikhail Gorbachev.[113]

When Volvovsky first read *Exodus* on that life-transforming night in the late 1960s, he knew little about the book's publishing history or about the mechanics of its transmission as part of the Soviet dissident samizdat. Later, he garnered pieces of information about *Exodus* in Russia. He learned that there were a few Russian-language translations of Uris's novel (including one that was miraculously produced by a veteran Soviet Prisoner of Zion, Avraham Shifrin, while he served time in a Gulag camp in Dubravlag), and he estimated that several hundred copies of these translations circulated among Soviet Jews. Yet he never knew very much about Leon Uris until he met the author at a Boston event on October 16, 1988, about half a year after he was finally allowed to leave Russia. In fact, from his first reading, he was sure about just one thing concerning *Exodus*—the book could only have been written by an American Jew.

Ideas of return (physical return to Eretz Israel, or emotional return to Jewish identity) tend to be taken for granted by Israelis, Volvovsky explains. Only Diaspora Jews can fully grasp the ironies and the inspiring power laden within Zionist calls of return, he believes. *Exodus* would never have been written with such depth and enthusiasm had not its author been on his own journey of Jewish pride and empowerment. Thus, from the first word he read in the translated, samizdat version of *Exodus* it was clear to Volvovsky that the novel's author was an American. His insight throws light on the fundamental dynamic of *Exodus:* even though Israel was the imaginative center of Uris's novel, *Exodus* was primarily an event in the ethnic identity of Diaspora Jews.

It was also a long-playing event. In this particular case, the dialogue between the American author who rediscovered his Jewish roots en route to writing an international best seller and a Soviet refusenik from Gorky who endured fourteen years of persecution before his request to settle in Israel was finally authorized, lasted decades.

In October 1988, Volvovsky was thrilled to receive an Action for Soviet Jewry award along with Leon Uris. The two spoke privately for a few minutes and Uris confessed that he sometimes regretted having written a book that caused so many Prisoners of Zion to suffer. Nonplussed, Volvovsky replied that *Exodus* helped free Soviet Jews.

The brief interview did not satisfy all of Volvovsky's questions. Twenty years after the 1988 Boston meeting, when I interviewed the ex-refusenik in Jerusalem, he asked me whether it were true that all of Uris's wives were goyim. Speaking in a tone that mixed admiration and puzzlement, Volvovsky asked, "how could it be that *Exodus* was written by a man married to a Danish American Christian?" I replied that if I had come to understand anything about *Exodus*, it was that Uris wrote the novel precisely because of his mixed marriage, because his all-American marriage at the end of World War II left dangling too many identity loose ends.

As I relayed some details about Uris's biography, it was fascinating to observe the look of recognition on the face of a man who spent a few years in the Gulag for, among other bugaboos, distributing samizdat editions of *Exodus*. Volvovsky identifies key elements in Uris's story as being essentially similar to leading components in his own journey as an assimilated Soviet who recovered his Jewish identity. In what is surely the most insightful comment I've ever heard about Uris and his novel, this ex-Soviet dissident cast *Exodus* as a kind of ethnic global community and as a remedy to the 1950s silence that descended upon the Jews in the American suburbs and behind the Iron Curtain. "I think a lot about Uris," Volvovsky said. "He knew he was Jewish; he must have felt very Jewish; but he was surrounded by goyim. I guess when a writer has nobody to speak to, he speaks with his readers."

After winning freedom from the tottering Soviet Union, Volvovsky settled in Israel with his family. He is deeply proud of the Jewish commitments and educational and professional accomplishments of his two grown-up children (at the time of our interview, one was a manager of the *Jerusalem Post*'s website). His humorous comments about his children's Israeli upbringing recalls the worldly pragmatism of *Exodus* characters—in the Gulag, he refused to speak anything but Hebrew to his Soviet interrogators, whereas in Israel he made sure that his two children knew Russian and English, to give them a leg up in the high-tech economy. A good-natured, intelligent and wise man, Volvovsky was one of the more recognized figures in Israel's last large wave of immigration, which swept in several hundreds of thousands of Russian Jews after the Soviet Union collapsed. As much as anyone else today, he is Israel's Everyman.

For the last few decades, he has gone by a new first name, abandoning the Russian Leonid, which means lion cub, and substituting the Hebrew equivalent. In selecting his new Jewish-Israeli identity, Volvovsky wanted a name that was more than the translated equivalent of his Russian birth name. He proudly adopted the name of Uris's hero in *Exodus*. Today he is Ari Volvovsky, after Ari Ben Canaan.

Acknowledgments

I OWE THIS BOOK TO A HAIRCUT.

The lowest moment in its writing occurred after my return to our Galilee home after a research and writing stint in Austin, Texas, and New York City. I had yet to meet several extraordinary Israelis, of different backgrounds, who swear that *Exodus* changed their lives; so, at home in Israel, the *Exodus* subject was ironically losing its immediacy. Stalled in an attempt to get from one chapter to the next, I drove down our mountain to the barbershop in Karmiel. The thought was that if I was losing hair anyway about *Exodus*, it might as well be done professionally.

Hagi, the barber, keeps a small, no-frills shop in the most run-down part of Karmiel, a Galilee town, but he invariably livens up the setting by regaling customers with stories from his life, which began in Lebanon and included a stint in Baltimore. Clipping away, Hagi mentioned during this haircut that while in his early twenties, half a century before, he had worked as a bellboy in a hotel in Haifa. I interrupted and said that I had heard of the hotel because the cast of the film *Exodus* had stayed in it during the shooting of the film. Like too many things I say, this comment came as a meaningless, pedantic non sequitur. Honestly, who in Israel has had time in the past fifty years to remember a movie that was not produced for the enlightenment and inspiration of the country's own population?

Faster than you can say Eva Marie Saint, the scissors stopped cutting. That not being the sort of silence that comforts you in a barbershop chair, I asked Hagi whether there was any sort of problem. He hesitated for a second, and then opened a table drawer, the one under the assorted, mostly unused hairbrushes that generations of men in barbershops have assumed is used to stash some illicit who-knows-what (condoms, a pistol, severed ears, the possibilities are endless). Out came a photograph of Hagi standing in bellboy dress at a table where various *Exodus* film stars are seated. I was so flabbergasted I ignored interesting details in the photograph (Sal Mineo, one might infer from this photograph, appears to have had a good time in Israel). But that was just the start.

Before I understood what was happening and why, Hagi was scrutinizing me for credibility, and overcoming fifty years of unease about a petty theft. He then pulled out something else from the table drawer—a copy of the *Exodus* film script! He explained that it had been left behind in one of the hotel rooms that he had been assigned to clean. The text had "confidential" warnings plastered all over it, but he was unable at the time to withstand temptation, and he pocketed the document; after half a century, he reasoned that the statute of limitations had expired on this liberty he had exercised as a bellboy. He was now ready to offer the forbidden fruit of his hotel employment to the scientific research community. I, naturally, concurred with his decision.

The reader might have noticed in this book a few instances in which having an original *Exodus* film script reinforced specific analytic points, though its usefulness in this respect had limits (the script apparently had belonged to an actor, who ripped out several pages on which he or she had no lines). Its utility exceeded this verification function. Obtaining the document transported a sense of the excitement Leon Uris's story generated across time and space, to a barbershop located just a few miles from our distant Galilee home. Hagi's eyes sparkled when he recalled his text-pilfering story, and I later came to recognize that same gleam on the faces of many Israelis of his generation who, as children or teenagers, surreptitiously flitted about the set encampments Preminger created in the country, which were entirely unlike anything Israelis had ever seen.

The hastily written, skimpy script projected just a fraction of the extraordinary detail and atmosphere that Preminger managed to pack into his film—but that fact was revealing. The script reenergized my research into how Uris's story exercised delayed but extremely strong responses. After he came to Israel, Otto Preminger obviously found much more in the *Exodus* story than he had expected to explore.

The same thing can be said both about my trip to Hagi's barbershop that day and broadly about my own research about Leon Uris and *Exodus*.

Upon the completion of this project, I have, in addition to Hagi, many people to thank for providing support needed for it to happen. Any errors in this text are my responsibility alone.

The Harry Ransom Center, at the University of Texas at Austin, holds Leon Uris's papers among its spectacular research resources. I thank Richard Workman and all other members of the center.

The Max Stern College of Emek Yezreel, my professional home, provided, as always, inspiration and practical support, starting with its president, and my own boss and mentor for the past decade, Professor Aliza Shenhar. Other senior college administrators, including Mika Kaptur, who authorized various requests, and Yoram Raz, who has his own memories of Preminger's film sets, helped with this book. I thank Shiri Berger, who in addition to helping us build a General Studies department from scratch, found time to drive here and there to help me on this project when my ankle was in a cast. Aviva Rafael, Hava Rembrand, and the rest of our college's superb library staff were, as ever, extraordinarily helpful.

Deborah Dash Moore, Frederick G. L. Huetwell Professor of History at the University of Michigan, read an early, raw version of this book before she had met me. I appreciated this collegial gesture, and the book profited on many levels from her thoughtful responses. Over the years I have had the privilege of maintaining contact with Jonathan Sarna, Joseph H. and Belle R. Braun Professor of American Jewish History at Brandeis University. With many others, I remain in debt to Sarna's learning and enthusiasm, and his advice about this project was very useful.

At an early stage in this project I sent an e-mail to one of my favorite college teachers from Cornell University's history department, R. Laurence Moore, the university's Howard A. Neuman Professor in American Studies. The e-mail related to an article on narratives we had discussed in a senior seminar at Cornell a quarter century earlier. The encouraging diligence of Moore's reply proved that nothing had changed in his distinguished department's learning ethos in twenty-five years. In this connection I should mention that lectures and writing produced by the department's Bryce & Edith M. Bowmar Professor in Humanistic Studies, Dominick LaCapra, initiated, for me, many years of reading and thinking about history and narrative.

I thank the University of Hartford's Maurice Greenberg Center for Judaic Studies and its indefatigable director, Richard Freund, for the invitations to teach a number of semesters and mini-semesters, which stimulated questions and interests related to this book. Thanks are due also to the Melton Center for Jewish Studies at the Ohio State University and its scholarly director, Matt Goldish, and to the large, lively history department at the Ohio State University, chaired ably by Peter Hahn, for providing an appealing professional home during the year when this book was brought to press.

I have received teaching and research awards and support over the years from the Joint Distribution Committee, the Schusterman Foundation, the American-Israeli Cooperation Enterprise, the American Jewish Archives, the Jewish Federation of Greater Hartford, and the Memorial Foundation for Jewish Culture. I thank them all.

I am not, in these acknowledgments, elaborating upon the help that friends and associates on kibbutzim, universities, the Israel Defense Forces, the Arab-Jewish "Galil" School, and many other places and institutions in Israel have furnished me, occasionally in relation to specific issues that arise in my professional work in Jewish History, and more generally. It suffices to say that this book, among other things, would never have happened if not for our shared love for learning and for our country.

Wayne State University Press was wonderful throughout the various stages of this book's publication. I owe very special thanks to the Press's editor-in-chief, Kathryn Wildfong, whose support for this project proved invincible.

Thanks to my father, David Silver, and stepmother, Ann Schwartz, are owed in innumerable ways, but I should mention that their generous loan of a Manhattan apartment jump-started the writing of this book.

Above all, thanks to the gang on Tuval—Melanie, Eitan, Galit, Talia, and Lior. Oh, and for Jimi, our wonder dog, with whom I tried out ideas and passages in our walks on the side of the mountain, many thanks for never having a word to say in criticism.

Notes

Introduction

1. The literature on post-Zionism is extensive. A programmatic essay announcing methodological intent to produce "new history" of Israel is: Benny Morris, "The New Historiography: Israel Confronts its Past," reprinted in Benny Morris, *1948 and After: Israel and the Palestinians* (Oxford: Clarendon Press, 1994), 1–48; originally in *Tikkun* 3, no. 6 (1988): 19–23, 99–102. A sample of early work in this critical history movement is: Simha Flapan, *The Birth of Israel: Myths and Realities* (New York: Pantheon Books, 1987); Baruch Kimmerling, *Zionism and Territory: The Socio-Territorial Dimensions of Zionist Politics* (Berkeley: Institute of International Studies, University of California, 1983); Avi Shlaim, *Collusion across the Jordan* (Oxford: Clarendon, 1988); Benny Morris, *Birth of the Palestinian Refugee Problem, 1947–1949* (New York: Cambridge University Press, 1987); Ilan Pappé, *Britain and the Arab-Israeli Conflict, 1948–1951* (New York: St. Martin's Press, 1988); Ilan Pappé, *The Making of the Arab-Israeli Conflict, 1947–1951* (New York: I. B. Tauris, 1994).

2. Morris, *Birth of the Palestinian Refugee Problem*.

3. By conceptualizing the 1948 war and its aftermath as an issue of narratives, one recent volume makes some headway in this direction: Robert Rotberg, ed., *Israeli and Palestinian Narratives of Conflict: History's Double Helix* (Bloomington: Indiana University Press, 2006).

4. In his groundbreaking *Birth of the Palestinian Refugee Problem*, Morris complained about the lack of availability of Arab-language sources. His claims in this respect are challenged by Efraim Karsh, *Fabricating Israeli History: The "New Historians"* (London: Frank Cass, 1997), 5–7.

5. Morris discussed the new historians' responsiveness to standard Zionist accounts of the 1948 Independence War in his "The New Historiography" essay. In more recent newspaper interviews and reports he appears to have moved closer, emotionally and ideologically, to this old narrative.

See Ari Shavit, "Mehakim l'barbarim" ("Waiting for the Barbarians"), *Haaretz* magazine, January 9, 2004; Scott Wilson, "Israel Revisited: Benny Morris, Veteran 'New Historian' of the Modern Jewish State's Founding, Finds Himself Ideologically Back Where It All Began," *Washington Post*, March 11, 2007, D1.

6. For differing views of Plan D: Morris, *Birth of the Palestinian Refugee Problem*; Walid Khalidi, "Plan Dalet: Master Plan for the Conquest of Palestine," *Journal of Palestine Studies* 18, no. 1, Special Issue: Palestine 1948 (1988): 4–33; Pappé, *The Making of the Arab-Israeli Conflict*, 87–99.

7. Pappé, *The Making of the Arab-Israeli Conflict*, 94.

8. The *New York Times* fiction bestseller lists: October 12, 1958; November 8, 1958; December 2, 1958; March 8, 1959; May 1, 1959. *New York Herald Tribune* bestseller lists: October 17, 1958; November 23, 1958; February 1, 1959; May 14, 1959; July 12, 1959; August 2, 1959.

9. *Shreveport Times*, September 27, 1959.

10. Aviva Halamish, "*Exodus*: A Film That Changed History" [Hebrew], in *Cinema and Memory: A Dangerous Relationship?* ed. Haim Bresheeth, Shlomo Sand, and Moshe Zimmermann (Jerusalem: Merkaz Zalman Shazar, 2004), 341.

11. Two articles that challenge factual descriptions in the *Exodus* novel are: Jeremy Salt, "Fact and Fiction in the Middle Eastern Novels of Leon Uris," *Journal of Palestinian Studies* 14, no. 3 (1985): 54–63; and Halamish, "*Exodus*: A Film That Changed History." Scholarly publications relating to the *Exodus* book and film, and Uris's life and writing, include: Kathleen Shine Cain, *Leon Uris: A Critical Companion* (Westport, CT: Greenwood Press, 1998); Rachel Weissbrod, "*Exodus* as a Zionist Melodrama," *Israel Studies* 4, no. 1 (1999): 129–52; Deborah Dash Moore, *To the Golden Cities: Pursuing the American Jewish Dream in Miami and L.A.* (Cambridge, MA: Harvard University Press, 1996), 248–60; Andrew Furman, "Embattled Uris: A Look Back at *Exodus*," in Andrew Furman, *Israel through the Jewish-American Imagination: A Survey of Jewish-American Literature on Israel, 1928–1955* (Albany: State University of New York Press, 1997), 39–57; Stephen Whitfield, "Israel as Reel: The Depiction of Israel in Mainstream American Films," in *Envisioning Israel: The Changing Ideals and Images of North American Jews,* ed. Allon Gal (Detroit: Wayne State University Press, 1996), 293–308; Foster Hirsch, *Otto Preminger: The Man Who Would Be King* (New York: Alfred A. Knopf, 2007), 321–42; Halamish, "*Exodus*: A Film That Changed History."

12. Halamish, "*Exodus*: A Film That Changed History."

13. Furman, "Embattled Uris," 46–53.

14. Benedict Anderson, *Imagined Communities: Reflections on the Origin and Spread of Nationalism* (London: Verso, 1991); Ernest Gellner, *Na-*

tionalism (London: Weidenfeld and Nicolson, 1997); Eric Hobsbawm and Terence Ranger, eds., *The Invention of Tradition* (Cambridge: Cambridge University Press, 1984).

Chapter 1

1. See Uris's remarks on Steinbeck in an address delivered at the Smithsonian Institution, October 24, 1988; Leon Uris Papers (hereafter LUP), located in the Harry Ransom Humanities Research Center at the University of Texas at Austin, 181.9.

2. See the final chapter, "After *Exodus*."

3. Ernst Pawel, *The Labyrinth of Exile: A Life of Theodor Herzl* (New York: Farrar, Straus, Giroux, 1989).

4. From the mid-nineteenth century onward, Jewish journals were a prime vehicle in the growth of Jewish political consciousness. See Eli Lederhendler, *The Road to Modern Jewish Politics* (New York: Oxford University Press, 1989), 119–33. Also G. Kressel, *A History of Hebrew Journalism in Eretz Israel* (Jerusalem: Hasifriya Hatzionit, 1964) [Hebrew].

5. Anita Shapira, *Berl: The Biography of a Socialist Zionist, Berl Katznelson, 1887–1944* (New York: Cambridge University Press, 1984), 137–50; Shmuel Katz, *Lone Wolf: A Biography of Vladimir (Ze'ev) Jabotinsky* (New York: Barricade Books, 1996), 32–37.

6. Michael Berkowitz, *Western Jewry and the Zionist Project, 1914– 1933* (Cambridge: Cambridge University Press, 1997), 99.

7. Michael Brown, *The Israeli-American Connection: Its Roots in the Yishuv, 1914–1945* (Detroit: Wayne State University Press, 1996).

8. Tom Segev, *One Palestine, Complete: Jews and Arabs under the British Mandate* (New York: Henry Holt, 2001), 217–20.

9. Ben Halpern, *A Clash of Heroes: Brandeis, Weizmann, and American Zionism* (New York: Oxford University Press, 1987).

10. Peter Grose, *Israel in the Mind of America* (New York: Schocken, 1984), 74.

11. Herbert Parzen, "The Magnes-Weizmann-Einstein Controversy," *Jewish Social Studies* 32 (July 1970): 187–213.

12. Berkowitz, *Western Jewry*, 51.

13. Matthew Silver, *First Contact: Origins of the American-Israeli Connection* (West Hartford, CT: Graduate Group, 2006), 164.

14. Deborah Dash Moore, *At Home in America: Second Generation New York Jews* (New York: Columbia University Press, 1981); Melvin Urofsky, *American Zionism from Herzl to the Holocaust* (Garden City, NY: Anchor Press, 1975), 299–372.

15. Ezra Mendelsohn, *The Jews of East Central Europe between the World Wars* (Bloomington: Indiana University Press, 1983), 68–83.

16. For examples of the interesting but neglected work of these two fig-

ures: Jessie Sampter, *The Emek* (New York: Bloch Publishing, 1927); Jessie Sampter, ed., *Modern Palestine* (New York: Hadassah, the Women's Zionist Organization of America, 1933); Maurice Samuel, *Harvest in the Desert* (Philadelphia: Jewish Publication Society of America, 1944). Sampter spent the last years of her life in Rehovot, and left behind unpublished manuscripts that are filled with information and insights about American Zionism and life in Mandatory Palestine—the oblivion that envelopes these draft texts symbolizes the dynamic traced above. See Matthew Silver, "A Cultural Model for America—Holy Land Studies," in *America and Zion: Essays and Papers in Memory of Moshe Davis,* ed. Eli Lederhendler and Jonathan Sarna (Detroit: Wayne State University Press, 2002), 179–80; Bertha Badt-Straus, *White Fire: The Life and Works of Jessie Sampter* (New York: Reconstructionist Press, 1956); Joyce Antler, *The Journey Home: Jewish Women and the American Century* (New York: Free Press 1997), 109–21.

17. Ralph Melnick, *The Life and Work of Ludwig Lewisohn: A Touch of Wildness* (Detroit: Wayne State University Press, 1998), 382.

18. Ibid., 407.

19. Urofsky, *American Zionism from Herzl to the Holocaust.*

20. Aaron Berman, *Nazism, the Jews, and American Zionism* (Detroit: Wayne State University Press, 1990); Menahem Kaufman, *Ambiguous Partnership: Non-Zionists and Zionists in America, 1939–1948* (Detroit: Wayne State University Press, 1991); David Shpiro, *From Philanthropy to Activism: The Political Transformation of American Zionism in the Holocaust Years* (New York: Pergamon Press, 1994).

21. Emanuel Neumann, *In the Arena: An Autobiographical Memoir* (New York: Herzl Press, 1976).

22. David Wyman and Rafael Medoff, *A Race against Death: Peter Bergson, America, and the Holocaust (*New York: New Press, 2002); Judith Baumel, *The "Bergson Boys" and the Origins of Contemporary Zionist Militancy* (Syracuse, NY: Syracuse University Press, 2005).

23. Stephen Whitfield, "The Politics of Pageantry, 1936–1946," *American Jewish History* 84, no. 3 (1996): 221.

24. Wyman and Medoff, *A Race against Death,* 71–73; Moore, *To the Golden Cities,* 15–16; Whitfield, "The Politics of Pageantry," 234–44.

25. Whitfield, "The Politics of Pageantry," 242.

26. Ibid., 244.

27. The following information on *A Flag Is Born* relies on Rafael Medoff, "Ben Hecht's 'A Flag Is Born': A Play That Changed History," published by the David S. Wyman Institute for Holocaust Studies, April 2004, at http://www.wymaninstitute.org/articles/2004-04-flagisborn.php.

28. Hecht, incidentally, is credited with virtually inventing the gangster film genre—see Whitfield, "The Politics of Pageantry," 235.

29. Ben Hecht, *A Child of the Century* (New York: Simon and Schuster, 1954); Whitfield, "The Politics of Pageantry," 235–36.

30. For the origins of Hecht's connection with the Bergson group, see Hillel Kook's reminiscence in Wyman, *A Race against Death,* 89, and Hecht's account in Hecht, *Child of the Century,* 516.

31. Medoff, "Ben Hecht's 'A Flag Is Born.'"

32. Whitfield, "The Politics of Pageantry," 248.

33. Ultimately, Hecht's flamboyantly anti-British publicity work—in one open letter, the writer celebrated Irgun terror attacks on British targets in Palestine, saying that each was a "little holiday" for Jews in America— "tarnished much of the good will that 'A Flag Is Born' had earned." Whitfield, "The Politics of Pageantry," 250.

34. Ibid.

35. Wyman, *A Race against Death,* 103.

36. Whitfield, "The Politics of Pageantry," 250–51.

37. This difference between the 1946 pageant and Uris's *Exodus* is illustrated by the circumstances of the two brooding, semisuicidal concentration camp survivors, David in *A Flag Is Born,* and Dov Landau in *Exodus*—unlike the situation of the prestate pageant, *Exodus*'s narrative portrayed the transformation of the young survivor as a heroic Israeli.

38. Deborah Dash Moore, "Reconsidering the Rosenbergs: Symbol and Substance in Second Generation American Jewish Consciousness," *Journal of American Ethnic History* 8, no. 1 (1988): 21–37; Bruce Afran, "The American Republic vs. Julius and Ethel Rosenberg," in *Jews on Trial,* ed. Robert Garber (Jersey City, NJ: Ktav, 2005), 163–201.

39. Loyalty, anxiety, and foreign policy, issues relating to the America-Israel connection in the 1950s, are discussed in Zvi Ganin, *Uneasy Relationship: American Jewish Leadership and Israel, 1948–1957* (Syracuse, NY: Syracuse University Press, 2005); Peter Hahn, *Caught in the Middle East: U.S. Policy toward the Arab-Israeli Conflict, 1945–1961* (Chapel Hill: University of North Carolina Press, 2004); Douglas Little, *American Orientalism: The United States and the Middle East since 1945* (Chapel Hill: University of North Carolina Press, 2002), 77–92; Robert Kaplan, *The Arabists: The Romance of an American Elite* (New York: Free Press, 1993).

40. Grose, *Israel in the Mind of America,* 303. For an interpretation stressing President Eisenhower's "limited understanding of American Jewry's attitude and concern for Israel," see Isaac Alteras, "Eisenhower, American Jewry, and Israel," *American Jewish Archives* 37, no. 2 (1985): 257–74.

41. J. J. Goldberg, *Jewish Power: Inside the American Jewish Establishment* (Reading, MA: Addison-Wesley, 1996), 153. See also Isaiah Kenen, *Israel's Defense Line: Her Friends and Foes in Washington* (Buffalo, NY: Prometheus Books, 1981).

42. Kenen, *Israel's Defense Line,* 110.

43. Ganin, *Uneasy Relationship,* 131–41.

44. Ariel Feldestein, *Ben-Gurion, Zionism and American Jewry, 1948–1963* (London: Routledge, 2006).

45. For the Ben-Gurion/Blaustein correspondence, see Ganin, *Uneasy Relationship*, 81–104. Also Yossi Beilin, *His Brother's Keeper: Israel and Diaspora Jewry in the Twenty-First Century* (New York: Schocken Books, 2000).

46. Ganin, *Uneasy Relationship*, 103–4.

47. For the waning of organized American Zionism after 1948: Melvin Urofsky, "A Cause in Search of Itself: American Zionism after the State," in *American Jewish History*, vol. 8, ed. Jeffrey Gurock (New York: Routledge, 1998), 451–63; Melvin Urofsky, *We Are One! American Jewry and Israel* (Garden City, NY: Anchor Press, 1978), 1–322; Marc Lee Raphael, *Abba Hillel Silver* (New York: Holmes and Meier, 1989); Mark Raider, Jonathan Sarna, and Ronald Zweig, eds., *Abba Hillel Silver and American Zionism* (London: Frank Cass, 1997).

48. Zohar Segev, "American Zionists in the State of Israel in the 1950s—A Liberal, Political Option," *Iyunim B'Tkumat Yisrael* 12 (2002): 493–519 [Hebrew]; Zohar Segev, "American Zionists' Place in Israel after Statehood: From Involved Partners to Outside Supporters," *American Jewish History* 93, no. 3 (2007): 277–302.

49. For discussions of Rabbi Silver's motivations and decisions, see Michael Meyer, "Abba Hillel Silver as Zionist within the Camp of Reform Judaism," *Journal of Israeli History* 17, no. 1 (1996); 9–31; Hasia Diner, "Zion and America: The Formative Visions of Abba Hillel Silver," *Journal of Israeli History* 17, no. 1 (1996): 45–69, and reprinted in the Raider, Sarna, and Zweig volume.

50. Albert Gordon, *Jews in Suburbia* (Boston: Beacon Press, 1959), 224–25.

51. For influence of this survey: Peter Medding, "Segmented Ethnicity and the New Jewish Politics," *Studies in Contemporary Jewry* 3 (1987): 34.

52. Marshall Sklare and Joseph Greenblum, *Jewish Identity on the Suburban Frontier: A Study of Group Survival in the Open Society* (New York: Basic Books, 1967), 322.

53. Ibid., 214–49. When the Lakeville researchers posed the question, "If the Arab nations should succeed in carrying out their threat to destroy Israel, would you feel a very deep, some, or no personal sense of loss?" 90 percent of the respondents confirmed that they would have a sense of loss; of these, 65 percent said it would be a "very deep" sense of loss" (p. 215).

54. Goldberg, *Jewish Power*, 147–48.

55. Philip Roth, *Goodbye, Columbus* (New York: World, 1959).

56. Riv-Ellen Prell, "Community and the Discourse of Elegy: The Postwar Suburban Debate," in *Imagining the American Jewish Community*, ed. Jack Wertheimer (Hanover, NH: University Press of New England and

the Jewish Theological Seminary of America, 2007), 67–90.

57. Prell's argument about the nostalgic orientation of Jewish self-validation in the suburbanizing 1950s follows points raised in Eli Lederhendler, *New York Jews and the Decline of Urban Ethnicity, 1950–1970* (Syracuse, NY: Syracuse University Press, 2001).

58. Karen Brodkin, *How Jews Became White Folks and What That Says about Race in America* (New Brunswick, NJ: Rutgers University Press, 1998); Eric Goldstein, *The Price of Whiteness: Jews, Race, and American Identity* (Princeton, NJ: Princeton University Press, 2006).

59. Norman Podhoretz, "My Negro Problem—And Ours," *Commentary* 35 (February 1963): 93–101; Michael Staub, *Torn at the Roots: The Crisis of Jewish Liberalism in Postwar America* (New York: Columbia University Press, 2002), 70–75.

60. Brodkin, *How Jews Became White Folks*, 162. Another scholar puts the point in general terms: "The young Jewish woman's image was shaped by men to express their struggles with American Jewish life." Riv-Ellen Prell, "Cinderellas Who (Almost) Never Became Princesses: Subversive Representations of Jewish Women in Postwar Popular Novels," in *Talking Back: Images of Jewish Women in American Popular Culture,* ed. Joyce Antler (Hanover, NH: University Press of New England, 1998), 124.

61. Alfred Kazin, *A Walker in the City* (New York: Harcourt, Brace, 1951); Lederhendler, *New York Jews and the Decline of Urban Ethnicity.*

62. For a discussion of the decline of Jewish "urban utopia" in this period, see Lederhendler, *New York Jews and the Decline of Urban Ethnicity.*

63. Jeremy D. Popkin, "A Forgotten Forerunner: Zelda Popkin's Novels of the Holocaust and the 1948 War," *Shofar: An Interdisciplinary Journal of Jewish Studies* 20, no. 1 (2001): 50–51.

64. Zelda Popkin, *Quiet Street* (1951; Lincoln: University of Nebraska Press, 2002).

65. Background biographical information draws on Jeremy Popkin's article "A Forgotten Forerunner," 36–60.

66. See, for instance, Bartov's *Regel Echat B'hutz* [One Leg Out] (Tel Aviv: Am Oved, 1994) [Hebrew].

67. Popkin, "A Forgotten Forerunner," 45.

68. Mel Scult, *Judaism Faces the Twentieth Century: A Biography of Mordechai M. Kaplan* (Detroit: Wayne State University Press, 1993), 316. Scult writes that "Kaplan had significant involvement with the organized Zionist movement in America"; he was, however, ambivalent about the depth of his daughter Judith's passion for Zionism.

69. David Kaufman, *Shul with a Pool: The "Synagogue Center" in American Jewish History* (Hanover: University Press of New England, 1999); Moore, *At Home in America,* 133–47.

70. Mordecai Kaplan, *A New Zionism* (New York: Herzl Press, 1959).

Chapter 2

1. Kathleen Shine Cain, *Leon Uris: A Critical Companion* (Westport, CT: Greenwood Press, 1998). One example of the disinterest in Uris's biography can be found in Halamish's essay *"Exodus:* A Film That Changed History," which cogently exposes gaps between the *Exodus* story's portrayal of facts and the actual history of illegal immigration and other Zionist efforts. This article (p. 346) identifies Uris as a "military correspondent in Israel" at the time of the 1956 Sinai Campaign—as shown in this chapter, this way of characterizing Uris's work in Israel, during his crucial research trip that produced *Exodus,* is rather misleading.

2. Uris Riga speech, LUP 149.6.

3. Information in this section is culled from an unpublished memoir prepared by Uris's father: "William Uris Yerushalmi Memoir," LUP 185.4.

4. Information here about Uris's parents is based on descriptions in Leon Uris, *Mitla Pass* (New York: Doubleday, 1988).

5. Ibid., 219–89.

6. See the inside cover page, "Leon Uris Says," in paperback editions of *Exodus.* In private correspondence, Uris frequently attested that one aim of *Exodus* was the "complete destruction" of "apologetic" descriptions of "psychologically tormented" characters in American Jewish fiction authored by Herman Wouk, Norman Mailer, and others. Uris letter to his father, June 25, 1956, LUP 137.7; Uris letter to his father, September 17, 1957, LUP 137.8.

7. Uris, *Mitla Pass,* 219–89.

8. Analyses of American Jewish writing through World War II emphasize ways in which notions of America as a welcoming home for Jewish success were explored with varying degrees of enthusiasm. See, for instance, Lewis Fried, ed., *Handbook of American-Jewish Literature: An Analytical Guide to Topics, Themes, and Sources* (New York: Greenwood Press, 1988), 1–57.

9. Information in this paragraph is from "William Uris Yerushalmi Memoir," LUP 185.4

10. Ibid.

11. Leon Uris, *QB VII* (Garden City, NY: Doubleday, 1970). This novel attributes part of the success enjoyed by the autobiographical, Uris-like character (Abraham Cady) to the teaching provided by an English editor-publisher named David Shawcross.

12. Uris Riga speech: Dor le'dor mission, October 15, 1989, LUP 149.6.

13. Ibid.

14. "William Uris Yerushalmi Memoir," LUP 185.4

15. Leon Uris, *Battle Cry* (New York: Putnam, 1953).

16. Kenneth Davis, *Two-Bit Culture: The Paperbacking of America* (Boston: Houghton Mifflin, 1984).

17. Ibid., 146, 178.

18. Ibid., 121–23.

19. Ibid., 253.

20. Ibid., 126.

21. Deborah Dash Moore, *GI Jews: How World War II Changed a Generation* (Cambridge MA: Belknap Press, 2004).

22. Uris, *Battle Cry,* 414–15.

23. See the *Battle Cry* drafts, LUP 15, 16.

24. Eliezer Yerushalmi was an important chronicler of the Holocaust. See his *Pinkas Shavli: A Diary from a Lithuanian Diary* (Jerusalem: Mosad Bialik, 1958) [Hebrew].

25. Eliezer Yerushalmi, "Leon Uris in Israel," *Ma'ariv,* April 20, 1956 [Hebrew].

26. Ibid.

27. Uris letter to his father, May 13, 1956, LUP 137.7.

28. Uris Riga speech, LUP 149.6.

29. Aaron Yerushalmi's *Hellenic Interlude* manuscript is located in LUP 1.4–1.6.

30. Jewish Book Guild of America to Uris, June 4, 1947, LUP, 1.6.

31. Aaron Yerushalmi, *Hellenic Interlude,* LUP 1.4–1.6. It bears mention that Aaron Yerushalmi's riveting, published Hebrew version of his war experiences, *Shlosha sh'barchu* (Tel Aviv: Ayanot, 1957) does not emphasize the hardships endured specifically by *Jewish* POWs in Nazi occupied areas and in Germany. The preface to the Hebrew volume contains a note about 1,600 soldiers from the Palestine Brigade who were captured on April 28, 1941, in Greece; the text itself contains little information about these soldiers and does not provide information about the narrator's (Aaron's) life and relatives in the Jewish prestate community in Palestine, the Yishuv. This published Hebrew version contains some of the references to anti-Semitic jailhouse propaganda cited in the 1947 manuscript that Leon Uris tried to sell. The most conspicuous "Israeli" addition to the 1957 Hebrew memoir is Yerushalmi's suggestion that he was betrayed after one of his escapes in Greece by a Palestinian Arab who also served in the British army.

Later in his life, Aaron Yerushalmi published fiction, including disparaging pieces about American Jewish life (see his *Beaufort* collection of stories [Tel Aviv: Golan, 1991], 57–96).

32. Aaron Yerushalmi, *Shlosha sh'barchu* [*Three Who Escaped*] (Tel Aviv: Ayanot, 1957).

33. Leon Uris, *The Angry Hills* (New York: Random House, 1955).

34. For reviews of *The Angry Hills:* LUP 168.

35. Uris letter to his father, January 24, 1975, LUP 138.2.

36. Eliezer Yerushalmi's *Pinkas Shavli* was published in 1958 (the year of *Exodus*'s release) under Yad Vashem auspices as an inaugural volume in a ghetto chronicle series. Whereas Leon Uris stressed heroic uprisings and other militant responses to Nazi oppression, Yerushalmi's *Pinkas* provides a realistic, day-to-day account of coping strategies in a Holocaust ghetto

and shuns literary dramatization—in this sense, I suggest, the uncle and nephew were engaged in mirror-image writing about the Holocaust.

37. Uris letter to his father, undated—apparently April 1956, LUP 137.7.

38. The Holocaust, one sociologist writes, "played an extremely important role" in the strengthening both of an "anti-Diaspora" ethos in post-1948 Israel and of the native-born sabra's "sense of superiority." Oz Almog, *The Sabra: The Creation of the New Jew* (Berkeley: University of California Press 2000), 82. For a description of negative conceptualizations of Diaspora (*Galut*) life, which heavily influenced Zionist thinking, see Arnold Eisen, *Galut: Modern Jewish Reflection on Homelessness and Homecoming* (Bloomington: Indiana University Press, 1986). For a critical discussion in Hebrew of the Zionist conceptualization of the "negation of the Diaspora," see Raz-Krakotzkin, "Galut me'toh ribonut: L'bikoret 'shlilat hagalut' b'tarbut hayisraalit," *Theory and Criticism* 4 (1993): 23–55; (1994): 113–32.

39. Almog, *The Sabra*, 82.

40. Uris letter to his father, March 4, 1958, LUP 137.8.

41. Ibid.

42. The term *Irgun* is a shorthand version of the Hebrew HaIrgun HaTzva'I HaLe'umi B'Eretz Yisrael (National Military Organization of the Land of Israel) and is also called *Etzel*. The right-wing militia was affiliated with the Revisionist Zionist movement and operated from 1931 to 1948.

43. For a survey of some of the dates and terms used in evolving observances of Holocaust Remembrance Day in Israel, and the attitudes these calendar days and names reflect, see Matthew Wagner, "An Anchor for National Mourning," *Jerusalem Post,* April 28, 2008.

44. Historical information in this section draws upon Aviva Halamish's study, which is the most thorough history of the *Exodus* ship episode. The Hebrew version, *Exodus: HaSippur ha-Amiti* (Tel Aviv: Tel-Aviv University, 1990), is authoritative, but for quotations here I have used the study's English translation: Aviva Halamish, *The* Exodus *Affair: Holocaust Survivors and the Struggle for Palestine* (Syracuse, NY: Syracuse University Press, 1998). Other *Exodus* ship accounts used in this section are cited in these notes.

45. Halamish, *The* Exodus *Affair,* 78. Evidence suggesting that Yigal Allon was the prototype for Ari Ben Canaan is circumstantial but draws upon an extremely enthusiastic report about a meeting with the Palmach hero Uris sent to his father on March 8, 1956, in the period when he was starting research for *Exodus.* See Uris letter to his father, March 8, 1956, LUP 137.2. For speculation about other real-life figures who might have served as models for *Exodus*'s sabra hero, see Halamish, *Exodus:* The Film That Changed History," 345–46.

46. Ruth Gruber, Exodus *1947: The Ship That Launched a Nation*

(1948; New York: Times Books, 1999), 51.

47. Halamish, *The* Exodus *Affair,* 167.

48. As Emmanuel Sivan shows, in the 1948 struggle the differences between these two categories, native-born sabras and Jewish youths who had been socialized in the prestate Yishuv, were minimal. Emmanuel Sivan, *Dor Tashah: Mitos, Deyokan, Ve-Zikaron* (Tel Aviv: Ma'arakhot, 1991) [Hebrew].

49. Except where noted, information about Americans on the *Exodus* is drawn from Halamish, *The* Exodus *Affair,* 15–25.

50. Gruber, Exodus *1947,* 85.

51. Ibid.

52. Halamish, *The* Exodus *Affair,* 23.

53. Uris letter to his father, September 25, 1956, LUP 137.7.

54. Information about *Exodus*'s passengers relies on Halamish, *The* Exodus *Affair,* 43–52.

55. Gruber, Exodus *1947,* 139.

56. The ensuing discussion about circumstances in DP camps and surveys of survivor inclinations draws from Yosef Grodzinsky, *Good Human Material* (Tel Aviv: Hed Artsi, 1998) [Hebrew].

57. Ibid., 143.

58. Ibid., 99.

59. Ibid., 114.

60. Ibid., 115.

61. Halamish, *The* Exodus *Affair,* 261–62.

62. Ibid.

63. Ibid., 248.

64. Foster Hirsch, *Otto Preminger: The Man Who Would Be King* (New York: Alfred A. Knopf, 2007), 15.

65. Ibid., 23.

66. Ibid., 47.

67. This and subsequent references in this study to the *Exodus* film script are taken from the March 22, 1960, version. My thanks to Hagi, formerly of the Zion Hotel, Haifa, for help in obtaining this script.

68. Ibid.

69. Tom Segev, *The Seventh Million: The Israelis and the Holocaust* (New York: Hill and Wang, 1993), 130.

70. Halamish, *The* Exodus *Affair,* 79.

71. Ibid., 67–68.

72. Ibid., 67. Interestingly, the much-photographed sign held on the ship's side by ma'apalim conveyed only the English name, "Hagannah Ship/Exodus 1947. The Hebrew, which lacks the universal appeal of the English, was superimposed in later versions of the photo (for an explanation, see the Hebrew version of Segev, *The Seventh Million* (Jerusalem: Keter, 1991), 117.

73. Halamish, *The* Exodus *Affair,* 69.

74. Ibid., 198.

75. Segev, *Seventh Million* (English), 131–32.

76. Information about this meeting drawn from Halamish, *The* Exodus *Affair,* 197.

77. *Pittsburgh Post Gazette,* February 23, 1959, LUP 170.

78. Uris Riga speech, October 15, 1989, LUP 149.6.

79. Leon Uris, *Trinity* (Garden City, NY: Doubleday, 1976).

80. One example of such speculation about *Exodus*'s success being manipulated by hidden forces is Midge Decter's 1961 *Commentary* review of Uris's writing—this future neocon luminary wrote that the *Exodus* novel's "early sales were modest though steady, and then somehow suddenly mushroomed beyond a publisher's wildest fantasies" (what exactly did the "somehow" in this remark refer to?). Midge Decter, "Popular Jews," *Commentary* (October 1961): 358. Another example was the writer Meyer Levin, who groused in 1959 that *Exodus* was breaking sales records thanks to the well-oiled machinery of the Hadassah organization. *Southern Israelite,* June 11, 1959, LUP 170.

81. Uris letter to his father, undated, late 1955, LUP 137.7.

82. As soon as he took up writing after his discharge from the marines, Uris confided to his half-sister Essie about his hopes to "make a million" from best-selling fiction. See his undated letters to Essie in LUP 137.5.

83. Uris letter to his father, January 19, 1956, LUP 137.7.

84. Willi Frischauer, *Behind the Scenes of Otto Preminger* (New York: Morrow, 1973), 179.

85. Schary never publicly suggested that his input on *Exodus* was particularly important. His silence regarding *Exodus* in his memoir, *Heyday,* is suggestive, since normal self-interest or spiteful motives would have encouraged him to highlight his proactive role in signing up Uris for *Exodus,* had there been one—after all, Schary was ousted as MGM chief in 1956, and the studio subsequently blundered when it surrendered the rights to *Exodus,* a profitable product, to Preminger and United Artists. For his part, Uris admired Schary as a man with spine. As far as Uris was concerned, Schary held his ground both in liberal politics and in a film studio that was crawling with cheap sycophants. Dore Schary, *Heyday: An Autobiography* (Boston: Little, Brown, 1979).

86. Uris letter to his father, February 8, 1956, LUP 137.7.

87. Uris letter to Esther Kofsky, undated, 1948, LUP 137.5.

88. LUP 156.1.

89. Ibid.

90. Ibid.

91. "William Uris Yerushalmi Memoir," LUP 185.4.

92. LUP 25.1.

93. Among other titles, Uris read *Forgotten Ally,* by the journalist Pierre Van Passen; J. C. Hurewitz's *Struggle for Palestine;* Sumner Welles's *We Need Not Fail;* Joseph Tenenbaum's *Underground: The Story of a People;*

and treatises and pamphlets on Labor Zionist farm collectives written by Eliezer Joffe and Shmuel Dayan and on Israel's Knesset by Moshe Rosetti. LUP 25.1, 25.2, 25.3.

94. Ibid.

95. Uris letter to his father, March 31, 1956, LUP 137.7.

96. LUP 168.

97. *L'Isha* July 25, 1956 [Hebrew], LUP 168.

98. Uris letter to his father, April [undated] 1956, LUP 137.7.

99. Uris letter to his father, April 27, 1956, LUP 137.7.

100. LUP 25.3.

101. Hartuv's daughter died in 2001 in a tragic accident when a Jerusalem banquet hall collapsed. Or Heller, "Goodnight, Ayelet," *Ma'ariv* (NRG), May 29, 2001.

102. LUP 25.3.

103. From United Artists release, undated, LUP 25.7.

104. LUP 25.3, 25.7.

105. Uris letter to his father, May 14, 1956.

106. Uris letter to his father, June 25, 1956, LUP 137.7; Uris letter to his father, September 17, 1957, LUP 137.8.

107. Uris letter to editor, September 25, 1956, LUP 137.7.

108. Ibid.

109. Ibid.

110. Uris letters to his father, July 23, 1956; September 20, 1956, LUP 137.7.

111. Uris letter to his father September 20, 1956, ibid.

112. Uris letters to his father, February 2, 1957; March 13, 1957, LUP 137.8.

113. Uris letter to his father, March 13, 1957, ibid.

114. Uris letter to William Bradbury, managing editor, Doubleday and Company, April 22, 1957, LUP 135.6.

115. Uris letter to his father, April 25, 1957, LUP 137.8.

116. Ibid.

117. Uris letter to his father September 25, 1956, LUP 137.7.

118. Motti Golani, *Israel in Search of a War: The Sinai Campaign, 1955–1956* (Brighton: Sussex Academic Press, 1998).

119. For an interpretation pointing to an array of motives—family repatriation, property recovery and crop cultivation, ideological hostility, and more—underlying the border crossings in the 1950s, see Benny Morris, *Israel's Border Wars, 1949–1956* (Oxford: Clarendon Press, 1993).

120. Golani, *Israel in Search of a War*, 181.

121. Mordechai Bar-On, *The Gates of Gaza: Israel's Road to Suez and Back, 1955–1957* (New York: St. Martin's Press, 1994), 17.

122. Golani, *Israel in Search of a War*, 183.

123. Ibid., 188–89.

124. Bar-On, *Gates of Gaza*, 244.

125. Ibid., 319–21.

126. Ibid., 244.

127. Uris cable to *Philadelphia Inquirer*, undated, late October 1956, LUP 25.6.

128. Ibid.

129. Uris's 1956 war adventure can be compared to Saul Bellow's experiences and responses during the Six Day War. See Eli Lederhendler, *New York Jews and the Decline of Urban Ethnicity, 1950–1970* (Syracuse, NY: Syracuse University Press, 2001), 189–90.

130. For Uris's Sinai Campaign dispatches, see "Blitz Described by Noted Author," *San Francisco Examiner*, November 14, 1956, and London *Internews* report, in LUP 168, LUP 25.6.

131. Uris, *Mitla Pass*.

132. See discussion of Uris's *The Haj* in the final chapter of this book.

133. Uris's unpublished autobiographical memoir, LUP 152.1.

134. Uris letter to Bradbury, April 22, 1957, LUP 135.6.

135. For Uris settling in Encino, see letters in LUP 137.8 (in particular, December 10, 1957, Uris letter to father).

136. Uris letter to his father, April 25, 1957, LUP 137.8.

137. Ibid.

138. Uris letter to Bradbury, June 4, 1958, LUP 135.6.

139. Geoffrey Godsell, *Christian Science Monitor*, December 4, 1958. LUP 168.

140. Leon Uris, *Mila 18* (Garden City, NY: Doubleday, 1961).

141. Uris letter to Doubleday editor, April 30, 1959, LUP 137.7.

142. Nachman Ben-Yehuda, *The Masada Myth: Collective Memory and Mythmaking in Israel* (Madison: University of Wisconsin Press, 1995).

143. Uris letter to Doubleday editor, April 30, 1959, LUP 137.7.

144. Leon Uris, *Exodus Revisited* (Garden City, NY: Doubleday, 1960).

145. Letter from Moshe Pearlman to Uris, July 22, 1958, LUP 135.6.

146. For Pearlman and his work in Ben-Gurion's office: David Ben-Gurion, *Ben Gurion Looks Back in Talks with Moshe Pearlman* (New York: Simon and Schuster, 1965).

147. Letter from Pearlman to Uris, July 22, 1958.

148. Bradbury letter to Samuel Vaughan, August 13, 1958, LUP 168.

149. Ibid.

150. Uris, *QB VII*.

151. Deborah Lipstadt, *History on Trial: My Day in Court with David Irving* (New York: Ecco, 2005).

152. Transcript: Wladyslaw Alexander Dering v. Leon Uris and Purnell Sons, High Court of Justice, Queen's Bench Division, 13th April 1964, LUP 69.

153. Ibid.

154. Joseph Tenenbaum, *Underground: The Story of a People* (New York: Philosophical Library, 1952).

155. Joseph Tenenbaum, *Ben Milhamah v'Shalom* [*Between War and Peace*] (Jerusalem, 1960), 40–93 [Hebrew].

156. Ibid., 273.

157. Uris's unpublished autobiographical memoir, LUP 152.1.

158. For an account of the trial: Mavis Hill and Norman Williams, *Auschwitz in England: A Record of a Libel Action* (London: MacGibbon and Kee, 1965).

Chapter 3

1. Jonathan Sarna, "The Cult of Synthesis in American Jewish Culture," *Jewish Social Studies* 5 (Fall/Winter 1998/1999): 52–79.

2. Charles Liebman and Steven Cohen, *Two Worlds of Judaism: The Israeli and American Experiences* (New Haven, CT: Yale University Press, 1990).

3. The differences in the 1950s political-cultural life of these two post-Holocaust Jewish centers are striking. For analyses of American Jewish life in this period: Arthur Goren, "A 'Golden Decade' for American Jews, 1945–1955," *Studies in Contemporary Jewry* 8 (1992): 3–20; Deborah Dash Moore, *To the Golden Cities: Pursuing the American Jewish Dream in Miami and L.A.* (New York: Free Press, 1994). Conversely, a sample of the politics and culture of Israel in this period is: Tom Segev, *1949: The First Israelis* (New York: Free Press, 1986); Eli Amir, *Tarnagol Kaparot* (Tel Aviv: Am Oved, 1983) [Hebrew].

4. Peter Grose, *Israel in the Mind of America* (New York: Schocken, 1984); Moshe Davis, "The Holy Land Idea in American Spiritual History," in *With Eyes Toward Zion*, vol. 1, ed. Moshe Davis (New York, 1977), 3–34; Michael Brown, "Moshe Davis and the New Field of America-Holy Land Studies," in *America and Zion: Essays and Papers in Memory of Moshe Davis*, ed. Eli Lederhendler and Jonathan Sarna (Detroit: Wayne State University Press, 2002), 39–48. For an important recent scholarly contribution to this examination of connections between America's founding and biblical, Hebraic culture: Shalom Goldman, *God's Sacred Tongue: Hebrew and the American Imagination* (Chapel Hill: University of North Carolina Press, 2004).

5. The Sephardic-Ashkenazi clashes in 1950s ma'abarot are portrayed poignantly in novels such as Amir, *Tarnagol Kaparot;* Sami Michal, *Shavim VeShavim Yoter* (Tel Aviv: Bustan, 1974); and Shimon Ballas, *HaMa'abarah* (Tel Aviv: Am Oved, 1964). See also Nancy Berg, *Exile from Exile* (Albany: State University of New York Press, 1996), 71–105. For the "German"-"Russian" (uptown-downtown) story in late nineteenth-century and early twentieth-century New York, see Esther Panitz, "The Polarity of American Jewish Attitudes toward Immigration (1870–1891)," in *The Jewish Experience in America*, vol. 4, ed. Abraham Karp (Waltham, MA: American Jewish Historical Society, 1969); and Moses Rischin, *The*

Promised City: New York's Jews, 1870–1914 (Cambridge MA: Harvard University Press, 1962), 95–114.

6. Jonathan Sarna, "A Projection of America as It Ought to Be: Zion in the Mind's Eye of American Jews," in *Envisioning Israel: The Changing Ideals and Images of North American Jews,* ed. Allon Gal (Detroit: Wayne State University Press, 1996), 41–59.

7. "William Uris Yerushalmi Memoir," LUP 185.4.

8. Uris letter to Esther Kofsky, October 23, 1944, LUP 137.2.

9. Ibid.

10. Ibid., December 8, 1944.

11. Ibid., December 12, 1944.

12. Ibid., January, undated, 1945.

13. Ibid., October 20, 1945.

14. Ibid.

15. Uris did not publish anything until 1951. His first published piece was about college football and appeared in *Esquire*; it proposed new methods for the selection of the all-American team. Leon Uris, "All-American Razz-Matazz," *Esquire, the Magazine for Men,* January 1951, 92.

16. Uris letter to Esther Kofsky, undated, LUP 137.5.

17. Ibid.

18. Ibid.

19. Ibid.

20. Ibid.

21. For a study that elaborates upon this point in a discussion of other texts: Paul Breines, *Tough Jews: Political Fantasies and the Moral Dilemma of American Jewry* (New York: Basic Books, 1990).

22. Andrew Furman, "Embattled Uris: A Look Back at *Exodus,*" in Andrew Furman, *Israel through the Jewish-American Imagination: A Survey of Jewish-American Literature on Israel, 1928–1955* (Albany: State University of New York Press, 1997), 52.

23. Ibid., 53.

24. LUP 18.6.

25. Ibid.

26. Ibid.

27. Uris letter to his father, September 17, 1957, LUP 137.8.

28. Ibid.

29. For a memoir of events at Ramot Naphtali: Varda Sholmon, *Ramot Naphtali in Battle* (Tel Aviv: Hakibbutz Hameuchad, 1984) [Hebrew]. In the notes Uris prepared before he drafted *Exodus,* the evacuation of children from Manara and Ramot Naphtali are prominently mentioned. LUP 18.5.

30. The structure of the Kitty-Ari romance traced here lends some justification to Rachel Weissbrod's classification of *Exodus* as a "melodrama." Rachel Weissbrod, "Exodus as a Zionist Melodrama," *Israel Studies* 4, no. 1 (1999): 129–52.

31. Ruth Wisse, *If I Am Not for Myself . . . : The Liberal Betrayal of the Jews* (New York: Free Press, 1992), 148–49.

32. David Sorkin, *The Transformation of German Jewry, 1780–1840* (New York: Oxford University Press, 1987).

33. For discussion of such criticism of *Exodus*'s main love affair, see Furman, "Embattled Uris," 46–53.

34. *Southwest Jewish Press,* October 1959, LUP 170.

35. Will Herberg, *Protestant, Catholic, Jew: An Essay in American Religious Sociology* (Garden City, NY: Anchor Books, 1955).

36. For a discussion of the emergence of this term, *Judeo-Christian civilization*: Mark Silk, "Notes on the Judeo-Christian Tradition in America," *American Quarterly* 36 (Spring 1984): 65–85. For the theory of invented tradition: Eric Hobsbawm and Terence Ranger, eds., *The Invention of Tradition* (New York: Cambridge University Press, 1983).

37. Edward Shapiro, *A Time for Healing: American Jewry since World War II* (Baltimore: Johns Hopkins University Press, 1992), 234.

38. Sol Liptzin, *The Jew in American Literature* (New York: Bloch Publishing, 1966), 224–25; see also Furman, "Embattled Uris," 40.

39. Bernard Malamud, *The Assistant* (New York: Farrar, Straus and Cudahy, 1957).

40. Herman Wouk, *Marjorie Morningstar* (Garden City, NY: Doubleday, 1955).

41. Uris letter to Doubleday editor, April 30, 1959 ("In my opinion, *Marjorie Morningstar* was a book harmful to the best interests of the Jewish people," Uris exclaimed in this letter), LUP 135.7.

42. The money came to total about one million dollars. In addition, Preminger insisted on using Weisgal, whose bifurcated snow-white hair looked like Ben-Gurion's, for a cameo in the film scene depicting the joyous celebratory response of a packed Jerusalem square to the UN partition decision. Weisgal, playing Israel's prime minister, stands silently on a balcony, alongside Abba Khoushy's secretary, Milka, who assisted in the arrangement of the filmmaker's Haifa wedding and who plays Golda Meir. By the time Preminger got to the shooting of the partition resolution scene, Weisgal was in London for business meetings. Preminger dragged him back to Israel to put him on the balcony. Weisgal happily recalled: "I didn't think it was too great a sacrifice for a million dollars, and I was by far the highest paid actor in the production." Meyer Weisgal, *Meyer Weisgal . . . So Far: An Autobiography* (New York: Random House, 1971), 313–15. For more information about the Preminger-Bryce wedding, see Foster Hirsch, *Otto Preminger: The Man Who Would Be King* (New York: Alfred A. Knopf, 2007), 329.

43. Rachel Weissbrod, "*Exodus* as a Zionist Melodrama," *Israel Studies* 4, no. 1 (1999).

44. Hirsch, *Otto Preminger,* 340–42.

45. During later stages of the shooting, the disaffected Newman simply

stopped responding to Preminger's direction, fellow actors recalled. Ibid., 332–33.

46. Information here draws from Anita Shapira, *Yigal Allon: The Spring of His Life* (Tel Aviv: Hakibbutz Hameuchad, 2004) [Hebrew]; the English version of this biography is Anita Shapira, *Yigal Allon, Native Son: A Biography* (Philadelphia: University of Pennsylvania Press, 2008). For discussion of whether Allon was a prototype for Ari Ben Canaan, see footnote 45 of the preceding chapter.

47. Shabtai Teveth, *Moshe Dayan* (London: Weidenfeld and Nicolson, 1972).

48. *Exodus* film script, 164.

49. Daniel Bell, *The End of Ideology: On the Exhaustion of Political Ideas in the Fifties* (New York: Free Press, 1962); Walt Whitman Rostow, *The Stages of Economic Growth: A Non-Communist Manifesto* (Cambridge: Cambridge University Press, 1965).

50. One-fourth of Jerusalem's 160,000 inhabitants were coaxed into serving as extras in this balcony scene—as inducement, Preminger's staff held a lottery, promising cash prizes of 20,000 Israeli pounds and six free trips to the film's opening in New York. Preminger worked on the filming for twelve hours, and the stress led to a bitter public altercation with actor Lee J. Cobb, who delivers the promise of fair play to Arabs cited above. As the crowd lingered in the middle of the night, Preminger recharged its energy by announcing the capture of Adolf Eichmann. For all these reasons, Preminger's recent biographer opines that the "milling crowd is among the most wired in film history." Hirsch, *Otto Preminger,* 340, 334–36.

51. Stephen Whitfield, "Israel as Reel: The Depiction of Israel in Mainstream American Films," in *Envisioning Israel: The Changing Ideals and Images of North American Jews,* ed. Allon Gal (Detroit: Wayne State University Press, 1996), 296.

52. Ibid., 307.

53. Moore, *To the Golden Cities,* 259.

54. Uri Avneri, "Don't Let the State of Israel Certify the Perpetuation of Literary Abomination," *Ha-'Olam Ha-zeh,* March 9, 1960 [Hebrew].

Chapter 4

1. Rachel Weissbrod, "*Exodus* as a Zionist Melodrama," *Israel Studies* 4, no. 1 (1999): 130.

2. Speaking at the Smithsonian Institution on October 24, 1988, Uris testified that reading Steinbeck as a youngster taught him that "my loneliness was universal." LUP 181.9.

3. Emily Miller Budick, *Fiction and Historical Consciousness: The American Romance Tradition* (New Haven, CT: Yale University Press, 1989), x.

4. John Lukacs, "*The Great Gatsby*? Yes, a Historical Novel," in *Nov-*

el History: Historians and Novelists Confront America's Past (and Each Other), ed. Mark Carnes (New York: Simon and Schuster, 2001), 243.

5. Samuel Freedman, "Separating the Political Myths from the Facts in Israel Studies," *New York Times*, February 16, 2005.

6. *Shreveport Times*, September 27, 1959, LUP 169.

7. Kenneth Davis, *Two-Bit Culture: The Paperbacking of America* (Boston: Houghton Mifflin, 1984), 266.

8. Lewis Glenn letter to Uris, August 26, 1959, LUP 138.5.

9. Nancy Goldberg letter to Uris, August 4, 1959, LUP 138.3.

10. Uris letter to Nancy Goldberg, August 11, 1959, LUP 138.3.

11. Joyce Hoffman letter to Uris, January 14, 1959, LUP 138.3.

12. Joy Goldsmith letter to Uris, April 8, 1959, LUP 138.3.

13. Harriete Giber letter to Uris, March 1959, LUP 138.5.

14. Uris letter to his father, December 3, 1957, LUP 137.8.

15. Inge Hirschfeld letter to Uris, undated, summer 1959, LUP 138.3.

16. Ralph Goldman letter to Uris, August 6, 1959, LUP 138.3.

17. Uris letter to Ralph Goldman, August 17, 1959, LUP 138.3.

18. Herzlia Levin letter to Uris, July 20, 1959, LUP 138.5.

19. Louis Forgash letter to Uris, undated, LUP 138.5.

20. Nathan Izbicky letter to Uris, undated, March 1959, LUP 138.5.

21. Uris letter to Nathan Izbicky, undated, March 1959, LUP 138.5.

22. Ronald Dunn letter to Uris, January 6, 1961, LUP 138.3.

23. Walter Lowdermilk letter to Uris, February 10, 1959, LUP 138.5; Walter Lowdermilk, *Palestine: Land of Promise* (New York: Harper and Brothers, 1944).

24. For records of these speaking requests and engagements: LUP 145.7, 145.8.

25. "Exodus Draws Tourists to Israel," December 13, 1959, LUP 168.

26. Ibid.

27. *Exodus* El Al materials, LUP 25.7.

28. Dan Wakefield, *The Nation*, April 11, 1959, LUP 169.

29. Maxwell Geismar, *Saturday Review*, September 27, 1958, LUP 169.

30. Harold Ribalow, *Pioneer Women's Journal*, January 1959, LUP 169.

31. Midge Decter, "Popular Jews," *Commentary* (October 1961): 358–59.

32. Ibid.

33. Geoffrey Godsell, *Christian Science Monitor*, December 4, 1958, LUP 169.

34. Marie Malmin Myer, *Christianity Today*, February 29, 1960, LUP 169.

35. *Catholic Star Herald*, March 16, 1960, LUP 169.

36. Allan Gray, *Michigan Christian Advocate*, July 18, 1959, LUP 169.

37. Uris, "The Faith You Have Kept," LUP 181.3.

38. Roth's comments in this section are from Philip Roth, "Some New

Jewish Stereotypes," 1961 speech delivered at Loyola University (Chicago) for a symposium on the "Needs and Images of Man," sponsored by the Anti-Defamation League of B'nai Brith and Loyola, in Philip Roth, *Reading Myself and Others* (New York: Farrar, Straus and Giroux, 1975), 137–47.

39. Avneri's comments in this section are from Uri Avneri, "Don't Let the State of Israel Certify the Perpetuation of Literary Abomination," *Ha-'Olam Ha-zeh*, March 9, 1960 [Hebrew].

40. Weissbrod writes that in Israel, "the political fringes attacked Uris for distorting history and for what they perceived as flawed Zionist ideology, and the literary establishment refused to grant *Exodus* any recognition. Weissbrod, "*Exodus* as Zionist Melodrama," 144.

41. For the Canaanite movement and Avneri's connections to it, see James Diamond, *Homeland or Holy Land: The "Canaanite" Critique of Israel* (Bloomington: Indiana University Press, 1986), 93–95.

42. *Ha-'Olam Ha-zeh*, edition 830.

43. On the contrary: *Exodus*'s premiere screening in Israel, at the Tzafon theater in Tel Aviv on June 21 1961, stirred tremendous energy and excitement in Israel. Ben-Gurion, who in this period did not attend any sessions of the Eichmann trial, attended the premiere of *Exodus*. Some film viewers in Israel were reportedly "ambivalent" about *Exodus*'s Americanization of their country's founding, but generally the movie, and its propaganda value, was deeply appreciated in the Jewish state. Aviva Halamish, "*Exodus: A Film That Changed History*" [Hebrew], in *Cinema and Memory: A Dangerous Relationship?* ed. Haim Bresheeth, Shlomo Sand, and Moshe Zimmermann (Jerusalem: Merkaz Zalman Shazar, 2004), 347–49.

44. Erskine Childers, "The Other Exodus," *The Spectator*, May 12 1961, 672–75; reprinted in Walid Khalidi, ed., *From Haven to Conquest* (Beirut: Institute for Palestine Studies, 1971), 795–803.

45. Erskine Childers, *Common Sense about the Arab World* (London: Victor Gollancz, 1960).

46. Childers, "The Other Exodus."

47. Uris letter to his father, May 4, 1956, LUP 137.7.

48. Students' letter to Uris, July 12, 1959, LUP 138.5.

49. Uris undated letter to students, late July 1959, LUP 138.5.

50. For an online translation of Dayan's eulogy: http://en.wikipedia.org/wiki/Roi_Rutenberg. For a discussion and another translation of this eulogy: Benny Morris, *Righteous Victims: A History of the Zionist-Arab Conflict, 1881–1999* (New York: Alfred A Knopf, 1999), 287–88.

51. Benny Morris, *The Birth of the Palestinian Refugee Problem Revisited* (New York: Cambridge University Press, 2004), 423–36; Shapira, *Yigal Allon: The Spring of His Life* (Tel Aviv, 2004), 372–76 [Hebrew]; Alon Kadish, Avraham Sela, and Arnon Golan, *Kibush Lod, Yuli 1948* (Tel Aviv: Misrad Habitachon [Israel Defense Ministry], 2000) [Hebrew].

52. From Uris's notes on the 1948 war, LUP 18.5. Uris's one-sided ac-

count should be compared to Morris, *Birth of the Palestinian Refugee Problem Revisited*, 99–109. On Morris's multidimensional account, over 60,000 Arab residents left Haifa due to the "cumulative effect" of the early departure of the community's upper- and middle-class elites, continued sniping and bombing, mounting unemployment, Haganah and Irgun pressure tactics, and, toward the end of the sequence, the Arab Higher Committee's decision to encourage the exodus. Not Israeli strategic planning ("Plan D"), nor any other single factor, explains this central phenomenon in the Palestinian tragedy, the Naqba; and in the causal chain, elements of Jewish coercion and of Arab collapse interrelate with a complexity that renders problematic retrospective blame games, suggests Benny Morris.

53. Uris letter to his father, December 3, 1957, LUP 137.8.

54. For differing viewpoints on Haj Amin al-Husseini and the Zionist movement: Ilan Pappé, *Aristocracy of the Land: The Husayni Family* (Jerusalem: Mosad Bialik, 2002) [Hebrew]; Shabtai Teveth, *Ben-Gurion and the Palestinian Arabs: From Peace to War* (Tel Aviv: Schocken, 1985) [Hebrew].

55. Teveth, *Ben-Gurion and the Palestinian Arabs*, 221–42.

56. Haj Amin maneuvered deftly following the Nebi Mousa disturbances of 1920. He tried to convince the British that they were a spontaneous uprising; owing partly to his active participation in the peaceful observances of the same holiday in 1921, British officials seemed drawn to his point of view. This topic is surveyed in detail in Pappé, *Aristocracy of the Land: The Husayni Family*, 219–44 [Hebrew].

57. Jeremy Salt, "Fact and Fiction in the Middle Eastern Novels of Leon Uris," *Journal of Palestinian Studies* 14, no. 3 (1985): 54–63.

58. Elias Khoury, *Gate of the Sun: Bab al-Shams* (Brooklyn, NY: Archipelago Books, 2006).

59. Thomas Friedman, "Sabra and Shatila Massacre: The Four Days," *New York Times*, September 26, 1982.

60. The parallel description in *Exodus* refers to a Nazi criminal named Heinen, "who perfected a method of killing several people in a row with one bullet, always trying to beat his previous record."

61. Robert Rotberg, ed., *Israeli and Palestinian Narratives of Conflict: History's Double Helix* (Bloomington: Indiana University Press, 2006); Peace Research Institute in the Middle East, *Learning Each Other's Historical Narrative: Palestinians and Israelis* (Be'er Sheva': Ben-Gurion University, 2003); Peace Research Institute in the Middle East, *Learning Each Other's Historical Narrative: Palestinians and Israelis* (Beit Jala: Ben-Gurion University, 2006).

62. Disappointingly, Yizhar's work on the 1948 war (including his monumental *Days of Tziklag*) has not been translated into English. The selections of "Hirbet" I translated in this section are taken from the 1990 edition of Yizhar's *Stories of the Plain* collection.

63. For an excellent discussion of Hirbet that examines Yizhar's biog-

raphy as well as responses to the story: Anita Shapira, "Hirbet Hizah: Between Remembrance and Forgetting," *Jewish Social Studies* 7, no. 1 (2000): 1–62. Another interesting discussion, which highlights how Yizhar's story departed from contemporary Israeli conceptualizations of the 1948 experience, is included in an essay by Nurith Gertz on Israeli media during the War of Independence: Nurith Gertz, *On What Melts Away* (Tel Aviv Am Oved, 1997) [Hebrew].

64. Shapira, "Hirbet Hizah."

65. 1981 UJA remarks, LUP 181.6.

66. Draft manuscript, *Beirut*, LUP 46.

67. Leon Uris, *The Haj* (Garden City, NY: Doubleday, 1984).

68. It bears mention that Uris deploys this mechanical Freudianism in his critique of Jewish traditionalism (and his own family heritage) in his autobiographical novel *Mitla Pass*.

69. For one critique of *The Haj*, which brands its depictions of Arab characters "an ugly misrepresentation," see Elise Salem Manganaro, "Voicing the Arab: Multivocality and Ideology in Leon Uris' *The Haj*," *Melus* 15, no. 4 (1988): 3–13.

70. Salt, "Fact and Fiction."

71. In addition to these claims about the novel's veracity, and its use by U.S. government officials as a Middle East primer, Uris wrote the following about *The Haj* in an autobiographical fragment: "I knew I would be called a racist by some but I felt even more strongly that the Western democracies were naïve about the danger they [Arab extremists] pose to our very existence. I decided to write it like I saw it with no apologies. It was the toughest decision I ever had to make as a writer. . . . The writing and completion of the novel was a trip through hell. I would get into my office at noon and by two I was sleeping on my couch. I was in a state of depression most of the book because its revelations tortured me. I also knew I had to tell the truth on every line and every page, and I did tell the truth although it was ugly." LUP 152.1.

72. For an analysis that appeals to multisided dynamics in the Palestinian exodus and that rejects claims about a cohesively planned and executed expulsion plan, see Benny Morris, *Birth of the Palestinian Refugee Problem, 1947–1949* (New York: Cambridge University Press, 1987). For arguments claiming that the Palestinian exodus was deliberately planned or orchestrated by the political-military leadership of the Yishuv/Israel, see Walid Khalidi, "Plan Dalet: Master Plan for the Conquest of Palestine," *Journal of Palestine Studies* 18, no. 1, Special Issue: Palestine 1948 (1988): 4–33; Ilan Pappé, *The Making of the Arab-Israeli Conflict, 1947–1951* (New York: I. B. Tauris, 1994), 87–99.

As to Israel's offer to absorb 100,000 refugees, in his *Birth of the Palestinian Refugee Problem* Benny Morris describes the proposal as being mostly disingenuous (among other things, Israel would have deducted 30,000 Palestinians who had already returned to the country, so the offer did not really refer to 100,000 new returnees), though he portrays its diplomatic context, summer 1949 meetings at Lausanne, as the "best and perhaps only chance for a solution of the refugee problem" (p. 285).

73. Hirsch, *Otto Preminger*, 342.

74. Ibid., 284.

75. For the legal papers: LUP 156.1.

76. For the author's financials: LUP 157.4.

77. Hirsch, *Otto Preminger*, 284.

78. LUP 168.

79. Ibid.

80. Uris dissembled whenever he spoke about this unhappy scriptwriting experience. For instance, he told Preminger's biographer that he "never wrote a line" for the *Exodus* film. "I was taken off the picture before I wrote one single line of screenplay, because of a personality clash—a moral clash." Hirsch, *Otto Preminger*, 321.

81. For Uris's incomplete draft screenplay for *Exodus:* LUP 26.1.

82. Hirsch, *Otto Preminger*, 322.

83. Otto Preminger, *Preminger: An Autobiography* (Garden City, NY: Doubleday, 1977), 198.

84. Ibid., 196–98; Hirsch, *Otto Preminger*, 284. LUP 25.7.

85. Gerald Pratley, *The Cinema of Otto Preminger* (New York: A. S. Barnes, 1971), 135.

86. Hirsch, *Otto Preminger*, 321.

87. Bruce Cook, *Dalton Trumbo* (New York, 1977), 274; Stephen Whitfield, "Israel as Reel: The Depiction of Israel in Mainstream American Films," in *Envisioning Israel: The Changing Ideals and Images of North American Jews,* ed. Allon Gal (Detroit: Wayne State University Press, 1996), 297.

88. Hirsch, *Otto Preminger*, 324.

89. *Exodus* film script.

90. Information about Mathilda Krim and Meyer Weisgal draws from Meyer Weisgal, *Meyer Weisgal . . . So Far: An Autobiography* (New York: Random House, 1971), 313–15. Some details are also taken from Tom Segev, *1967* (Tel Aviv: Keter, 2005), 131–34 [Hebrew].

91. Segev, *1967*, 320–21.

92. *Exodus* film script, 156.

93. Preminger, *Preminger: An Autobiography,* 201; Whitfield, "Israel as Reel: The Depiction of Israel," 300; Deborah Dash Moore, *To the Golden Cities: Pursuing the American Jewish Dream in Miami and L.A.* (New York: Free Press, 1994), 256–57.

94. Hirsch writes perceptively about this funeral oration: "Trumbo's writing for this climactic moment, both blessing and prophecy, is far from incandescent, but it rises to a lyrical pitch Newman's inner-directed style does not begin to accommodate. Newman fails the film at this moment." Hirsch, *Otto Preminger*, 341.

95. Meir Shalev, *The Blue Mountain* (New York: Aaron Asher Books, 1991).

96. For one overview of the broad topic of Jewish responses to Israel: Yosef Gorni, *The State of Israel in Jewish Public Thought: The Quest for Collective Identity* (New York: New York University Press, 1994).

97. Michael Staub, *Torn at the Roots: The Crisis of Jewish Liberalism in Postwar America* (New York: Columbia University Press, 2002), 280–308.

98. Staub quotes a Breira founding statement (December 1973): "This is the reason we join together now: we deplore those pressures in American Jewish life which make open discussion of these and other vital issues [relating to Israeli war and peace topics] virtually synonymous with heresy." Staub, *Torn at the Roots*, 281.

99. Steven Rosenthal, *Irreconcilable Differences: The Waning of the American Jewish Love Affair with Israel* (Hanover, NH: University Press of New England, 2001), 28–30.

100. Michael Lerner, "Twenty Years on the West Bank," *Tikkun* 2, no. 2 (1987): 55.

101. Michael Lerner, "The Pathology of the Occupation," *Tikkun* 4–5 (September–October 1989): 41–48.

102. David Biale, *Power and Powerlessness in Jewish History* (New York: Schocken Books, 1986).

103. Ibid., 6.

104. Biale explained (p. 164) that "the task for contemporary Jewish political theory is . . . not to try to resurrect a 'classical' Zionism but rather to forge a new vocabulary based on contemporary realities." Elsewhere (p. 234) he borrowed from Bernard Avishai's recent volume (Bernard Avishai, *The Tragedy of Zionism: Revolution and Democracy in the Land of Israel,* New York: Farrar Straus Giroux, 1985) when he used the new term "post-Zionism."

105. Biale, *Power and Powerlessness in Jewish History,* 156.

106. Ibid., 164.

107. For a recent discussion of this perceptual frame: Rotberg, *Israeli and Palestinian Narratives of Conflict: History's Double Helix.*

108. Mordechai Bar-On, "Conflicting Narratives or Narratives of Conflict: Can the Zionist and Palestinian Narratives of the 1948 War Be Bridged," in Rotberg, *Israeli and Palestinian Narratives,* 143. For an effort to defend the feasibility of "bridge" narratives, see Ilan Pappé, "The Bridging Narrative Concept" in the same volume, 194–204.

109. To date, two of these booklets have been translated into English: Peace Research Institute in the Middle East, *Learning Each Other's Historical Narrative: Palestinians and Israelis* (2003); Peace Research Institute in the Middle East, *Learning Each Other's Historical Narrative: Palestinians and Israelis* (2006).

110. Subsequent details about Volvovsky are drawn from an interview

with him on April 28, 2008, in Jerusalem.

111. Edwin McDowell, "'Exodus' in Samizdat: Still Popular and Still Subversive," *New York Times,* book review, April 26, 1987.

112. See Maxwell Geismar's evaluation, cited in note 29 of this chapter, LUP 169.

113. *Congressional Record,* Senate, November 14, 1985, S 15409.

Index